Boardman Robinson

SELF-PORTRAIT

BOARDMAN ROBINSON

by Albert Christ-Janer

WITH CHAPTERS BY
ARNOLD BLANCH & ADOLF DEHN

Crescat Scientia Vita Excolatur

THE UNIVERSITY OF CHICAGO PRESS

The University of Chicago Press · Chicago 37
Agent: Cambridge University Press · London

89562

To MISS VEE

89562

INTRODUCTION

Jo DAVIDSON, Boardman Robinson, and Sinclair Lewis—two vast beards with a thin, red-topped face between them—left the meeting of the Institute of Arts and Letters and gathered at a secluded table in the Plaza Cafe at Fifty-ninth Street, to continue over their glasses a discussion of artists, the capriciousness of reputation, and the uncertainties of lasting fame.

Intermingled with bantering, Lewis and Davidson carried on an argument concerning the names in the world of the arts which they regarded, among their contemporaries, as being firmly intrenched in gilt-edged security. Robinson, for his part, was the amused and entertained listener; by and large, he agreed with the novelist that it was impossible to evaluate with any ultimate consequence the artists of today. "We'll leave that job to posterity," he said.

"Jo, you are a great success," prodded Lewis, "but I don't believe that your fame will endure always. It will be up and down, probably. How can you be sure where it will be in the next revival—whatever will be revived?"

The sculptor was indulgent toward himself. "When we come right down to it, Red, we are probably much better than we are supposed to be."

"Well, what basis for judgment do we have for thinking that the names we discussed in the meeting, the names that came up for membership, will be worth a tinker's dam tomorrow?" argued Lewis. "Should we use a utilitarian standard, for example, and say that a name known to the greatest number of people and doing the most immediate good for them is the one to which the future will give a big hand?"

At that moment the three were aware that an excellently tailored figure of handsome proportions was approaching their table. The man came forward and, with obvious sincerity and politeness, addressed his greeting to Jo Davidson, who, because of his distinguished appearance, had caught the eyes of numerous people in the room.

"I shall take only a moment, Mr. Davidson, but I want to tell you how much I admire your sculpture. Because I model in clay whenever I have free time, your work has been a great inspiration to me." Davidson acknowledged the compliment with a bob of his head, and the visitor gracefully excused himself, declining an offer to join the group at the table. He shook hands with the sculptor, included Lewis and Robinson in his glance when he spoke a warm word of appreciation, and returned to his own party at a table in the opposite end of the cafe.

Jo Davidson turned a questioning and uncertain look upon his companions. "Who was that?" he rumbled.

"Don't tell me you don't know!" Lewis was incredulous. "You believe that because you have spent years at your business, because you have traveled and done dozens of prominent people in clay, you're pretty well known, don't you?" The writer grinned at Davidson. "Compared to that man who just now shook your hand you are unknown. I venture to say that more people have his framed and autographed photograph in their homes than will, in all time, look at all the sculpture you'll ever do."

"There may be some truth in what he says, Jo," smiled Robinson as the sculptor stared doubtfully at him. "That man is Nelson Eddy."

This book is not an attempt to evaluate the work of a living artist. A critical essay of Boardman Robinson's accomplishments seems not to fit into the scheme of this biography; such a study will be made, probably, at another time, the work of other hands.

A certain degree of judgment, naturally, must be exercised in the compilation and the presentation of the material contained in such a book as this: some incidents of the life were omitted, while others are stressed at the expense of those which are reduced to understatement; choices of the work of this artist show to advantage certain trends, while others are minimized. In so far as this process of weighing and selecting is necessarily based upon judgment, to that degree is criticism involved.

As the life of this man unfolded itself, given color by his words and dramatized by the stories about him, which delight his friends and acquaintances who like to tell about him, it became apparent that no straightforward, factual accounting could be made of the experiences which have contributed to make this man what he is or to explain this artist and his creations.

To have begun this story with a date would have been dull and unprofitable. There are more important things than the fact, the date of the occasion. The factual things of a man's life, who was conceived and born, fed and bedded by conscientious parents, guided and driven to manhood's stature; who was anxious at the hour of the birth of his children, spurred by unrelenting custom to provide his family with daily bread, bruited about from one job to another more demanding;

who managed, by hook and by crook, to maintain his life and sanity and to attain the best share of his promised three score years and ten—the facts about such a man can be listed neatly and precisely in a chronology, which might go to prove that the man is, somehow, like any man. But the words of this book were not written to prove anything, least of all that this artist is like any man.

This story about the life of Boardman Robinson is, so far as memory and search into history can make it, a true story. Yet the story aspires to be a tale. Perhaps that aspiration will reveal more about the man than the fact that he lived at the corner of Tenth Avenue and West Twenty-fourth Street in 1925.

Here is a man who hopes to be, as he says, "not too good, too moral, nor too weak." He has a range of interests and abilities which is uncommonly broad; he has a personality which is remarkably interesting.

And how great an artist is he? Let the artist speak for himself. Look at the pictures. This is a picture-book, first and foremost; and anything else in it is only an attempt to complete an understanding of these pictures.

Art is not life. It is a statement about life. In his pictures a statement has been made by Boardman Robinson. The transitory qualities of life he has translated into the illusion called "art," which is permanent. And so in his way and from the facts of his time he has created illusion, or art, which other men will search in order to find the truth, a deeper reality.

A. C.-J.

ACKNOWLEDGMENTS

To BOARDMAN and Sally Robinson, to whom I am deeply indebted for their patient and never failing help in compiling the factual material for this volume.

To my friends and to the friends of Boardman Robinson, who enriched the pages of this biography in various ways: Franklin P. Adams, Thomas Hart Benton, Arnold Blanch, Edgar Britton, Adolf Dehn, Lamar Dodd, Otis Dozier, Helen Farr, Daniel Fitzpatrick, Francis Froelicher, Percy Hagerman, Mrs. Meredith Hare, Antoinette Kraushaar, Doris Lee, Sinclair Lewis, Lewis Mumford, Paul Parker, Bartlett Robinson, Virginia Sorenson, J. Duncan Spaeth, Robert Ulich, Mitchell Wilder, and Walker Winslow.

To George Biddle, whose introduction to Boardman Robinson's *Ninety-three Drawings* focused biographical interest upon Robinson.

To Warren Chappell, whose labor of love brought forth a well-designed book.

To the director and to the members of the staff of the University of Chicago Press, who spared no effort to produce this work.

To the owners and collectors of the work of Boardman Robinson, who assisted in the compilation of the facts incorporated in the catalogue.

To Dean Lloyd C. Emmons, Michigan State College, for his encouraging interest in the development of this work.

To my wife, Virginia Morgan Christ-Janer, to Barbara Hanna, Barbara Wilson, Marion Goss, and Rosemary Howland for their painstaking and constant attention to the details of filing, typewriting, correcting, and other nerve-racking and backbreaking jobs.

PROLOGUE

HE WAS reminded of a winter's day in southern France, that day when Boardman Robinson journeyed back to Penarth in Wales, and to intimations of his boyhood. It was his sentimental journey.

The sun shone full and bright, interrupted twice at high noon by pelting rain, which drove down from cold, gray clouds. Though it was only September the first and a good and pleasant season, Robinson felt a chill. It may have been the excitement. As his train drew into Cardiff, he became almost reluctant to go on. The scenes he had come to review, in which his father had played the leading role, had once enthralled him. He sensed intuitively that this visit might show him the folly of retrospection. A subtle disappointment could be his reward for this attempt to reanimate what had been once lively and complete, now over thirty years ago.

At the Cardiff station Robinson made close connection with the Taff Vale and smiled at the innocent appeal with which the name sought to make more comfortable this dilapidated and dirty coach-train. He stared out of the grimy window, half-conscious of scenes which had a strange familiarity, half-thinking of his relief that this was the last leg of his trip. When he stepped off the car at Penarth, the sun was bright again, and great clouds, their sides pure and white, were piling up behind the horizon hills.

He threw a glance around as he sought out his Gladstone and found the aspect reassuring; the station stirred a recognition in him, the street had some resemblance to a picture stored in his memory. But, like the remembrance of a dream, there was no distinction in the details. Robinson noted that during his absence the monumental arch of the depot entryway had been scaled down.

The center of the village was left behind as Robinson hurried from the train. As he turned into a lane, lined on each side with a vine-hidden wall, he was aware of the fast beat of his heart. When he heard voices, he looked to his left and thought, "Those small boys running and shouting there on the green—why, they might be my brother Scott and me!"

Walking at a fast pace, he reached the house. He stooped to set down the heavy bag and peered closely at the posts of the gateway, trustfully searching for traces of his defacement of the stone which once bore, in black paint, the mystic words, "Canara House." But he saw that the coping had been replaced, and he thought that his self-mocking smile was too small to cover his disappointment. After all, it was only a mark he had put into the stone, but the initials had always seemed to make this spot his own. It was home.

Turning his glance up the pathway, Robinson viewed the old house. Smaller, a good deal smaller, it was than he remembered it. The color was not just right; perhaps it had not been so obvious before. Though the distance was short from those posts to the door of the house, he knew it was too long a way for him to walk and not lose the spell. He had not quite forgotten many things about this picture; the drawing would perhaps grow clearer as he moved on the edge of reality and of memory.

He sat down on a stone garden-bench, near the gate; his thoughts turned back. There, in that large oak, he and Scott had made their tree-house and whiled the hours away. After Robinson had lighted his pipe, his fingers stroked the rough edge of the bench. Turning, he noticed the figure of a woman moving near the house, a maid probably; he became suddenly aware of the fact that he, an unknown man, seated there in the privacy of the garden, might appear to be, in the minds of the householders, a questionable character.

1923

Slowly he strode toward the house, up the long path, each step a venture. He approached the figure and explained that he used to live here—would he be permitted to go around to the back? Without a word the maid disappeared, and pretty soon an untidy woman with sleepers in her eyes appeared and asked his name. She was not reassured when he said "Robinson," though she said she had lived here for twenty years or more. When he asked her permission to visit the back garden, she grudgingly gave it.

He went down the side passage, opened the trellis gate, and saw it was all still the same; there were the small trees and the profusion of vines and Mother's conservatory—no, that was gone. In its place stood a two-story ell. Luxuriant with growing things, the garden was well kept and fragrant, as it used to be.

He crossed the grass plot and, passing through an opening in the wall, he came upon the Sherwood house. They were still at Number Six. Two women were working in the vegetables, and an old man sat in a lawn chair near by. Robinson walked up and awkwardly told them his surname. Miraculously, he thought, the women seemed to know him at once and called excitedly, "Papa!" And Papa creaked from his chair to stalk forward as though his pants were too tight in the crotch.

The old man took Robinson's hand in twisted fingers and, though his eyes were perfectly expressionless, he assured the artist that he remembered him and asked about Lydia Jane and Jennie and Scott. Then, after he had unclosed some heavy platitudes about the state of the world, he recited a plaint that had to do with his asthma. He was on the verge of going into the horrid details of his ailment when one of the women, whom the artist took to be a Mrs. Sherwood of another generation, shut him off with questions about the Robinson family and with agreeably complacent remarks about her own. In her quick chatter she acquainted Boardman with news and tales of persons whose faces he mentally snatched out of his past.

Phyllis, the youngest, was to be married soon, but Blanche, who was no longer at home, had remained single and worked in London. Uncle Munro was dead. The Davis family had disap-

peared, though little Nellie, the peculiar one, had been seen recently near Penarth. Old Nell had married her snob-postman and left him a child, who worked near Morgan's in a tobacco shop.

The Lloyds had gone away, no one knew where; old Mrs. Raymond lived with her only son, up near the church; little Captain Jones, widowed, was believed still to be the deputy dockmaster at Barry. His pink-eyed girls "didn't turn out awfully well, not awfully well," neither of them. Captain Black died and left his ship to his son, an unworthy spawn of a fine, upright man. The Reverend Davis—dead. Only the Sherwoods, it seemed, were steady, permanent, virtuous, complete, and immortal.

Presently the Sherwood women served their guest China tea and Devonshire cream with scones. He thanked them and promised to take their messages to his mother. Slowly he walked back through the opening in the wall, crossed the brief garden path, and passed through the trellis gate. As he did so, he sensed rather than saw the presence of the maid peering at him from behind a window curtain. Crossing the front lawn, he reached the stone bench on which he had earlier placed his hat and bag.

With resolution he gathered his things and turned away to continue up the hill. The Munro's house was there still, and though the image of *her* gave Robinson a slight thrill he could not recall her name. Ah, well, it was not her name that used to turn his bowels to water when she came into view. He passed old Dr. Webb's home and turned, to come abruptly upon the churchyard. He stood, resting a moment, and saw the gate open to the small plot of graves. It was with difficulty that he found the stone, a small but dignified gray one.

From the meager display of flowers at Crosslings, the flower shop near the station, Robinson had selected a large handful of cornflowers. With them in the crook of his arm he walked slowly through the pattern of aisles which designed the graveyard. He stepped up to the aged stone, finding the inscription deep and clear: "Captain John Henry Robinson, born 1840, died 1890." With a wide sweep of his arm, Boardman Robinson strewed the flowers upon the gradual mound. The colors intensified the warmth of the gray stone.

The Somerset shore and the little islands over in the blue-gray channel seemed to glide in and out among the cloud shadows. Robinson made his way down from the churchyard. He did not notice that the Gladstone bag was heavy. He was reassured.

Boardman was his father's son; that conviction he had known when he was able to distinguish the deep voice and follow the measured and powerful movement of the sea captain with his eyes. Even later, when he felt the impact of the father's dominant will and was given his share of the sharp cut of the captain's temper, the lad was not repulsed. His admiration for the strength in Captain Robinson's bearded face and his respect for the pride in the old man's eye which welcomed his daily life, his home, and his ship made a deep mark in the boy's heart. That mark made Boardman a fascinated, if not a devoted, son.

He had seen his father last in Wales, in the house in Penarth. The strong, short nose, the high forehead, the powerful hands, the vibrant tone of his voice, the heavy and dark-red beard, the suit of blue broadcloth—the man filled the home with security and with promise of better things tomorrow. Boardman did not forget the man, nor did he forget the evenings, in the home near Cardiff, when other sea-captains urged John Robinson to sing the songs of the sea while they joined in, with rich voices and with instruments:

There were three brothers in merry Scotland,
In merry Scotland there were three;
And they did cast lots which of them should go,
    Should go,
    Should go,
And turn robber all on the salt sea.

The lot it fell upon Henry Martyn,
The youngest of all the three;
That he should turn robber all on the salt sea,
    The salt sea,
    The salt sea,
For to maintain his two brothers and he.

With these memories fresh in his mind, Robinson wrote a report that evening of this visit to his father's grave. His mother, his brother, and his sister in New York received an account from Penarth:

Hail, John Robinson! You have been here a long time, my dear, a longer time probably than it will be 'til we shall join you. (The tears did not come then but, inexplicably, now.) As I stood there I had an almost complete sensation of being my own father and of dropping cornflowers upon his father's grave. . . . .
Children are somehow near-sighted, I suppose. I had remembered that the church-yard was high, but I had not the faintest recollection of the great prospect it revealed over toward Cardiff. The tide was out and on the other side, at the foot of the docks, the mud gleamed purple in the dazzling sun. And behind and above Cardiff, black and crimson and gold, great cranes and tips and towers and steeples and notched houses could be seen; and beyond were the incredibly green hills, near and high and above that again, up and up, ending in vast towers of cumulous clouds piled up against a Mediterranean blue. It would have made Turner pitch his palette over the cliff and follow it in despair.

It was the first of September, 1923.

PROEM

THE central meaning, the dominant note of the immortality ode, is Wordsworth's refusal to allow the disillusionment of riper years, born of experience of human wrong, suffering, misery and injustice, to embitter him as poet and artist and to engender a settled mood of cynicism and despair.

Though

> touched with due abhorrence of *their* guilt
> For whose dire ends tears flow, and blood is spilt,
>   And Justice labors in extremity,

he yet affirms that liberty has been the scope of his song

>   which did not shrink from hope
> In the worst moment of these evil days.

And so Wordsworth prefaces the poem in which he portrays three moments of the artist's life, and in which the second moment describes the transitoriness of the rainbow and the passing of the glory from the earth, with the closing lines of an earlier poem:

> My heart leaps up when I behold
>   a rainbow in the sky.
> So was it when my life began
> So is it now I am a man
> So be it when I shall grow old
>   Or let me die.

The child is father to the man
And I could wish my days to be
Bound each to each by natural piety.

Here is the peculiarly Wordsworthian application of this truth to conduct: a man makes shipwreck of his life unless he carries into his maturity and old age the intuitions of his childhood, so that there shall be no tragic disruption, no break with his past, no revolution—but evolution. Piety in the ancient classic sense did not mean going to church and saying your prayers, it meant respect for your ancestors, and Wordsworth would bind together his days by this feeling of respect for the ancestral voices of his boyhood, its joys and raptures and its deepest intuitions. So again at the close there flashes upon the inward eye the image of the rainbow with which the poem opened, but now it is charged with new meaning, it is a symbol of youth and age linked by the bridge of hope that beckons to the man of cheerful yesterdays and confident tomorrows.

And the third moment, that completes the whole and binds the three together, is not one of *dis*covery, but of *re*covery of

>   truths that wake,
> To perish never.

J. DUNCAN SPAETH

PART ONE

There was a time when meadow, grove and stream,

The earth, and every common sight,

To me did seem

Appareled in celestial light,

The glory and the freshness of a dream.

1

JOHN HENRY ROBINSON was an Irishman, whose grandfather had escaped from Dublin during Lord Edmund FitzGerald's rebellion and had found refuge in Nova Scotia in 1810. His father's father, originally a Catholic whose individualistic spirit had turned him away from the church, had brought that imperial strength to the clan which made his sons and grandsons seek their work amid the uncertainties of wave and weather. So it was a natural thing that John Robinson, grown tall and brawny and hungry for adventure and ready for a man's responsibility, should be master of his own ship when he had turned just nineteen, master of a sailing vessel and not a steamer. Later, after his retirement, when he was approached with alluring offers to captain a ship with boilers and engines, he refused, roaring, "I won't be bossed by a damned Scotch engineer!"

Like many young natives of Nova Scotia, the youthful sailor set out to prove again that, according to most Nova Scotians' thinking, the peninsula should have added a "fourteenth state" to the original thirteen colonies. When civil war threatened the Union he enlisted, in 1861, in the First Massachusetts Volunteers. Within a few months he had earned a second lieutenant's commission, had fought through the Battle of Gettysburg, and, shortly thereafter, had left the army to join the navy as a pilot. It has been, for eighty years, a subject for argument among his descendants as to whether or not he surrendered his place in the Army of the North with the full knowledge and consent of his commanding officer; there seem to be reasons for assuming that John Robinson, a man used to giving orders, was not happy in receiving them. However, be that as it may, his sea experience was valuable to the hard-pressed naval forces of the North, and he served as a pilot until the end of the war.

After peace came to the states, Robinson returned to Nova Scotia and to his job as captain of a merchant vessel. With his merchantman he sailed round the world six times and doubled the Horn twenty-one times before he quit the deck at the age of forty-five. A list of the ports at which he docked reads like pages from a maritime gazetteer.

An old Connecticut family, of which the great Boston theologian, Theodore Parker, was an illustrious member, had moved to Nova Scotia when John Robinson returned from his war service. A maternal great-grandfather, William Parker, had been granted a deed of land upon the peninsula in lieu of payment for his soldiering under Wolfe at Quebec. Major Edward Parker took advantage of this royal grant, thereby providing the opportunity for John Robinson to meet Lydia Jane Parker, the Major's eldest granddaughter.

The cut of the figure of the sea captain looked right and fascinating to Lydia Jane. After a lengthy courtship, because the Captain was so long at sea, so seldom home, John Henry married Lydia Jane. "Jennie," he called her.

Lydia Parker Robinson brought forth three children, of whom Boardman was the first. She was a forceful woman, a mate fit for her robust husband, a personality with graded and subtle col-

1876–1904

oring, a mind radical, keen, and always questioning. Though she was not politically minded, nor did she actively participate in any movements, she was sympathetic with all who advanced the right of women to do more than the routine labor of the household.

Boardman's early impressions of his mother assured him that, while it is not important to answer questions, it is essential to ask them. He was invited to become a contributing member of a family that applauded stimulating talk. His home was one in which ideas were held to be important.

Good thinking habits were impressed on Boardman's mind through those influences brought to bear upon him by his mother. Because the eldest of the Robinson brood saw less of his father than did the others, his mother's character worked strongly upon him. The dramatic appearances of Captain Robinson, the potent flavor of his tales of the ports of China and Africa, the mystery of his life upon the seas, made stirring days in the first years of the lad's life. But the time of his development through adolescence was given form by his mother's work and love.

They were happy years, evenly moving with the incoming and the outgoing of the tides in the Bay of Fundy. In the deep orchards, aromatic with blossoms in the late spring, the children increased the size of their world. They wandered in the fruitful valley, watched the vast meadows which stretched toward the east, dotted with pasturing flocks. It was Evangeline's land.

After the day's work, Lydia Jane Robinson read to her children from Longfellow's story that included their valley, the Annapolis; they would demand a repetition of the lines which described the homes in which they and Grandfather Parker lived:

> Dikes, that the hands of the farmers had raised
>   with labor incessant,
> Shut out the turbulent tides; but at stated seasons
>   the floodgates
> Opened, and welcomed the sea to wander at will
>   o'er the meadows
>   . . . . aloft on the mountains
> Sea-fogs pitched their tents, and the mists from
>   the mighty Atlantic
> Looked on the happy valley but ne'er from their
>   station descended.

But the children did not understand until later why their mother's voice was deep and vibrant when she concluded:

> There the richest was poor, and the poorest lived
>   in abundance.

It seemed to be a favorite line of hers.

In Nova Scotia, Boardman knew a security which daily enfolded him in a calm embrace. Such surety is an estate for the child, a prison for the

adult, and only those who are empty look back with yearning.

The mother was a devout Baptist. The concepts of her religion and the strictness of her morality, while not definitively adopted by her children, were not forgotten. Although Boardman learned quickly that lasting lessons come through experience and self-realization, his mother's precepts served him well while he was learning. The healthy appetites of his youth, the vigorous demands of his young manhood, were tempered by the wisdom he brought from his Nova Scotia home.

An abiding relationship grew up between Boardman and his brother Scott. The younger boy was the quiet, studious kind, often a sufficient adversary for the foil of his brother's quick and impulsive wit. They found one another interesting and got on in mutual respect.

When Boardman was six years old, he was sent to a public school for a few months during the year 1882. The training he received there was only incidental to that which he had been given at home.

One day Captain Robinson returned from one of his extended trips with an idea that set his children's minds afire with high imaginings. They would come with him, he said, and Mother, too. And they would sail around the world!

The eldest was discussed. Could Boardman leave his schooling for a year, maybe two? No, it would handicap him later; the school would have to be considered first. The boy was stunned to think of it; to go to school, to study grammar and arithmetic, to go to live with Grandfather Parker —all of that, instead of sailing round the world.

It seemed too much for a lad to bear. Boardman was inconsolable. But he went to Grandfather's house, and he watched Captain Robinson and Jennie wave a goodbye. Only Boardman knew, though, what disappointment means to a boy who must study grammar instead of sailing for the Horn and the China seas. He watched the horizon line long after the masts had gone down and away into the gray.

Life with Grandfather was easy and pleasant. School days passed, and Boardman was more interested as he came to know numbers and letters and their arrangements. They made sense, finally, and he forgot the poignant sting in his eyes the day he watched the ship sail out of the bay. He heard from distant places—Canton, Hong Kong, Manila, Montevideo, Rio de Janeiro—and tried to imagine that Scott was now, as they told him, two inches taller. Often he would close his eyes and restore the picture of Mother to the fore of his mind: black hair, a heavy roll at the nape of the full neck; a dark and heavy line over each dark eye; the sure and swift hands moving, not resting. The image grew faint, no matter how he tried to fix it firm.

Grandfather Parker was a good farmer, and his prosperity made him the bountiful host in the largest house in the little village of Somerset. A kindly

man, he was nevertheless a frugal manager who attended to the well-being of his crops and his herds. Boardman learned to work in the barns and often, in the frost-white mornings when he huddled against the belly of a milch cow for warmth, he would hear Grandfather's admonition over the rhythmic sounds of the milking, "Now strip the teats, son, strip the teats."

From Cardiff, a place Boardman found on the map in "Wales," there came news. The Captain had ordered the ship to lower sail; he had found a new home for a family that was in need of reunion, education, stability, and calm days. So Grandfather Parker decided that he himself would take Boardman; and the two set out for Cardiff, in the pleasant season, in 1885.

Matthew Arnold once examined the lives of men who had accomplished much in the various arts. He found that, in most cases, they had had experiences of sudden and various changes in their early, formative years; most of them had developed in childhood the attitude of taking very little for granted. Perhaps this trip had such an influence on Boardman, for he was most impressionable at that time and appreciated the drama of the trip to the full. It was exciting, and it was an adventure for the boy to find his new home and to renew acquaintance with Scott, with his sister Jennie, and with his father and mother.

A faint line fixed firm upon the waves, a line which grew and became color; then the passengers pressed toward the deck. "Land! Ireland!" It was something he could not have dreamed. "Bristol Channel," said Grandfather, the next day. "Soon we'll be in Liverpool, son." Then finally from the deck he saw a large, bearded man and next to him a figure that he knew must be Mother; there was Sister, and Scott. Scott *was* tall! When he and Grandfather stepped off the gangplank, he tried to be less excited than he felt.

In "Canara House," in Penarth, near Cardiff, Boardman grew to almost fifteen. He and his brother and sister attended numerous private schools—"board-schools"—and learned, among other things, that, although they spoke a similar language, they did not understand Welsh or English ways. The young Robinsons adapted themselves quickly to the new places, however; and the first year had not passed before they were well acquainted with new friends and with new scenes. They were very popular because they had many stories to tell.

Boardman was especially taken with the new scene, the docks and ships, the busy life of the folk who made a living by unburdening the vessels which brought a thousand things from all ports of the world. He was, of course, impatiently awaiting the day when he would be a sea captain, with his own ship and the freedom to sail to those distant places which sparkled through his father's stories. He learned the songs the sailors sang.

Upon the path of the cliff, haunted by pirates and smugglers, the children lugged alabaster, Boardman and Scott sweating and groaning. The thickets of briar and hawthorne grew dense along the edge of the high precipice. The heavy clay was carried home, young shoulders straining at the load, to plaster the "passage." And from the treasured sea chest of old Uncle George—that chest which smelled of strange and faraway things which set children's minds aflame with incredible fancies —came the sea boots that Boardman wore on those special occasions when the haunts of the pirates were raided.

The "red path" of deep sienna clay was always the route to the back door of the house, and the "red path" also led out and away to Pontevedra and Pichucalco and In Shan and to those worlds which children were ever permitted to inhabit.

More frequently, now, Boardman saw his father. He watched him play his part in a fine setting among the fellow-captains, who regarded John Robinson with a tinge of envy and with a secret desire to be as much the sea captain as he was. Their eyes filled with respect bordering on awe when Robinson prophesied the weather, for he was held to have supernatural sight for storms and for calms. Because he was an observant student of the tides, his predictions often came true. There was the story of the two ships which set out, against the advice of Captain Robinson; both foundered in a raging storm, within sight of the shore, and all their sailormen drowned. Not a man-jack lived to tell the tale.

Great and fearful stories of the moods of the oceans filled the rooms of "Canara House" those winter evenings when sailors, home from the sea, recounted their most dangerous voyages. The children listened avidly to stories of ships becalmed and ships torn by the violence of tornados, ships tossed in the deeps of mountainous waves and ships sodden in deadly calms.

Strange lands were lighted by an unholy glow when a skilled tongue spun tales with transparent threads of phosphorescent stuff. The impossible became real, just there before their eyes. Those lands were peopled by Taalians and Slavs and Yabassians with whom Boardman became intimately acquainted. And so, when he came to read it, he was not at all surprised that

> In Xanadu did Kubla Khan
> A stately pleasure-dome decree:
> Where Alph, the sacred river, ran
> Through caverns measureless to man
> Down to a sunless sea.
> So twice five miles of fertile ground
> With walls and towers were girdled round:
> And here were gardens bright with sinuous rills
> Where blossomed many an incense-bearing tree;
> And here were forests ancient as the hills,
> Enfolding sunny spots of greenery.

In fact, to him it was an old, old story.

For Boardman, "Canara House" was the theater which played the best of comedy and tragedy. The actors trooped in and out, cast characters and mountebanks, specialists in buffoonery and Thespians blown with dignity; their repertory was read not from any book but from their lives. In each act of every play Captain Robinson played a stellar role.

Dogmatic opinions were spears which were shattered upon shields of iron will. Religion, politics, and criticism of those who were in high places—these sober matters were not neglected. The "Welsh problem" was a *pièce d'occasion*.

In the Captain's mind there existed a neat balance of skepticism and rocklike belief. He expressed both in unhesitating terms. Four clergymen were frequent visitors at the house, the victims of their host's wit and the recipients of his older suits of clothes.

As the boy watched his father draft sails and sailing boats, he admired his clever hand. He heard him read from Shakespeare. The Captain was a reading man, one who carried "a flask of whiskey in one pocket and a volume of Dante in the other," as he often boasted.

(4)

All this, to be sure, was before the Skipper became a teetotaler. Once he dreamed a dream in which there were two pictures of his life: one prosperous and happy, in which he was full with success; the other a ruinous one, in which he went down to a tragic end in a drunkard's grave. The Captain went above deck, driven in haste from his nightmare-haunted cabin and ordered his men to toss overboard every bottle of spirituous liquor and never to drink aboard his ship again.

John Henry Robinson died an abstemious man, in the prime of his years, on January 22, 1890.

Bequeathing an inheritance of the spirit to his son, he remained vivid in fast colors. The sailor lives strong in the frame of the artist, who never works better than when he is painting a character which is blood-kin to the personality of the man who, to him, is the original sea captain.

Shortly after the death of her husband, the mother took the children from the cliffs near Cardiff and returned to Nova Scotia. The chapter written in Penarth was closed. It was to be re-opened only for a glance when Boardman Robinson made his sentimental journey there over thirty years later.

2

With her three and with the whole responsibility of the new situation heavy on her shoulders, the widow found a refuge in the comfortable scenes of the peninsula. The immediate problems were urgent; bread and butter had to be earned, and Mrs. Robinson set to with determination, resolute in her pride and her independence. Her strength was sufficient.

Boardman, aware of the new perplexities which had beset the family, accepted the time when it was his obligation to do a man's duty. With willingness he stepped forward to take up his job. The solicitude with which Robinson dealt with his own children found its roots in this, his early introduction to the matters of pater familias.

The orientation of the Robinson children to their new circumstances was not accomplished without a few tears; Boardman and Scott came in, now and then, in the evening with shirts torn and knuckles stained. In Wales they had been the Yankees, and it was only historically correct that they should have to fight the Revolution on the American side. Now, among their cousins in Boston and in play with their friends in Nova Scotia,

they were dubbed "British"; they fought the Revolution over again. Boardman quickly analyzed the position of the minority and saw that it requires more in stoutness than it offers in consolation. As a consequence, he has been wary of the partisanship and competitive ways of civilized man. A psychologist might say he was "conditioned."

Lydia Jane Robinson did not neglect the schooling of her children, though for a time she could do no more than have them attend classes in a small school in Berwick, Nova Scotia. Fortunately for them, they came under the influence of a man whom Robinson today calls a great man. This teacher, a farmer and craftsman when he was not in the schoolroom, by chance had the name Robinson, though he was not related by blood to the John Robinson family. This teacher, who helped to develop the characters of the children whom he taught, believed in the virtues of an accurate mind. Boardman, at an age to profit by such guidance, marked his lessons well. The training he received was fundamental in the unfolding of certain important qualities in Robinson's intellectual equipment: he studied Latin, arithmetic, and the king's English.

At the close of the school year in 1894, when Boardman was eighteen, he decided to leave Nova Scotia. At home he could be of little help to his mother; the opportunities for earning substantial sums were small; and his education could hardly be carried further. So he set out for Boston. The insurance which had helped the family after the death of the father was now spent, and Boardman tried to find a job which would enable him to send money to his mother and, at the same time, give him time to enter a training-school.

In Boston, Boardman received a few meals and much advice from his numerous relatives; and, after working at odd tasks and saving a small sum, he enrolled in the Massachusetts Normal Art School, an institution established for the training of teachers, craftsman, and artisans. Most fortunately for him, Boardman selected E. Wilbur Dean Hamilton as his instructor. Munsell, the creator of the famous color-theory which is known today by his name, was also a teacher in the school. Hamilton, a brilliant teacher, one who was aware of the

1876–
1904

most advanced trends in European painting, was the person who inspired young Robinson.

Up to this point Boardman had had no training in the skills and techniques of painting. He had shown an early interest in drawing and illustrating, but it was nothing more than one might find in any intelligent boy who is interested in books and pictures. His first skill was developed by Hamilton; his initial perceptions were created by this excellent teacher. The class work consisted of drafting, still-life drawing and painting, the study of anatomy, and design. In the subsequent three years at the school, Boardman studied the history of art, principles of architecture and building construction, machine drawing, historic ornament, and life-drawing. Robinson refers to this today as an adequate and all-around training, much better than that which he was to receive in France a number of years later. And he also escaped, as George Biddle says, "a novitiate at the Boston Museum of Fine Arts under the devastating chill and dry rot of Benson, Tarbell, and Philip Hale." He was under a bright star, and, as Robinson remarks now, it was more luck than planning which made his study in Boston so profitable to him.

Outside the technical aspects of his education, however, the most significant contribution to the youth's development did not come from his contemporaries. He loved books, and he read voraciously. As a boy he had, as a matter of course, found the books which were widely read: *Remarkable Men and Events*, a compilation of biographical sketches calculated to inspire the youth; and *Zig-Zag Journeys in Classic Lands*, a Cook's tour and geographical table d'hôte, with illustrations by F. O. C. Darley. But John Robinson's son was impressed by Dante and Shakespeare, by John Bunyan and Dickens. Fortunately for art and poetry, a man always may conceivably be more thoroughly conditioned by Stratford-on-Avon in the sixteenth and seventeenth century than by his next-door neighbor whose name may be George F. Babbitt.

In Nova Scotia, Robinson had subscribed to *Harper's Young People*, which featured the drawings of Howard Pyle, Reginald Birch, and other popular illustrators. The Winslow Homer drawings he saw frequently in *Harper's*. Nearly all of Rob-

inson's impressions of pictures, until he arrived in Boston, were in black-and-white.

It was while Robinson was obtaining a library card at the Boston Library, in 1896, that he first saw Puvis de Chavannes's murals and those by John Singer Sargent. Though he was mightily

bored by the work which decorates the upper flights of the library, Robinson had obtained enough information from Hamilton to give him a full appreciation of the Frenchman's work. "Though today their significance may be somewhat negligible," Robinson reflects, "the murals were full of important things for America in the nineties." It was the first monumental and decorative work he had seen.

Soon more able to find his way around in Boston, the young student discovered the Boston Museum of Fine Arts in its old Gothic home on Copley

Square. It was here he had his introduction to the paintings of Millet, whose work is so adequately represented in the museum. He was especially pleased with the three pictures, "The New Born Calf," "Bathers," and "The Sower." Though he visited the classes at the Museum School, Robinson was keen enough to see that much of the work was academic and constrained, much more so than that which was being done under Hamilton at the Normal Art School. So he continued to work under Hamilton for three years and was reasonably satisfied with his progress.

The young art student occupied himself with various jobs during his years in Boston. Reading gas meters paid the rent, and often, as he climbed from yard to yard, from porch to porch, an appropriate line or two would come to mind: "O meter! . . . . , Who are a light to guide, a rod to check the erring. . . . ." And in the summer he packed his things and went off to a resort hotel in New Hampshire, as assistant to the headwaiter. His great opportunity came on the day that the manager of the hotel, who maintained an ingratiating smile for his guests and a fierce scowl for his employees, became violently impatient with the headwaiter, dismissed him and all his grandeur, and appointed Robinson to the regal position in the dining-room. The new headwaiter, however, could not arrogate the icy authority that his new station required of him. The manager developed a frustrated personality by the end of the summer, because each time he became incoherent in his rage at his inadequate headwaiter, he was barely able to sputter, "Go pack your bag, you are dismissed!" Robinson would answer truthfully, "I have no bag." Faced with such an insoluble state of affairs, the manager would retire to his office, completely foiled.

One fine Boston day, in the spring of 1896, Robinson was engrossed in a book while he was sitting on the seat of the elevator cage which he happened to be operating at the time. He was not aware, until some moments had passed, that he was being observed by two well-dressed and attractive women, who had come into the shopping district to do their marketing. The young man was somewhat embarrassed when one of the women asked him what it was he found so absorbing.

It was an auspicious moment for Boardman. The interest and friendliness of the women did much to change the course of his life. The poetess, Hannah

Parker Kimball, and Mrs. David P. Kimball, her sister-in-law, both benevolent and well to do, urged him to continue his schooling; they helped him while he was a student in Boston and finally made it possible for him to make his trip to France. It was Shelley he was reading that morning, and he has maintained a kindly attitude ever since toward the romantic lyricist.

The foundation laid by Hamilton was by then broad and firm, and he and Robinson decided that, if it were possible, the structure of the latter's training should be completed in Europe. Backed by the promises and the aid of the Kimballs, Boardman made his plans to spend the following two years in Paris.

In the summer of 1898, Robinson persuaded two students to throw in their lot with his. When the three added their resources, they discovered that there was a way that the most impecunious could take to Paris. They shipped on a cattle boat, "nurse-maids to eight hundred twenty head of Texas longhorns," Robinson recalls.

On board ship the trio was told that one Sanford, a Yale athlete, who, Robinson learned, had been on the Eli team for six years, would give out the orders. The three friends grew to hate his violent and specific directions with burning in their chests. Because the longhorns were meek, poor sailors who wished only to be let alone, the fortnight went by uneventfully, and the boat docked at Liverpool.

Upon his arrival in France, Robinson announced the advent of his day of decision. He would be an artist. With a poor purse but with a greater poverty of experience, he faced all that was strange to him with youthful courage. There was much to learn. But, naïve though he was, he was altogether certain of his will and strength. He knew he had selected the way of his heart's desire, though he was not to be told the full price of that way until years later. Enough then, as he surveyed the delightful and intimate fields of Normandy, the neat gardens surrounded by wide thickets, that he was young and eager. Then he remembered his mother's readings, "the houses . . . . such as the peasants of Normandy built . . . . , " and he was certain that dreams come true.

A sensible mind and an active imagination told

**1876–
1904**

him that what was ahead would require some sacrifice. But sacrifice is easy when it is not called by name; Robinson did not pause to think it out. He had come here to begin his life as an artist.

In that year, 1898, Robinson was a giant figure, full of the vitality which flows from health and youth. He was twenty-two. The large head, topped by a thick mop of red hair, was held high and defiantly. His movements were quick and sure, revealing the deep confidence which supported him. One could see he was lucky.

Paris, when Robinson first saw it, explained why it was the center of the world of art. Full and wise and old but well preserved in her seductive charm, hospitable with the privacy a charming hostess will extend her guests, Paris was the mother of the restive who were comfortable nowhere else. And the young American, walking in the vicinity of the Rue des Apennins, filled his lungs with clear Sunday-morning air and, finding his way to the treelined Avenue des Champs Elysées, watched the procession of smart carriages. He returned to his hotel, "de l'Univers et de Portugal," and tried to rest, but the close walls confined him; he descended to the street again, excited with adventure, and walked. The day being such an event, he threw aside economy and drank a bock at the Café des deux Magots, a quiet place in which the genteel atmosphere was shattered for only a moment when one of the waiters, accused by a patron of having come by his pocket-book dishonestly, heaved a pile of plates on the floor in outraged righteousness. Then Robinson looked at his watch and saw that it was already seven o'clock in the evening.

In this Paris, Robinson concluded that he carried the total responsibility for himself. He did not learn a better lesson. He balanced self-reliance with searching and seeking, and he stepped over the threshold into maturity.

Finding a room up six flights of stairs, just off the Cimetière Montparnasse, in the Rue Delambre, Robinson distributed his things and felt at home. Dressed in corduroy trousers and wearing a flowing black tie, he might have been there from the very beginning.

When he went about, however, and visited the art schools, he was not so sure; things were different than they had been in the Normal Art School in Boston. Much of the spirit of the schools was dry and academic, and their influence was unprofitable in other ways. Robinson painted for a time at Colarossi's and, like most American students, entered the portals, at least, of the famous Julian's in the Rue du Dragon. He took away his disappointment.

At one time Robinson was admitted to the class of Leon Gérôme, at the École des Beaux Arts, but he was informed that he would not be eligible for *concours*. Gérôme, an impressively tall and handsome man, sprinkled gold dust carefully from a seashell upon his flourishing signature, while the *massière* took the usual ten francs admission from the prospective student. Robinson felt he had received his money's worth.

As his initiation into the class, the American bought the *masse*, a round of drinks made of hot rum punch. He was badly overcharged, of course; but he did manage with some adroitness to avoid the customary hazing. When he departed, he had empty pockets and deflated hopes.

"Gérôme, contrary to much opinion I heard at the time, was no draftsman; he was merely an expert," says Robinson, when thinking about this effort to begin his art training in Paris. "There seemed to be damned small interest in art in any of the schools."

Aside from these disillusioning visits to the academies, Robinson had no contact with them during his years in Paris; however, there was an occasion when he served as guide for an American visitor who wished to see the classes under the French masters.

Mr. Newton Carpenter, one of the staff members of the Art Institute of Chicago, came to Paris to study the schools. Robinson, lower in funds than usual, posed as one who knew Paris and offered to show Carpenter the sights and to introduce him to the Académie Julian. Carpenter entered the classroom, with his guide following, and gazed interestedly about the room without so much as removing his hat. One of the members of the class, staring coldly at the visitor, spoke a heavily accented sentence of welcome, "Take down your hat, you fat ———!" The episode did not amuse Mr. Carpenter, and the guide watched his client depart in embarrassment. Robinson looked reproachfully at the student who had cost him his new business.

The popularity of the *art nouveau* swept large areas of the art world, and young Robinson felt very much out of touch with its mode. And so, though he did invest small sums of the Kimball money for lessons, usually he kept his francs for more important things, such as wine and bread.

The galleries and the windows of discerning dealers, such as those of Durand-Ruel in the Rue Lafitte, were the best schools. These Robinson studied with eagerness and care. Thus the best part of his training came to him for nothing but his efforts. The museums, the windows, and the friends he made, who, like him, had come from all parts to learn—these were the best teachers.

The Louvre was to Robinson, as it was to most of the serious students in Paris, the golden opportunity. There he studied and restudied Giorgione's great "Fête champêtre" and Rembrandt's "Supper at Emmaus." It was then that the artist developed his love for the works of the Dutchman whose drawings had a profound effect upon him.

Chinese drawings and paintings impressed their qualities so indelibly upon Robinson's mind that,

many years later, when he attacked the problem of analyzing the mountains of Colorado, they were forever a guide to him.

Many an hour was spent in the Luxembourg Gallery, the benefits of which were more limited but where Robinson examined the works of Manet and Whistler. He came upon the paintings in the Caillebotte collection which presented the Impressionists. Though this rich gift, with the exception of the Cézannes, which were thought to be impossible, was but perfunctorily accepted by the French government, it was a shining jewel in an institution which considered these contemporary works, sadly enough, as *machin* art, a contrived and overly schemed stuff.

In newspapers such as *Figaro*, young students were invited by the drawings of Manet and Fo-

rain. The latter, the same Forain whose best drawing Vollard prized at a hundred francs but who held his breath if a customer tempted him with fifty, was a draftsman who caught and held Robinson's eye. His style of drawing, published in *Figaro*, affected the American for years after he saw the first.

Daumier was "out of the period" at the time in Paris; only the most discriminating and those sure of their tastes and confident in their judgments were concerned with him. His prints could be obtained for insignificant amounts, of course, even as late as 1925. But in Robinson, Daumier had one of his most ardent friends. Thinking of the great cartoonist, the young artist felt that, indeed, he had come to Paris just twenty years too late.

The summer of 1898 passed by on wings, each day being for Robinson a high and daring flight. He and his new friends, William King and Arthur Atkins, hit it off; and together they made a banquet of the thousand opportunities which served their appetites for music, pictures, and drama. Rich blood ran in their veins, and they were nourished.

Bill King, a musician who studied with Widor, the famed organist of St. Sulpice and the later hero of Albert Schweitzer, frequently mentioned the name of a friend, a girl from San Francisco, whom he regarded with affection and admiration. Both King and Atkins were natives of the Golden Gate city, and Robinson at first gave little credence to the praises these two sang of the girl; it was the sort of thing San Franciscans did for one another. Atkins and King, in turn, described the Nova Scotian to the girl in such elaborate terms that she was inclined to doubt the existence of such a figure: a red beard, a flowing cape, a large-brimmed black hat, a blue flash of the eye, a sweeping manner, a name like *Boardman*.

Sally Whitney, a student of Rodin, had come to Paris with talent, ambition, and with complete evidence of the hearty disapproval of her family. It was not a usual thing that a girl should have sincere aims to be a professional sculptor; to leave her home; to travel and live alone—to live alone in Paris! But, to use the familiar phrase with which Doris Lee once described her, "with her whim of iron" she set about to do what she believed she

1876–
1904

should. She worked hard in Rodin's classes, made beautifully strong drawings, and won the praise of the Master.

Atkins and King introduced them, Sally and Boardman. And Sally felt her heart forgiving the beard and the manner and the black hat and the flash, but not the *Boardman*, certainly not for "every day." It was she who first called him "Michael." Michael he is today, or "Mike," to all his intimates. And Michael and Sally were engaged to be married within a few short weeks, though they had to postpone the wedding ceremony for several years.

A gifted painter, Arthur Atkins, a nephew of the late Frederick Keppel, Sr., became closely associated with Robinson, and invited him to share with him the small apartment on the second story of the Keppel store on the Quai de l'Horloge. During 1899 the young artists absorbed the quality of the fine prints and drawings in the Keppel collection, especially those of Rembrandt and Whistler. This was the part of his education which Robinson might think of as his graduate work; it was of inestimable value to him, and it sharpened his taste.

Especially attractive were the musical programs which were almost daily features in the center where musicians of every nation were visitors or adopted natives. Frequently, Sally and Michael and Arthur would accompany Bill King when he went to St. Sulpice; they would sit in the high organ loft, studying the pattern of shell holes which German guns had cut into the old ceiling of the church in 1870, while they listened to the deep-throated harmonies of Johann Sebastian Bach's chorales with which Bill filled the great auditorium. And when the four attended the Christmas Eve service at St. Sulpice and heard the massed choirs sing the everlasting hymns, they counted their good fortunes and believed they were the happiest young people on earth.

Whenever they could manage to raise the money for tickets, the four would attend concerts. When they had a notice, one day, of the premier performance in Paris of Tchaikovsky's *Pathétique*, under the direction of a famous German conductor, they were among the first in the audience. Three young French music students, stirred by national-

istic emotions and perhaps by some aesthetic objections to the Russian's work, hissed sharply on the necks of Bill, Arthur, and Boardman; they, sitting just in front of the critical Frenchmen, bore with the noise for a few moments, then rose in a body and moved in on the hissers, took them firmly by their coat collars, and threw them out of the concert hall into the arms of waiting gendarmes. Sally applauded.

It was a grand summer for Mike and Sally. Plans for each day were spontaneous, and the pair worked hard and played with abandon.

Michael grew. From the depth of him there came a voice which prompted him, and in his mind there was a sign which guided him. With force came discernment. Lydia Jane Robinson's building was firm and sound. He wrote each week to his mother and to Scott and Jennie. In these letters he inclosed drawings, many of them, which illustrated the things that had attracted his attention and which would make his accounts more interesting to them. Drawing frequently, he learned to understand that you must draw everlastingly; in Keppel's library he ascertained from Leonardo what he was finding through experience: "You should often amuse yourself when you take a walk for recreation, in watching and taking note of the attitudes and actions of men as they talk and dispute, or laugh or come to blows with one another, both their actions and those of the bystanders who either intervene or stand looking on at these things."[1]

He was often to think of these lines, how true they are, when he later walked in the streets of New York, watched the "talk and dispute," the laughter and the fighting, and saw how all these things gave the breath of life to his pen and paper.

Much depended upon Sally; for there was some confusion in Robinson's eye these days, and he struggled to find his way—he studied new things and experienced new ideas. Sally, in many ways the more mature, was instrumental in bringing an integration to his ideas, which often needed organization. Robinson was not a patient young man.

Confirmed in reading, the artist became deeply interested in the writings of Balzac, de Maupassant, Meredith, Henry James, Emerson, and Walt Whitman. "When Lilacs Last in the Dooryard Bloomed" stepped up his pulse and brought a

[1] Leonardo da Vinci, *The Notebooks*, ed. Edward MacCurdy (New York, 1941–42), p. 886.

flush to his cheeks; it developed his enthusiasm for Whitman's power and conflict, which grew with the years. It was the realization of an old ambition when, in 1944, Robinson completed his paintings for *Leaves of Grass*.

Robinson, through Sally, had the opportunity of visiting frequently with Rodin, who helped him see the penetration which a drawing may make and who spoke of the value of drawing continually. The young artist got the habit of drawing as many write or speak; and he increased his ability to see as he came more and more to grips with nature, with which art is, in a way, in constant conflict.

3

Frederick Webb, a prepossessing dilettante who had a flair for doggerel low in style and irregular in measure, wanted to broaden his mind and travel around the world. His mother approved the idea but opposed Frederick's plea that he be allowed to go alone. She proceeded to hunt a traveling companion for him; Robinson considered her proposal a grand opportunity.

Though Robinson was not sure of the definition of his authority and though he could only guess at the scope of his jurisdiction, he was happy to tour the globe. In amiable spirits he and Webb packed up, in the autumn of 1898, and took a boat from southern France, which landed at Naples. The trip was just about right to put them in condition for the next lap, Robinson thought. But in Naples, after the travelers had gone for a sight-seeing trip to Carpaccio on the edge of Paestum, Webb encountered an English girl, who, it developed, was last year's love. And Webb's dreams of Athens, Bangkok, and the Pacific faded as thoughts of a cottage in Sussex turned his head. Robinson, who philosophically concluded that the world was well lost, prowled around in as many ruins as he could find.

All the bills were paid by Webb, of course, so when he rented a ground-floor apartment in Naples, his traveling companion thought it best to share it. The artist wandered around making sketches and became acquainted with the people. He was fascinated by the ease with which most Neapolitans met their problems. Apparently they were conscious of none of life's complexities at all.

Deciding that the yard needed attention, Webb asked Robinson to get some chap to set it in order.

The latter went out and found a young Neapolitan lying on a walk in the sun, and, because the lad was husky, Robinson decided he would do for the job. He politely asked the recumbent figure if he would come and rake the leaves.

"Mama!" called the Neapolitan to a full-blown, middle-aged woman resting her arms on the casement of a window of the third story, "Mam.... ma! Cia pane in cas'?" ("Any bread in the house?")

"Si, c'e sta....," answered the mother unconcernedly.

The young man turned a dark and drowsy eye on Robinson, shook his head slowly, "No....tsk, tsk, tsk....," apologetic but conclusive. He threw an arm over his eyes and went back to sleep.

Robinson managed to interest Webb in Pompeii and the ruins; and, as the weeks went by they studied the great monuments of Rome and, finally, of Florence. Robinson was stirred by the indescribable beauty of the Tuscan city. "For me it was far more appealing than Rome," he recalls. The great work of Masaccio absorbed him, and he sat for hours viewing the Giotto Campanile. He touched the past; he tried to imagine the city of the fifteenth century. "Slowly his artistic personality was maturing," says George Biddle. "In his case it was to mature very gradually indeed, not finally crystallizing until his intellectual tastes had fused with the stark realities of life through his newspaper cartoons a decade and a half later."

Now Robinson saw he must return to Paris, for it was clear that his "services" to Webb could not continue indefinitely. He was ready to take up his work again, and his funds were at low ebb. Shortly after he had put his things in order in Paris, he took a boat for Boston. Because he felt that he had accomplished some of the things he had set out to do, he returned to his family a more confident man. In Boston he found odd jobs to do and remained there for about eight months, during which time he worked on a plaster model of the city which, in 1900, was sent to the Paris Exposition. But he discovered that, after he had known the happy and mellow flavor of Paris, the cold fare of Boston was unpalatable.

However, these months were enriched when, through his friendship with Edward Burlingame

BOARDMAN ROBINSON: *Part One*

1876–1904

Hill and Gregory Mason, Robinson became acquainted with William Vaughn Moody, the Hoosier-born, Celtic poet and author of *The Great Divide*. Moody had a great influence upon the artist and, during the hours they spent together, the painter advanced his knowledge of life and the arts. Frequently Moody read aloud to Robinson from some of his own work; these noble rhythms profoundly moved the artist:

> I stood within the heart of God
> It seemed a place that I had known:
> (I was blood-sister to the clod,
> Blood-brother to the stone.)
>
> I found my love and labor there,
> My house, my raiment, meat and wine,
> My ancient rage, my old despair,—
> Yea, all things that were mine.

Moody, quick with generosity, showed his kindness in many practical ways, lent money to the young painter, and introduced him to his friends in Boston.

Early in 1901 Robinson, according to a plan which he and Sally Whitney had arranged, boarded the train for San Francisco, where Sally was then visiting with her parents. He slept for six nights upon a bouncing coach-seat, wore a large hole in the seat of his one pair of trousers, and arrived in San Francisco a disheartened mass of fatigue.

It was immediately necessary for the artist to find a job and make a living on the West Coast. He knew no one there except Sally and King, who had returned for a visit to his home, and, consequently, he had some discouraging days while he searched for a place to work. However, he had a great enthusiasm and energy; he soon became acquainted with a number of influential people who aided him. Sally and William King were his constant companions; together the three mourned the death of their old friend of Paris days, Arthur Atkins.

Robinson met Bruce Porter, one of the students of John LaFarge and co-founder of the *Lark*, who had earlier married the daughter of William James. When Robinson met him, Porter, who was doing work in stained glass in San Francisco, asked Robinson to help him in executing a commission for the window of the Episcopal church at San Mateo. The influence of working with

Porter was deeply felt by the painter, and he developed an increasing sensitivity for subtle color.

Serious financial problems confronted Robinson despite the hard work he did to make his way. He followed up every idea that he could think of, but his pocket-book remained lean. Finally, he and the sculptor, Arthur Putnam, attempted to revive the San Francisco Art Students' League. Both he and Putnam felt strongly opposed to the academic Mark Hopkins tradition, which prevailed in that section of the country. They were able to persuade only a few students that they were right, however, so they received small wages for their

efforts. Putnam taught a class in sculpture; Robinson supervised the painting. The day when they had to close the doors of their school was a discouraging one indeed.

During bright days it was their custom to combine the funds they had in their pockets; the two artists would lay in a stock of crackers and a five-pound round of cheese against the dreary time when they had nothing else to eat. On lesser days they learned to frequent bars where for fifteen cents they could enjoy a glass of sherry or a stein of beer and all the lunch they wanted, since cold cuts, salads, pickles, and cheeses were gratis with the purchase of the drink. Their money dwindled, and one day they were unable to produce the small amount required for even one serving of beer. So Robinson knew that his time in California was drawing to an end.

When the artist received a letter one day from his former traveling companion's mother, Mrs. Annie Bertram Webb, he thought at first that it might be an invitation to go the rest of the way around the world. Though he was disappointed in that, he welcomed the news she sent. He was to return to Paris immediately, to act as her major-domo and general secretary. He left San Francisco on the first train out, and when he landed in Cherbourg, he was a happy young man.

Mrs. Webb, a kindly person, had many interests and was sympathetic with the arts and with artists. She gathered around her musicians, writers, and painters, and Robinson enjoyed their association. One of his friends during this year was Geraldine Farrar, who was also one of Mrs. Webb's protégés.

Robinson's arrangement with Mrs. Webb stipulated that he was to work half-time for her and devote himself, during his free hours, to painting. Time proved that this arrangement did not work out very happily; though he was in no position to quibble over details, he found himself more and more involved in his job as secretary.

Sally Whitney, in the meantime, had returned to France to continue her work with Rodin. She and her fiancé worked together many times and succeeded in being accepted in the Salon d'Automne, where both showed sculpture and paintings. For them it was a momentous occasion.

Rodin and Whistler were the gods at the turn of the century. Only the select of an inner circle had heard much of Cézanne and the new movement which had set artists upon a new road to adventure. Spiritually, it was a placid period.

In the years which dated from their meeting until the day of their marriage, on November 27, 1903, Sally Whitney and Robinson had come to

know one another thoroughly; their love for each other was no ephemeral thing, it was based upon understanding and was warmed by a deep fire. In the Château du Plessis-Trevise the couple began their life together, though, as Sally remarked, it certainly was not the most comfortable or intimate place for two sensible people to begin. In spite of the fact that finances were always a problem, they had a happy time.

During the first year of marriage, which proved to be the last year that Robinson and his bride were to live in Paris until many years later, the artist put the finishing touches upon his training; he worked both in painting and in sculpture. He managed to finance a studio, which was located on the Boulevard Rochechouart. From his window he could look down upon the Cirque Medrano, where Toulouse-Lautrec had made so many of his colorful drawings. In the quiet of this studio Robinson worked hard that year, painting nudes—in a rather academic manner, he recalls, but valuable for his vocabulary—and building up a larger-than-life form of St. Christopher, which was never cast. Robinson did not have the funds for the casting, and he avoided asking Mrs. Webb for the money to have the job done.

In 1904, with regret at leaving the Paris which had been the scene of so many glad years and yet with eagerness at the prospect of starting the work they had prepared for, the Robinsons took their leave of France. Their hopes were high. When they saw the harbor of New York from the deck of the "Staatendam," they felt they had come home. For them the earth and every common sight was colored by a youthful dream.

PART TWO

The Rainbow comes and goes,

And lovely is the Rose;

The Moon doth with delight

Look round her when the heavens are bare;

Waters on a starry night

Are beautiful and fair;

The sunshine is a glorious birth;

But yet I know, where'er I go,

That there hath passed away a glory from the earth.

1

BOARDMAN ROBINSON had noticed, now and and then, the transiency of the rainbow; he had observed the unabiding quality of the dew-drenched rose of Tyrian grain. By degrees the melting and the growing, the harvest and the white fields, had changed the things he knew. But in the years of youth the goodness of each day was sufficient unto itself.

There is no telling when the artist passed from his first moment to the second, so gradually did he move from the time when each morning promised an undiscovered thought or thing to the day which ground the old and familiar lesson into his consciousness and he lay down at night, sure that it was enough. Thus, because dates and occasions are only the momentary indications of what was and is and will be, there is no one act or scene when we can read the stage-business: "Flourish. Exit the Past, with train. Enter the Future."

The scope and the underlying meaning of the "Intimations of Immortality" will measure the length of the way that the best of men have traveled. It is not that an equation, or even a poem, can tell the full meaning of a complex life; were such condensation possible, the history of drama would be brief. As long as Hamlet lives, though, men will continue to discover that he is relating their biographies. And Wordsworth, because he could transcend himself and write the story of man in three moments, was therefore greater than the man who called him a "Laker."

Only in a manner of speaking could Robinson say that his youth had passed, when he and his wife set foot on the Dutch Line docks in New York. But, though he never lost his humor, he could look back a year later and say, "Where is the visionary gleam?"

When he was unable to make his living by his art during those first years in New York, Robinson had a wry smile for the student days when he thought he had a world to win.

The time that Robinson and Sally moved into a barn loft, in the summer of 1904, and caught the water which dripped from the rough ceiling in tins and pans marked the beginning of a new era in their lives. Underneath the smiles they showed to one another, they knew that era had begun. It was the difference between Paris and New York, between student days and grown-up days.

Robinson looked about him in New York and found attitudes toward art which ranged from indifference to ostentatious confidence. America was not then what it seems to be today: "art-conscious." In general, there was an apathetic ignorance about painting. Those who bought pictures were, by and large, indiscriminately eclectic in their choice of European *objets d'art*, usually of Renaissance vintage, which they purchased from knowing dealers. The finest American collections proved that Royal Cortissoz was right when he wrote that "it was plain from the records of the sales room that in America art was coming to be regarded more and more as a stable asset." The phrasing was meant to be complimentary.

As he began to realize that he would not be received with open arms, with gifts of robes and golden rings, Robinson was presented with the choice of assuming an expatriate resentment toward the provincialism of his countrymen or of bowing to the existing prejudices and giving in to popular demand. He accepted neither choice. He would not follow Whistler, nor would he become a Charles Dana Gibson. Robinson decided to remain in New York and work there until that which he had to give should be received.

He had much to learn. As Sally told him, he had lost the trick of the American character; he would have to find and master the manner of speaking to the people with his own voice. He had to walk about in the streets of New York, to watch for the things which Leonardo had written about: the people—angry and fighting, making peace and love, singing, walking, and standing silent. And while his wife worked, licking stamps in a publishing office and doing editorial work for an encyclopedia, Robinson roamed about in New York and made drawings. He sold not a one.

The Robinsons moved from one dilapidated rooming-house to another more sordid. Possessing nothing but a sense of humor, they were thus prevented from thinking themselves tragic.

There was simply no work for the young artist. After he had been rejected by juries of numerous exhibitions, he came slowly to the realization that he did not fit into the times and, furthermore, that he could not surrender to their demands.

The most prominent magazines were *Harper's*, *Scribner's*, the *Century*, and *Everybody's*. Robinson sent drawings to all of them and sold approximately a single work to each. It was not that some of the editors did not see their quality; it was simply that the public was not ready for his way of drawing. The illustrations which the editors demanded were impossible, thought Robinson, after he had

seen *Figaro*. So with wholehearted humor he went his way, doing his work with a high standard.

Robinson's manner of drawing at this time was somewhat similar to the work that Forain did in Paris. Because the Parisian *Figaro* had only a select group of readers, composed of those who wished to keep in touch with the advance guard in the literary and art world, it was not surprising to the artist that there was no American newspaper or magazine of such quality which would sell to the reading masses, even in New York.

Many of the American editors were unaware, of course, of the abilities of their most advanced illustrators. Instead of encouraging the development of new methods and brilliant styles, they asked artists like Robinson to illustrate books and stories in the manner of Harrison Fisher. It was almost demoralizing, but not quite. Robinson held fast to his ideal and, in the end, he prevailed. For this reason Warren Chappell has written of him, "Both as a pictorial reporter and as a political cartoonist, he changed the face of American newspaper drawing. He was, perhaps, the first American illustrator to believe strongly that any drawing is to be dealt with as a composition just as seriously as a painting is."[1]

Robinson said to the editors: "I do not think of making a cartoon, in your popular interpretation of that word; I try to make drawings, and I want to make these drawings what I see and understand in the works of the great draftsmen." He convinced no one but himself.

After the first year of insupportable reverses Robinson saw that to sustain his wife and himself he would have to seek employment outside the field of art. In 1905 he went out to find any work which would offer a living wage. When he applied to the Association for the Improvement of the Condition of the Poor in New York, he obtained a job as a field worker. The experience was a good one. For the next year Robinson studied human beings and their problems as before he had examined their arts. It was an opportunity for him to draw and learn; it was the time when he found out what it is to draw from *life*.

"This experience made a socialist of me, as it

[1] Warren Chappell, in *The Dolphin*, No. 4, Part 2 (New York: Limited Editions Club, winter, 1941).

1904–25   did of all those of our group who had a grain of sense," said Robinson, as he turned back to that period when he worked in the homes of the impoverished and the disheartened of a great city which seemed indifferent to them. The influence of this experience can hardly be overestimated.

After a year of satisfying work with the association, Robinson was promoted to a desk position, which was irksome to him, and he resigned. He never forgot, however, the "field," the poverty, the dismal aspect, and the frustrations which devoured the spirits of the wretched who suffered dire want. His memory of these things has been revealed in his work.

2

Arthur Turnure, *Vogue* publisher, was quick to spot a good illustration. When he paid twenty-five dollars for one of Robinson's drawings, the artist was jubilant. His star was ascending. When he saw that Turnure used the drawing for the cover, he was sure the star was a fixture in the firmament. He had no further doubts when the publisher offered him the art editorship at a salary of a hundred dollars a month. He remained on the *Vogue* staff until 1907. The magazine was not the prominent periodical then that it is today; the editor, with modest candor, referred to it as "the leading toilet paper in America." Edna Chase, a close friend of the Robinsons, worked as a clerk in the office in 1906; later, under Condé Nast, her worth was recognized, and she was made editor. The Robinsons became a part of Ilka's imperfect past when she later came to live with them during her mother's illness. Sally's heart opened to the child, for her own daughter Barbara had died in 1909.

Robinson's bank account fluctuated, during this period, from the few extra dollars which he and his wife were able to save, to a low level when they were informed by a stern cashier that they had overdrawn again. Their problems would have been worse had it not been for the impersonal and easy generosity of an old friend, Franklin P. Adams. Without being asked, he often came to the rescue and filled the Robinson larder. Adams was then working for the *New York Evening Mail*, and in his spare hours he labored over his *Tobogganing on Parnassus*, with scholarly dreams tucked away inside him which the artist and his wife encouraged.

"Adams is really a very serious soul, as all humorists are," said Robinson.

By the year 1907 things were on the upswing for Robinson, and, with new hope and confidence, he

W. J. FERGUSON

created a more powerful cartoon-drawing. The New York *Morning Telegraph*, a racing, sporting, and theater sheet, "the official organ of New York's race tracks, whore-houses, and barber shops," gave him the opportunity he had struggled for; he was urged to do as he pleased with the art section of the paper. The Sunday editors objected violently to the artist's work and went frequently to the editor-in-chief, W. E. Lewis, complaining about the nature of the work that Robinson was submitting to them. They argued that the drawings were beside the point and out of line with the editorial policy of the *Telegraph*. But Mr. Lewis, a somber, world-weary Missourian who liked Robinson, always defended him: "Oh, your paper is no good, anyway. Let Robinson alone; he's having a good time!" The art section was Robinson's domain, and, because the editor made it so, he has a claim for reward; for these drawings that Robinson made for the New York paper are today important source material for the students who study draftsmanship. He was considered a master of the pen and brush by his colleagues, men who later became well known. Says John Sloan, in his life-account, *Gist of Art:* "Boardman Robinson's illustrations in the New York *Morning Telegraph* were a great inspiration to me."[2]

His reputation as a black-and-white artist whose brilliance has not been surpassed in the history of American journalism was founded while Robinson was on the staff of this unique newspaper. He drew his impressions every day, seeking his subject matter from the streets of New York, looking for the things which were significant and replete with life and the richness thereof. In his scope he included also the cartoons for the theater section and for the illustrated Sunday edition.

Now the artist passed from what might be termed the Forain-influence to a quick and restive style of his own, which pierced the essence of the subject and permeated the drawing with rich meaning; it was soon recognized as one of distinction and high quality. He had a way of getting to the essence of a thing and presenting it with economy and force of line. He slashed out at complexity and pointed his pen at the heart of simplicity. Quickly the readers, as well as discriminating editors and publishers, were attracted to this power; and the name of Robinson was as secure in New York as names ever are in that town. His first victory in his profession was won.

During the three years that the artist worked on the *Telegraph* he was disciplined in the basic rule which is the guide of every good newspaper cartoonist: Fortune favors the bold. Minus boldness, the cartoonist is a mosquito; blessed with audacity,

[2] John Sloan, *Gist of Art* (New York, 1934), p. 1.

he becomes a rattler with fangs a yard long and bloody.

So it came about that, at the age of thirty-four, Robinson had won his place among the best in his field. He was sought out. In 1910 Paul Hanna, son of Mark Hanna, owner of the *Cleveland Leader*, came to the cartoonist with a generous offer. At the same time Horace Greeley's old newspaper, the *New York Tribune*, invited him to remain in New York and, as inducement, held out a fabulous salary. Robinson was all the while determined to remain in New York because he enjoyed the excitement of being in the heart of the publishing center; too, he and his wife appreciated the metropolitan life which gave them unlimited opportunities for self-education. He chose to continue on in the city, accepting the *Tribune*'s proposition.

The *Tribune* position was liberal not only in money but also in its stipulations concerning the artist's work. He was given carte blanche; "his office was to be his castle." Now, every newsman knows that no office is a castle, but he does not complain until it becomes a concourse. Robinson's, it turned out, was more like a castle; he did his drawings almost as he pleased. He was, however, aware of the fact that his leftist trends were frowned upon. He has come to think of that time on the New York daily as his most conservative period.

Whitelaw Reid, a war correspondent under Horace Greeley and one of the advanced and brilliant newsmen of his day, owned the *Tribune*. When Reid was sent as ambassador to the Court of St. James he deposited a large authority in the hands of two extremely conservative members of the editorial staff. It was with Clinton Gilbert, however, that Robinson, happily, did most of his work. Gilbert, a thoughtful liberal who was admired by his colleagues, maintained his place in the vanguard of the leading issues during a precarious span of years. Robinson and his companions in the *Tribune* offices, Franklin P. Adams and Heywood Broun, worked and played in fun and harmony. One of their colleagues, Royal Cortissoz, who was art critic for the *Tribune* at the time, still holds the same position today. As Guy Pène du Bois, who worked with him a year on the paper, phrases it,[3]

[3] *Artists Say the Silliest Things* (New York, 1940), p. 168.

1904–25 Cortissoz has "with the passage of time and the lengthening of experience grown mellower"; but he was greener on the vine when Robinson, Broun, and Adams raided his patch and found his flavor often a bit sour. They admired his integrity, nonetheless, and thought that perhaps he would turn out to be a better critic than journalist.

When Gilbert left for Washington, D.C., to syndicate a newsletter, the artist missed his support. The *Tribune*, shortly after the death of Whitelaw Reid, passed into the hands of his widow and his son, Ogden Reid. Mrs. Ogden Reid, an energetic and intelligent woman, maintained a strong voice in the meetings which determined the policies that the newspaper followed.

Though his own newspaper work was absorbing, Robinson found time to participate in certain educational activities. Frank Crowninshield, at the time the art editor of *Century Magazine*, a close friend of both Edna Chase and Robinson, grew worried about the state of the public taste. He and Robinson often discussed this deplorable condition, and, in 1911, they hit upon a plan which would improve the quality of the "art objects" which cluttered up the whatnot shelves in the homes of America. They decided to present an "Exhibition of Bad Taste." In a vacated storeroom on Thirty-second Street, across from the Astoria, the three aesthetic uplifters rounded up the most frightful articles of nonsense collected since the Crystal Palace Exhibition of 1851: a Venus de Milo with a clock cunningly placed in her stomach; a dustpan bordered with a relief of fat and frivolous angels; patchwork quilts daintily designed in pinks and lavenders; china-painting, à la mode; and the hundred and one things which had been unfortunately affected by the *art nouveau* period. To the sponsors' surprise the newspapers upset their calculations by speaking in disrespectful terms of the exhibition. Many editors were plainly piqued because the show appeared to them to be severely critical of their long-established ideas of interior decoration.

During these four years, 1910–14, Robinson met with success, not alone in the mundane sense but also in his artistic growth. He had not sacrificed his ideal of drawing as an offering to popular taste; rather, he had championed the cause of the

best that he could envision. In that arena where the force of excellence conflicts with the power of the common mind—that might to which Aldous Huxley refers as "the enormous stupidity of the average"—the fight goes seldom to the brave. Robinson was fortunate as well as valiant. He became aware, in France, that whatever qualities go

ETIENNE GIRARDOT

into the nature of an artist, quailing modesty is not one of them; now he stepped forward to have his say. The creator in any of the arts must set out to tell the world; he must speak out with conviction. Because creation is not altogether an intellectual business, he must rely upon the faith that what he feels, thinks, and says in his work is valuable. In his physical prime, Robinson was not lacking in this faith; his drawings developed a new brilliance.

Adolf Dehn, who was intensely interested in the work which he studied in the newspapers and magazines of this period, says: "Robinson's drawings were like young oaks in a forest of weary willows. They were vigorously disliked by most people, though an occasional editor and many artists knew that these cartoons and illustrations were also rare drawings. Particularly the young art student valued them, so that Robinson's direct influence on many of us was profound. Such artists as Reginald Marsh, Ivan Opfer, and David Fredenthal are a few of the many who would heartily concede this influence. In the field of cartooning to this day I see the hand of Robinson still at work. He created a style of cartoon which was vigorously and freely drawn, as against the cross-hatches of *Punch* and the old *Life*. The work of such men as Robert Minor, Clive Weed, Daniel Fitzpatrick, Rollin Kirby, Fred Ellis, Edmund Duffy, and Jacob Burck shows that they have looked at Robinson's drawings long and well. At first it was about the only good influence. Until now it has been the best one."

Many of the readers of the *Tribune* came to recognize this influence as they grew to admire Robinson's convictions. One of them wrote to the editor: "In that group of illustrations Robinson has attempted many things—political caricature, a glance at the manners and customs of the day, a shy at the stage in good natured portraiture, an echo here and there of foreign affairs—a various criticism of life. Some day all this will be of value to the historian who would catch a glimpse of us as we actually are."

Robinson was a prosperous, successful man. His work was growing in popularity, and he became well known in various circles in New York. His associations with literary personalities, actors, musicians, and artists added flavor to his life. He developed a range of his personality; he was sought out, he enjoyed his friends and made a reputation for his wit and his charm. As a New Yorker he was decidedly in the swim.

3

Vacation days were pleasant during those tranquil years. Just around the Second Cliff, near Scituate, Massachusetts, lay a rolling tract of green not larger than Boston Common. In the very center the Gillmore's tennis courts, a geometric plot of gray, relieved the smoothly flowing acres of

thick, well-tended grass. Over toward the east the Atlantic, in her best mood and moving gracefully, designed a border of cool blue, repeating here and there small units of triangular white with long and wavering lines trailing against an aqua background. Light salt air, sun-warmed and fresh, breathed over all the shore land, whispering a reassurance to Bostonians and New Yorkers that vacation days would not end in early September. Bicycles crawled up the sloping hills, then darted down, carrying girls with large flaring hats and lads with sailor-straws. Dark and light spotted the tennis courts, where Robinson and his friends had gathered; and the laughter of the players reached the guests, who lolled in wicker chairs on the bungalow veranda, near which O. Henry, the Gillmore's fat bulldog, lumbered about and snorted.

Mr. Gillmore called, "Here, here!" and the dog galloped across the lawn, wheezing and puffing. Gillmore pounded the fat ribs with the flat of his hand. O. Henry shut his eyes and grinned.

The host watched his guests while they gesticulated and moved about in animated conversation. "Regular word factory, this place," he grumbled to O. Henry, who yawned. Sauntering over to the group, he listened to his wife tell someone that the weather was always grand near Scituate, just grand.

Lying in a hammock, Inez Gillmore interrupted herself briefly to introduce her husband to the young woman who had arrived from the village. "Miss Cartwaith—you *are* a reporter from Boston? I think it's wonderful for women to do things —my husband, Mr. Gillmore. You've read his detective stories? My dear, Miss Cartwaith would like to interview some of our 'literary stars and artistic notables' and I was just telling her how we all happened to be here."

"You see, we Gillmores—that is, Rufus and I— were the pioneers," Mrs. Gillmore turned back to the reporter. "It was a case of one person inviting another, and of his friends inviting other friends until all the friends of even those we don't know very well come here to visit with our friends. It's rather involved sometimes, but we enjoy it, don't we, Rufus?"

"I was just telling Miss Cartwaith about our place and," the hostess spoke to her guest, "you

1904–25 will want to interview Will Irwin and Boardman Robinson. They are all down at the court, so there's no need of going there because they'll be up here in half an hour, so I may as well tell you about them, and you'll have your lead, won't you?"

Gillmore stretched his length on the grass, puffing at his pipe and preparing to prompt his wife. O. Henry approached to have his thick neck scratched.

"Those two, Robinson and Irwin," continued the hostess, "don't seem to look very much alike, but each calls the other by his own name—I mean Will calls Boardman Bill and Boardman calls Will Mike, you see, because Boardman is really Mike and not Boardman. No one ever calls him Boardman."

The reporter seemed confused, and O. Henry moaned softly as Gillmore stroked the bulldog's ear. Gillmore puffed placidly away.

"And you," he prompted.

"Oh, yes, I wonder what you think of this for a title, 'Phoebe, Ernest, and Cupid,'" Mrs. Gillmore resumed. "I am just finishing something, and I think that's a good title, don't you? I like it. We all work here. That's why we have rooms with typewriters upstairs, and very often you'll find writers working up there in the morning."

"Yeah, a regular word factory, this place," nodded Mr. Gillmore.

"You'll hear all about them when they come up from the tennis courts. Isn't it about time they finished their set, Rufus?"

"It's four-thirty," said Mr. Gillmore.

On the tennis courts a tournament was breaking up. Four figures were seen to leave the nets, racquets under their arms and jackets flung loosely over their shoulders. They walked up the incline, arguing and laughing, until they came within earshot, when Mrs. Gillmore's voice reached them: "There you are! Oh, Mr. Robinson, Mr. Irwin, come up. There's someone here to interview you."

"What! No one to see me? And me the winner of the invisible cup of Second Cliff," shouted Franklin P. Adams. "You may quote me as saying that I was lucky, that my opponent was in top form and he gave me a stiff battle. Carl Ruggles, the Winona Wonder, nearly did me in. But my superior footwork won me the match; and I guess I'm just smarter than he is, too," he concluded bashfully.

The foursome gathered around the lawn table, where Gillmore fixed drinks for them. In a happy mood, Irwin and Robinson dropped into wicker chairs, propped their chins with their knees, and turned to the reporter.

"Are we going to get our pictures in the paper?" asked Irwin gleefully.

O. Henry growled uneasily as Ruggles and Adams settled down near him and tickled his nose with spears of grass.

"Well, now," continued Irwin, "first of all, we don't think an artist should ever—that is, hardly ever—come before his public."

"Right," echoed Robinson. "He should be aloof, apart, and beyond. Though his work may belong to the people, he himself belongs . . . ."

"Best thing yet," broke in Irwin, "in light of such truth—though it be couched in a hackneyed phrase—is for you to interview him about me and me about him. Only let me explain: we are supposed to look like brothers. Notice it?"

Irwin scooped his scant sandy hair upward and proceeded to look as much like Robinson as possible. "Robinson's hair is so thick he can't do a thing with it; he doesn't even bother to comb it, I hear," Irwin confided to Miss Cartwaith.

"Well, go ahead. You talk about me," urged Robinson.

"You asked me, or you might have asked me, when did Robinson get the urge to draw funny faces . . . ." began Irwin.

"When I met Will Irwin," interrupted the cartoonist.

The reporter looked at Robinson. "Why does Mr. Irwin write?"

"I must confess I don't know," answered Robinson. "All his friends ask the same question." He turned to Irwin, "By the way, why do you write, Mike?" Robinson explained to Miss Cartwaith, "You see, he's Mike and I'm Will."

"I am misunderstood, not appreciated," Irwin looked sad. "There are cases in history—but never mind. I'm not sure I do look like Robinson, after all. Frankly, isn't there something in my face that Robinson's lacks?"

"Yes, one of my cigars," conceded Mr. Gillmore.

"I must say," the hostess intervened, "it seems

to me you are not being very fair with Miss Cart-waith. Why don't you interview Mr. Ruggles and Mr. Adams, instead? They are more interesting, anyway. Tell her, Carl, about the symphony orchestra you founded in Winona, Wisconsin—or was it Minnesota—which was, Miss Cartwaith, the biggest musical organization west of Milwaukee, or someplace in the vast west. Carl did a beautiful job, single handed, all alone, and he sold vegetables. Didn't you, Carl?"

Before Ruggles could arouse himself to this challenge, Mrs. Gillmore forgot about him and called gaily to a guest who had come from the house. "Oh, Miss Cartwaith, I want you to meet our highwayman, I mean a real ex-highwayman from the Panhandle. Miss Cartwaith, Mr. Al Jennings!"

Mr. Jennings acknowledged the introduction with a nod of his head, took a glass, and sat down near the reporter.

"I used to be a desperado, but I got converted," he said sincerely. "I never liked to kill people."

Seeing Miss Cartwaith's startled face, Robinson threw her a reassuring smile and asked Jennings, "Who was the last man you killed?"

"An Indian. I was riding alone, out there in Oklahoma, and this Indian was following me. Pretty soon I figured he aimed to get me in a tight spot and rob my carcass."

"And what did you do?" breathed Miss Cartwaith.

"I had to shoot the bastard," Al Jennings brooded, fixing his cold blue eyes on the tennis courts.

Sometime during 1910 Robinson became a member of the Players Club, at Gramercy Park, an organization so exclusive that it heartlessly turned away from its doors all drama critics. Here in this old home of Edwin Booth, the founding father and sustaining spirit of the club, Robinson met editors and publishers, whose friendship often provided him with excellent opportunities. He was in the Players for the fun of it, though, and not for business reasons. For many years the club was an important part of the cartoonist's life.

The Players Club was home for Allan Pollock, an English comedian, whose pet abominations were Billie Burke and Charles Frohman and who, after the war, brought to New York the *Bill of Divorcement* in which he played the leading role. His was a saturnine and gloomy character, per-

versely and intensely funny, which endeared him to all the members. He and Albert Sterner, one of Robinson's intimate friends, were frequently seen together in the lounge.

On an excursion trip to Bermuda, where they were to rest for a week, Rollin Kirby and Robinson discovered Pollock on board the boat and persuaded him to join them at the resort island for a period of complete relaxation and leisure. Upon their arrival the three moved into the largest room in the most elegant hotel in Bermuda, where, as Robinson says, they "reverted immediately to

carefree childhood." A Mr. Glaenzer, noted for his epicurean taste, a gourmet who meticulously superintended the preparation of each meal which he served to his guests, invited the New Yorkers to a lavish dinner. When the *pièce de résistance* was set before Pollock, he automatically sprayed it heavily with the salt shaker. Kirby noticed the stark horror on the host's face.

"Le diner est salé, Monsieur!" he protested with fluttering hands.

Pollock continued to ply the shaker, staring

1904–25

moodily at his plate, and said finally with maddening tranquillity, "I like salt." He applied the pepper with his left hand.

After a hectic week the comedian returned to New York and to the sheltering walls of the club, and he could not be inveigled by Kirby or Robinson to leave their security again. "You are wasting high time," he replied to further blandishments and invitations and remained in the lounge with Albert Sterner to listen to Otis Skinner and E. H. Sothern extol the sacred name of Booth, which they pronounced "Booth-ah."

Robinson's most ebullient companion, however, was Glenmore ("Stuffy") Davis, a press agent with a glimmering eye and a glittering bald head, whose charm was all that exceeded his unparalleled imaginative talent. Davis had never known the meaning of the word "surfeit" because of his splendid constitutional endowments. He belonged to the Lambs Club, and one evening he asked Robinson to join him for a round of drinks. Quite early in the morning they rode to the door of the club in a hansom cab, and Davis, hospitable and kindly, insisted that the cabby join him and Robinson at the bar. The driver expressed concern for his horse, the night air having set in, and so the passengers, ever mindful of the comfort of animals, unhitched the gelding and led him up the steps and on, triumphantly, through the sacred portals of the Lambs Club. Flushed with magnanimity, Davis registered all four at the desk and ordered service. But this kindly act was an uneventful one in the life of the press agent who staged his most magnificent gesture of compassion the day he drove a herd of elephants down to the beach at Coney Island and bathed them with bricks and salt water.

The most memorable occasions at the Players Club were the New Year's Eve celebrations, when the members gathered around in various degrees of sobriety to listen solemnly, stirred to grave tenderness, while Tommy Safford, sober as the church organist he was, accompanied himself on the piano, improvising:

> 'Twas brillig, and the slithy to-o-oves
> Did gyre and gimble in the wabe:
> All mimsy were the borogo-o-oves. . . . .

There was not a dry eye in the place.

In September, 1912, the breezes at Scituate, Massachusetts, were pleasant; the nation was basking in the sun of contentment. The scale of the gold standard was weighted by the unblinking faith of millions; the American home was safe, for God and His everlasting blessing had so ordained it; William Randolph Hearst invested in European real estate, crated it, and shipped it to California; the most durable Model T of the series was produced by Henry Ford at Detroit; Lincoln Steffens guarded the temples of integrity and threw good black dirt at those who slung mud at the structure of democracy.

"From there it looked like an expansive time," says Boardman Robinson. There were to be no more wars; even the soldiers believed it. Reform was rampant. Liberalism was so popular it frightened the liberals. On the Main Street of every Middletown, Optimists' Clubs lunched weekly in hotel dining-rooms. Progress forever was the general idea.

Bankers thought highly of homeowners who did not open charge accounts. The high-school attendance records pointed to the time when America's illiteracy percentage would be less than Germany's. Annoyed at being tripped, now and then, in its magnificent stride by belittling, carping trust-busters, big business recognized the bigger things which were still up ahead. America, the beautiful, was loved by the solid citizens and exploited by the aggressive.

Now, upheld by good judgment and backed by a respectable checking account, the Robinsons spoke seriously of building their own home. They discovered a corner lot in a restricted area in Forest Hills and consulted Harrie Thomas Lindeberg, a creative architect. Sally spent most of her time on this project and, after the plans were drawn, she supervised the construction of the building. As she remembers it today, "it was fun, but it didn't last."

Gregarious, interested, and happy with the world; feeling that art is, as John Sloan says, above all, a response to "the living of life," Robinson enjoyed the days at Forest Hills. The first son, John, now six years of age, helped Sally while she cared for his brother, Bartlett Whitney, who was born in 1912. In the new and beautiful home the memories of hard times faded quickly; the Robinsons were grateful for luxuries they had not hoped to possess. The mood of the period was reflected in summer vacations and the recreations which occupied the time of Americans during a year, for example, which was to be used as a standard for the "normal."

Called in illness and entertained with good will when he dropped in at the Robinsons' for an evening's talk, Dr. Frederick H. Bartlett, whose daughter Phyllis came to live with the artist's family for a year, was always welcome. His services to the family, for which he would accept no money, were manifold. Dr. Bartlett, whose friendship the Robinsons were delighted to acknowledge in the naming of their second son, shared Sally's hospitality with the many friends—Edna Chase, Heywood Broun, F. P. Adams, Walter Pritchard Eaton among them—who were frequent visitors at Forest Hills.

The work at the *Tribune*, offering security and freedom, gave Robinson time for thoughts about painting. He was in close touch with many of the artists whose studios were located in New York during the decade from 1905 to 1915.

4

The cartoonist had a deep sympathy for the new insurgency, which, coming in with the century, expressed itself in the now celebrated group, "the Eight." Though, as Martha Cheney very correctly points out in *Modern Art in America*,[4] "the fact must be stressed . . . . that he was a thorough independent," Robinson was a force which ran parallel to that of such men as Robert Henri, John Sloan, and George Luks, especially those three. After analyzing the work of Forain and Daumier, which had markedly impressed him in Paris ten years before the Eight held their famous exhibition, it was difficult for the artist to see what it was that so shocked the people that they would paste these painters with the appellation, "Ash Can School" or the "Revolutionary Black Gang."

Robinson, with a more extensive background than most of his contemporaries had had the opportunity to develop, because of his European experiences, was not then militantly "regionalistic," nor has he ever been; this attitude is clearly revealed in his lecture, "Regionalism in Art," which he gave on the occasion of the dedication of the Colorado Springs Fine Arts Center. He has always seen the value in doing his work close to the earth upon which he lived and labored. So, though

[4] (New York, 1939), p. 129.

he was completely in sympathy with the artists who portrayed the American scene, he was not intimately connected with them, nor were others who were sincerely interested in a healthy and functional art form for this country.

The cartoonist looked with suspicion upon Kenyon Cox and the National Academy group. But by temperament he was incapable of joining up with an opposition force. Even healthy and good movements, he thinks, are vitiated by organization. He likes to tell Lincoln Steffens' story about the devil and his earthly lieutenant who, walking one day in the streets of a great city, happened to see the arresting face of one human being whose features were aflame with a transcendent light. The devil's companion faltered in his step as he turned to his master and said: "Look! What are you going to do about that? There goes a man who has found a truth." The devil walked on in silence for a moment, then turned a reassuring smile upon his friend, "Don't worry, I'll have him organize it."

Robinson's relationship with the newspaper artists and the group of painters who were then most active in America was always one from which he derived a deep satisfaction. He went to many parties with his fellow-artists and listened often to George Bellows, who used to entertain at gatherings of artists with his renditions from *Pagliacci*. George Luks, an illustrator for the *New York World*, and John Sloan, who once worked for the *Philadelphia Inquirer*, drew their cartoons with the same lusty enthusiasm, the same outgoing tenderness for those things which live in the light of common day, that motivated the *Tribune* artist. And though Robinson never associated himself with a *movement*—he was not known as a painter at that time, anyway—he is a part of that important period in American art which marked the heated climax of the fight between the "dead" and the "alive." Fundamentally, this battle was a bout between sterile minds and forms rescued from the ashes against blood-fed brains and forms which would contain living ideas. It was not "Ash Can" artists against French-trained or, if you will, "Non-Ash Can" painters.

Certainly, not all artists who have contributed to the history of painting during the last thirty years were in full sympathy with Henri and his

1904–25 group. Like George Biddle, who inherited his mood from the French school and who still argued with the Philistines that "a fine passage of painting needs no moral or ulterior justification" and, consequently, looked down his nose at the American rebels—Sloan, Henri, Luks, and Bellows, some American artists were conscientiously not with the "Gang." And as time examines closely the work, for example, of two of the insurgents, Henri and Bellows, it finds that Bellows left much half-developed and that his teacher, Henri, frequently filled voids with the very adroitness of his brush. However, as Robinson says of Henri: "He was a great liberal, though his liberalism was seldom, to my mind, exemplified in his work." Inasmuch as art is a vision and technique is the handmaiden, the essence of what the courageous "Revolutionary" advocated became the controlling spirit of later American painting. "The greatest importance of the Henri group," according to Holger Cahill, "was in opening the eyes of American artists to the life around them, to contemporary and local subject matter."[5]

"There is so much talk today about the American Scene," complained Sloan in 1939. "If anyone started the painting of the American Scene it was our gang of newspapermen: Glackens, Luks, Shinn, and myself. . . . . But we didn't really start it. What about Homer, Eakins . . . . ?"[6] The chronicles of American painting support his implied contention, certainly.

It has always been quite useless to argue about regionalism. Such a conclusion may be reached after a close reading of nineteenth-century painting. America was a *pioneer land*, in the most basic interpretation of that overburdened phrase. Hence, though some few painters chose to remain in their native land and paint what they knew of it, most of the artists wearied of their confines of indifference and misinterpretation and went off to Europe, usually to Paris, in the latter half of the century. For every Raphael Peale, George Caleb Bingham, Winslow Homer, or Thomas Eakins, there was a plurality of "expatriates" who sought refuge in the refined atmosphere of the English portrait-

[5] "American Painting, 1865–1934," *Art in America in Modern Times* (New York, 1934), p. 32.

[6] Sloan, *op. cit.*, p. 3.

painter's studio, who traveled to Düsseldorf and Vienna to cultivate heavy tricks and elephantine ideas, or who Bohemianized on the Left Bank and picked up an impressionistic palette at a second-hand shop. Some of them, with European training, retained their senses, worked hard, produced fine paintings, and gave their valuable gift to America. On the other hand, some of the "native" artists, because they were bad painters, were inconsequential, and no amount of latter-day research and nationalistic pride will make them more than that.

It may be too early to get at the whole truth, facts being so unequal to the strain of bearing the total meaning of anything, but in so far as Ben Jonson's warning, "Art has an enemy called ignorance," applies here, more wisdom might be found if there had been less bitterness in the discussion about regionalism versus nonregionalism —or call it what you will—and a more accurate study made of the history of modern painting.

A painter is one who knows how to paint. Such a statement may be an oversimplification, but if it is interpreted sympathetically it may take the

sharp edge off the blade of intolerant dispute which hacks away at understanding. Paul Gauguin may have oversimplified it, also, when he said, "Art for Art's sake, why not? Art for Life's sake, why not? Art for Pleasure's sake, why not? What does it matter as long as it is art?" But what he meant is plain and right. So, looking back upon the work of the Eight, today's student of art will come to the conclusion that what high quality exists—and a good deal does remain—must be discovered in the manner in which these painters spoke in the vocabulary of the painter: with shapes, forms, values, colors, and textures. Time will tell.

The Armory show of 1913—officially designated "The International Exhibition of Modern Art"—was to men like Guy Pène du Bois, who lived through it, "an eruption only different from a volcano's in that it was made by man."[7] "It exploded like a bomb," adds Robinson. "It was amazing and stimulating."

In the old Sixty-ninth Regiment Armory, on February 17 of the "gold-standard" year, a group of generous contributors made possible the presentation of approximately sixteen hundred works of European artists. The curiosity of the Americans —a quality of mind so remarkable in them that the people of other nations apprehend it only with profound difficulty—became excited by the exhibition, and thousands upon thousands thronged through the doors of the Armory building. So huge were the milling crowds that the officials of the exhibition, seeking to give opportunity to those who wished to examine the *objets d'art* without suffering physical harm, raised the price of admission during the morning hours to a dollar. And, to the unbelieving eyes of the sponsors, the gate receipts were richly supplemented when thousands of dollars' worth of art was sold to collectors. The exhibition, subsequently, was shown in Chicago and in Boston, where vice-squads, jealous and worried dealers in antiques, provincial art students, conservative and fearful museum-board members, pietistic ministers of the gospel, and incredulous housewives worked themselves into a state where they were fit to be tied.

The newspapers said it was tremendous, using various phrasings, and Walter Pach, who acted as curator-interlocutor, was driven by desperation to employ an effective, if vague, comparison when he was asked for the thousandth time to reveal the figure in Marcel Duchamp's "Nude Descending a Staircase," "Can you see the moon in the Moonlight Sonata?" His answers to the curious questions amused Robinson immensely.

What this exhibition meant to America has been widely discussed, and, whatever the point of view toward it, there has been no disagreement about the importance of the meaning. In a way it was the beginning of "modern" art in this country. For many artists who had studied and traveled in Europe during the previous decade, it was the introduction to Cézanne. Robinson, for his part, was again impressed by the sculpture of Wilhelm Lehmbruck and by the painting of Frenchmen whose work he had never ceased to admire.

There are those who have charged that the healthy influence of the Eight was undermined by

[7] *Op. cit.*, p. 166.

the Armory show; they point out that the waves of post-Impressionist interest which arose after the exhibition submerged the movement which Henri and his friends and followers had heroically advanced. Others have said that, without the catholicizing and purifying powers of the cubist, abstract, and nonliterary painting which was most distinctive in the show, the trends of American art would have gone on toward purblind representation of subject matter with a disregard for the painterly. Either side of the argument bogs down in the mud of the a priori.

Reading the account of what happened to the Eight and to their followers, the exponents of the first position find a basis of fact for their contention. The eye of the young American student, for instance, continued to turn to Paris for more than

a decade after the Armory exhibition; the list of now prominent artists who completed their training in Europe up until almost 1930 is long, and the names are impressive. However, the essential and eternal soundness of the philosophy of Henri's and Sloan's teachings—that the artist must know of that which he speaks—possessed the power of truth; and most of the artists of the postwar period who received some valuable instruction in Europe —usually self-instruction—returned to their native land and worked out their destiny. This was a natural and a sensible procedure.

It would seem that the fundamental conflict was between the *dead* and the *alive*. Both the influences of the "Revolutionary Gang" and the repercus-

1904–25

sions of the Armory show made a united attack upon that dreadful hoax to which the American public had given its unthinking allegiance for such a long time that it had actually come to believe that academic, postiche ornament was the "beauty of art." The attack of the alive in art was successful; it achieved a victory all around.

Robinson made his contribution to this force of *life* in American art. While it is true that, even today, he is not placed in a remarkably prominent position among American painters, it may also be true that the final evaluation of the painters of our time will bring earned recognition to the man who, because he works quietly and confidently in Colorado, is not unduly concerned with the honors which are granted each season in the galleries of a distant city. He would want no apology to be made for him. He argues no case for himself. But the very quality of vitality and of truthful expression, as it has been revealed in American painting during these last five years, is that quality which is Robinson's own quality and that of the healthy movements in the history of our painting—the *alive* in art; the sincerity which comes from an understanding of the subject under consideration; the subjugation of skill to idea; the promotion of form over sentimental literalism; the conviction that even truth makes itself known only through the quality of the form.

Always the dynamics of art will bring about changes in the appearance of any individual's expression. And with the change and flow of time, whole eras of creation may be dismissed while the new one is acclaimed. But there needs to be, always, that awareness of the alive which Robinson, for one, always has maintained.

5

August, 1914, cracked like doom. Anxious eyes watched the European scene; wishful thoughts expressed a common illusion, "It will be over soon." But the realists knew that Viscount Grey's expression was prophetic and that the lamps would go out.

Because of the happiness they found in the "normal" years, the Robinsons, like most families in America, were unprepared for the shock. Soon they felt it. In the late summer of 1914 the cost of

the cable tolls to the *Tribune* had grown to astronomical proportions. The outgo of money staggered those who were financially responsible for the newspaper, and frantic efforts were made to reduce current operation expenses.

It was a brutal blow to the Robinsons when they realized that their home was in jeopardy; the cartoonist's job was insecure. Robinson's salary was such a drain that for the sake of the budget, reasoned the board of the *Tribune*, he would have to be ousted. The artist, without a contract, was caught. He left the paper, and, shortly after, the family sold its home and moved to Croton-on-the-Hudson, into a wreck of a building which had no water, no bath, and no furnace. They lived there for nine years. Not until 1930 were the Robinsons to know any degree of economic security again.

The artist began, as a free-lance illustrator, to work for the popular magazines, *Collier's, Harper's Weekly, Puck, Leslie's Weekly,* and *Scribner's.*

In March, 1915, Robinson was selected by the *Metropolitan Magazine*, owned by Harry Payne Whitney, to illustrate a series of articles upon the European war which were to be written by John Reed, a creative reporter and "a terrifically serious human being," as Robinson describes him. Among the "contributing editors" of this magazine were Theodore Roosevelt; Morris Hillquit, liberal Socialist; and Peter Dunne, the "Mr. Dooley" known to everyone.

The cartoonist's reputation, at the time he began this work with Reed, was reported thus by *Vanity Fair:* "He killed the old, badly drawn, cross-hatch-line cartoon, and developed a cartoon which was also a work of art. His big ideas and his big drawings have been reproduced more frequently in European papers than those of any other American artist. In method and grasp he belongs to the bold and simple school of Daumier. A few of his swift lines and a little of his grim, sardonic humor are more deadly than columns of editorials."[8]

The original plan of the *Metropolitan* was to send Robinson and Reed to the Western Front. John Reed had been, for a year, a war correspondent in Germany. Then the idea was advanced by Jusserand, the French ambassador to the United States, that the writer and his illustrator should go to

[8] "A Dozen of the Most Distinguished Illustrators," *Vanity Fair*, August, 1915.

France and report the progress of the war from the viewpoint of the Allies.

Robinson, with only his first papers filed, was not yet a naturalized citizen of the United States. He appealed to William Jennings Bryan, Secretary of State, who recommended that a passport be issued to the artist, but his application was denied him by the visa authorities. In the meantime, John Reed, viewed with grave suspicion by many leading citizens, was thoroughly denounced as a radical by Theodore Roosevelt, who sent his heated views in a letter to the French government. So, despite the promotions of Jusserand, Reed was denied permission to visit the French front, and Robinson had difficulties with his passport.

Determined to take advantage of the opportunity that the *Metropolitan* held out to them, Reed and Robinson appealed to the British consul for permission to enter Italy and to penetrate from there into the Balkans and Russia. They obtained visas and military permission and boarded an English liner bound for the port of Naples.

The account of this spectacular journalistic coup is recorded in John Reed's book, *The War in Eastern Europe*, which was published later by Charles Scribner's Sons. The artist's drawings reveal the drama of war-torn scenes which came to the amazed eyes of these daring correspondents. Daring they were. For months they were in frequent personal danger, especially in the territories of Serbia, Bulgaria, Rumania, Poland, and Russia. For seven months Reed and Robinson lived a precarious but absorbing life in lands which fascinated both.

In a letter sent from old Petrograd on June 25, 1915, Robinson wrote a colorful description to his son John:

"We have just landed here and I am still quivering with the emotion of the first bath in twenty-six days. We have been that time reaching Petersburg from Bucharest, the details of which extraordinary trip I can't tell you here because of the censorship—most unfortunately—for it is an amusing and distressing tale. . . . . My feet feel very well indeed but alas! I am afraid I am permanently flat-footed. We have been living for nearly three weeks on Kosher food—not always palatable, but generally wholesome. . . . .

"All that we have seen of the city in driving from the station looks equally ugly and forbidding. The country we have come through, however,

"The War in Eastern Europe"

1915

since leaving Galicia—though somewhat forbidding, too—is rather splendid in its interminable features—mostly second growth, often mixed with slender birch saplings—gleaming in white stripes through the red green of the pines. . . . .

"The river Neva—about as wide as the East River—flanked by massive granite parapets, cuts the city of Petra in two, and from everywhere along its banks offers a perspective of sinister magnificence. The winter palace of all the secular structures is the most architectually execrable. There ain't no sech animal; and yet it's strangely impressive in its dull, red, peeling, stuccoed, shambling way.

"As for the churches! Well—when the Church of the Resurrection of Jesus Christ dawned on my astonished eyes, I just shinnied up the nearest wall and jibbered. It looks more like the resurrection of Coney Island after a long term in hell. . . . . Most of the churches are of late Byzantine School and give you the early Byzantine pip to look at 'em. In the center of them usually rises a tower that's a cross between a French 'sâle petit villa de Banlieu' and a Ninth Avenue 'L' station surmounted by a lemon colored onion and surrounded on the main roof by a whole litter of other onions colored everything from indigo blue to Scotch plaid. However, there is one church, quite new, which is surmounted by a wonderful turquoise blue dome—shaped like a tulip bulb. We are right beside St. Isaacs—which is Italian, aggravated by a Russian architect—from which an enormous, velvety bell booms every once in a while, sometimes inciting to an excited and shrill clamor a whole nest of young bells. . . . ."

In a postscript the cartoonist made a sketch and appended this note: "Dear Billy—This is a Russian cab. The driver in his thick, padded coat is called an iztvostchick. Doesn't he look like one? Dad."

BOARDMAN ROBINSON: *Part Two*

1904–25

From Petersburg the two correspondents moved on through a maze of experiences. All the drawings that the artist made during this time were, of necessity, reconstructed from memory in hotel rooms, after each day's observations. To have drawn them on the spot might have meant court martial for the artist and for his companion. These accurate observations were sketched in pen and ink, the subjects freely translated with a skill developed during the years when Robinson was a "roving" artist for the *Telegraph*.

Finally, after a series of harrowing trials which were hardly ever without a side of humor, Robinson and Reed returned to Italy, and from there they set sail for Boston on the White Star Line.

Many of the drawings which the artist executed during those vital months on the Eastern Front are among his most excellent. The humor of bewhiskered Russian generals being ushered into battle by open carriage; the tragedy of the suffering of peasants who wallowed in filth and died in pestilence; the force of the brutal men on horses; the feeble resistance of the weak trampled under foot; the raw horror of war; the comic aspect of the dead who die without a show of dignity—all that and more came to the artist's eye in the guise of life and left his hand in the form of art. He did not bother with an unessential thought, nor did he draw an unnecessary line.

The *Metropolitan Magazine*[9] presented this work with pride and explained to its readers in simple phrasing what Robinson was about: "He maintains that a picture is *finished* as soon as the idea sought is expressed; to polish a surface and 'tickle it up' is at once inartistic and trivial." About the content of these drawings the editor added: "Robinson's magnificent pictures of the Eastern armies have given a new vision to Americans of what this part of the gigantic conflict is really like." Yes, as Robinson said, only the "romantic idealists" had a premonition of what war would be like when America came in for her share; the people, by and large, saw it most clearly in 1915 through the illustrations which set John Reed's words against a complementary, symphonious background.

What meaning this dramatic experience held for the artist is stated succinctly by George Biddle in his Introduction to *Ninety Three Drawings*:

As an event in Robinson's life it [the trip to the Eastern Front] is important for two reasons. Firstly, he came close to war, disease, famine and death, and by that *rencontre* he was inspired to do some of his very finest work. Secondly, it marks in the lives of Robinson and Reed a turning point, or if you prefer to put it, the definition of two parallel currents, that of art and that of social and political preoccupation.[10]

The artist, seeking ways to support himself and his family, was urged to go on a lecture tour with his news and pictures about the Balkans and Russia. There was a growing demand in the country to hear about a part of the world which, to the average citizen of Kansas City and Minneapolis, was vague and distant from him. The Pond Lecture Bureau invited Robinson to give a series of talks about his travels; he was sent to the cities of the Middle West, as far as South Dakota, where he presented "The War in Eastern Europe."

Having been scheduled to appear before the Buffalo Club, in upper New York State, Robinson made his appearance before the "solid mahogany" organization, a phrase which described not only the furniture of the establishment. The speaker began his lecture, aware that he was given a frigid reception because of the very name of his topic; all Russians had bombs tucked away in their boots, and they were persona non grata here. Though some of the men in the audience finally responded weakly to the artist's inimitable way of telling a story, the president of the club was unimpressed. When he returned to New York, the lecturer was asked by his manager, "What in the world did you do out in Buffalo?" The artist, who remembered only that he had been treated royally in the club bar after the question period, said he had had a grand time in Buffalo. "Well," answered Pond, with cold politeness, "will you please read this letter from the president; it may refresh your memory." Robinson read: "Dear Mr. Pond: Don't ever again send a lemon like Boardman Robinson out to Buffalo!"

6

It was during the year 1916 that Robinson began to contribute to the *Masses*. Ever since the year he had been a field worker for the Association for the Improvement of the Condition of the Poor, the cartoonist had indicated his deep concern for the problems of inequity in society. By

[9] *Metropolitan Magazine*, October, 1915, p. 28.
[10] (Colorado Springs, 1937), p. 10.

temperament he was a champion of the unfortunate, by sympathy an exponent of the rights of the minority, though he was acquainted with the rewards which come, usually, to the advocate of the few against the many. He was not a visionary who suffered from a masochistic complex; his interest in the cause of right, as he interpreted it, came from a compassionate heart. So when he viewed and considered all the "oppressions that are done under the sun and beheld the tears of the oppressed," he was not surprised, because he had learned early that "on the side of the oppressors there is power" and he had read enough of the story of man's inhumanity to man to know that those oppressed had been without a comforter for a good long while. No conceited illusions depressed his sense of humor; he has always retained the balance which is characteristic of a man of wit.

Robinson was sincere, however, when he made his drawings depicting the brutal onslaughts of the mighty against the weak. He had drawn them some years before Piet Vlag, the idealistic Dutchman with the accent which sounded so strange to the ears of his parochial young "radicals" of 1911, had hawked the first class-conscious magazine of America in Union Square, calling, "Messes! Messes! Messes!" From the first issue, the cartoonist was interested in the fate of the ragged little sheet; he watched its growth under the loving guidance of Horatio Winslow, the dreamy Latin scholar from Wisconsin, and was happy to see it arrive at an impressive maturity in 1912, when Max Eastman gave it the force of his ability and personality, presenting to New Yorkers a magazine "that is now a success"—an impressive twenty pages in big format with double-page cartoons.

John Sloan, the friend of good causes, began to work with Eastman, as the art editor; and before the exhibition at Sixty-ninth Street startled the nation with the works of the Europeans, the *Masses* had shown its own gallery of painters, who were devoted to both art and society. Their names make an impressive list: John Sloan, Robert Henri, William Glackens, Jo Davidson, George Bellows, Stuart Davis, H. Glintenkamp, Art Young, Cornelia Barnes, K. R. Chamberlain, and Robert Minor.

The editor-in-chief was not slow, on his end, to fill in the roster with names of writers and poets who had spoken for themselves and for the nation during the preceding three decades, men who have written a chapter of American literature: Lincoln Steffens, Will Herford, Howard Brubaker, Franklin P. Adams, Homer Croy, Upton Sinclair, John Reed, William Rose Benét, and Carl Sandburg. One of the few editorial mistakes that Eastman made, by the way, was his neglect of some of the early poems of Sandburg; but he quickly corrected this error when a few successful magazines published the work of the Illinois poet, who, in 1914, was awarded the Levinson prize for his now famous "Chicago." Eastman, a handsome and personable man, was capable of inspiring long-lived loyalties among people who had already, by 1912, gained prominence in the arts, and he had a way of encouraging and supporting the young talent that he was sure to discover. He was himself an able writer with a solid literary background, an editor who has few equals in the history of American journalism.

It was to such a man and to such a cause, a cause in which he had a balanced faith, that Robinson gave of his abilities. He enjoyed doing the work, and he did it for no rewards, as did the others who contributed to the *Masses* and to the later *Liberator* which supplanted the first named after the trial of 1917.

There were the scoffers who sat by, of course, and asked why

> They draw nude women for *The Masses*
> Thick, fat, ungainly lasses. . . . .
> How does that help the working classes?

And there were sincere critics, artists who felt as du Bois did that "the *Masses* draughtsman saw too little of the rich," that often their attacks appeared to be "directed toward the very people they aimed to defend."[11] The pages of the magazine may seem, today, to be somewhat indirect in their aid to the proletariat, and there is no doubt that few of the artists who made cartoons for its double spreads about J. P. Morgan were invited to weekly luncheons with the banker at the New York Yacht Club. The spirit of the magazine, nonetheless, was one which advanced genuine liberal polemic, in word and line; within its hospitable walls the publication invited Pablo Picasso and Reginald Wright

[11] Du Bois, *op. cit.*, p. 116.

1904–25

Kauffman to lie down together between the same editorial sheets. They presented the wholeness of America, in a sense—these artists who selected freely the subjects that indicated her diversity. And "when the *Masses* group touched these subjects, it was their combination of sophistication and naïveté that made what they said so difficult to resist," as Genevieve Taggard said[12] when she was distant enough to be objective and close enough to be informed. The detractors of the *Masses'* artists and writers forgot something of the essential character of the United States; they were unaware, evidently, that these poets and painters were unconsciously answering Walt Whitman when he asked, "Do you suppose the liberties and brawn of These States have to do only with delicate lady-words? With gloved gentleman-words?"

"Them Asses," as they gloried in being designated, kicked up their hind legs and landed squarely, nine times out of a dozen, against the rotund paunches of "respectibilians" and complacent publicans. Such treatment, though it was indelicate, brought sobriety to the citizens who were frequently somewhat unsteady from toasting with too many glasses, "America! America!"

The artists and the writers kicked and pranced; even for the smooth, firm hand of Max Eastman they were hard to hold in check. Finally came the day, inevitably, when they learned that a proverb may become a bromide, that truth repeats itself, that nothing succumbs like success. The war made intolerable what had been passed by as uncomfortable but innocuous; the words and the drawings of the magazines were frequently critical, in 1917, of the policies of the government. In the autumn of that year indictments were handed down by a federal grand jury charging Max Eastman and six members of his staff with having conspired, caused, or attempted to cause insubordination and refusal of duty in the military and naval forces of the United States of America. Floyd Dell, the managing editor, a liberal from Chicago; Josephine Bell, poet; John Reed, radical Communist; H. Glintenkamp, subversive cartoonist; Art Young, author of the famed drawing, "Having Their Fling"—all had serious charges brought against them. Robin-

[12] "May Days," *Nation*, CXXI (September 30, 1925), 353–56.

son was not included in the indictment after it was discovered how many "Christ-subjects" he had drawn, though he was under deep suspicion.

Defense attorneys were Morris Hillquit, one-time Socialist candidate for mayor of New York City, and Dudley Field Malone, former assistant secretary of state and then effective liberal. The trial was a stern affair, though Art Young, who was present at all the meetings of the court, was so unconcerned about his guilt that he slept quietly through the presentation of the case against him. Finally, after two mistrials and some adjustments of viewpoint on both sides, the charge was dismissed. An account of this trial in the June, 1918, issue of the *Liberator*, reveals a picture of the proceedings which made a clear page in the history of American jurisdiction.

Through all its growth and difficulties, the *Masses*—later the *Liberator*—drew to its support a remarkable number of the younger artists, men and women who have since established themselves because of their high competence: Arnold Blanch, Adolf Dehn, Wanda Gág, William Gropper, Morris Kantor, Reginald Marsh, and Maurice Sterne, to name only a few. Europeans, some of whom were to join the American artists in New York during the following two decades, contributed their drawings, along with the work of George Grosz, once one of the greatest liberals of them all.

Among all these artists it was probably Art Young with whom Robinson shared the most of his beliefs about the social-political order. A man of humor can never be thoroughly affiliated with any creed or tenet, but Young was convinced of the worth of socialism. He rested his profound belief in the humble man, and he loved America. "Art Young," said Robinson shortly after the death of the kindly man who wielded a two-edged sword of wit and strength against the evil he saw and opposed, "enjoyed the enmity of small and malicious people. Had he not been so intelligent and so honest, he might have been satisfied to be a congressman; I always told him he wore his collar just right. Yes, Young was really *sui generis*; he belonged."

Although many of the literary figures who contributed to the *Masses* were intimate friends of the artist, Robinson was especially devoted to the man who has been widely misunderstood at the same time that he has been praised for the wrong qualities. John Reed was not the playboy that he was described to be by Theodore Roosevelt, nor was he the dreadful and vicious anarchist that those who suspected the good of any foreign influence charged him to be. He was a man of serious convictions and an ardent advocate of the rights of the humble man. His friend composed "A Memory," when Reed died in Russia in 1920, which speaks of

a pose.

the affection in which the champion of liberalism was held by the artist who knew him as few ever did. This statement was published in the February, 1921, issue of the *Liberator*:

A little more than five years ago Jack Reed and I stood in the Kremlin, at Moscow, and contemplated that old cemetery under the ancient wall. Nicholas II was still on the throne of his fathers, and his minions were all about us—some of them, we knew, charged with the not difficult task of keeping their eyes on us.

The mutilated bones of that emperor now lie in an unknown grave, his empire has passed into history; and the mysterious powers of change—amid a multitude in tears and to the triumphing strains of The Internationale—having placed the splendid body of Jack Reed in the ground once sacred to the Romanoff, now stir in the heart of Russia, the capital of the world's workers.

The fact is grandiose enough, and could Jack have prefigured it, he would have smiled and shrugged, with an artist's admiration of the large movements of destiny, but it would not have seemed important to him. He would not have thought a thought, or done a deed, to escape a more humble end, or to achieve a happier state—if it would have interfered with the doing of his job as he saw it. That job he did with an immense and joyous energy, regardless of jolts and scars, and with a magnanimity possible only to a great spirit.—BOARDMAN ROBINSON.

7

In the studio which he had built within the framework of an old barn, Robinson worked, read,

and thought. The life at Croton-on-the-Hudson was quiet compared to the time when he went daily to the office of the *Tribune*. He spent hours with the children, "Billy" and Bart, while Sally took a turn again at sculpture in her studio, which she had established in the city, next door to that of Russel Wright, who at that time was on the point of starvation. "Perhaps it was this fact that ingrained in his mind the idea of food which, in turn, made him design the dishware which you see on every table these days," says Sally, thinking about the year when she made a sincere attempt to return to sculpture.

Robinson, always very much a home body, was content to be by himself, to read and make a great many drawings which did not sell.

The home that the Robinsons had made of the dilapidated house was a happy one. The old trees which surrounded it were heavy in the late spring and summer and the grass thick and fragrant. Old friends, John Reed and Robert Minor, lived just up the road; Max Eastman's studio was next to the one Robinson had remodeled. And often Morris Hillquit, Dudley Field Malone, and Doris Stevens would drop in to make a merry party.

Young artists, serious students who had been attracted by the ideals expounded by the *Masses* group, often came up to the heights to visit with the Robinsons. Wanda Gág, Adolf Dehn, and Arnold Blanch, recently graduated from the Minneapolis Art Institute School, had come to New York; and Dehn and Wanda Gág soon found their way to Croton to see the cartoonist whom they had admired when they read the *Masses* during their student days. Dehn had contributed, even before he arrived in New York, to the liberal magazine: "I believe Adolf is going to have something printed in the *Masses*,"[13] wrote Gág in her diary on July 7, 1917. He was a young man of "conscientious scruples"; Robinson remembers him, in 1918, as a "leader among his friends; kind, just, and interested in social movements as well as in art." Arnold Blanch did not meet Robinson until 1919, when he was a member of the cartoonist's first class in the Art Students League.

[13] Wanda Gág, *Growing Pains* (New York, 1940), p. 465.

1904–25 Happiest of all were the times when Charlie Chaplin would join the group and they would play charades, Chaplin impersonating a Ford car. "His shy amateurishness," recalls Robinson, "made his stuff very charming; he treated us as though we were experts and he a novice." The best of Chaplin's pantomimicry was required when he and Robinson gave a dramatic imitation of a well-advertised brand of Little Liver Pills which boasted, "We work while you sleep"; Chaplin represented the liver in distress. The comedian was a generous supporter of the *Masses* group, as he was of other liberal causes.

There was another time, nearly as amusing, when Rockwell Kent came to visit Robinson and they ate lunch without saying a word to one another. It seems that neither was capable of voicing an opinion about the other's work.

But there were days of a hue less bright. Since Robinson had boarded the ship which carried him and Reed to Italy, he had increased his education. He had come to close grips with some basic questions. In 1915, when E. P. Dutton had published the artist's *Cartoons of the War*, he had written a brief Foreword to the volume in which he had stated bluntly that, in all that he could make of it, Germany was guilty. Upon his return from Europe his views toward the war received close scrutiny, and he discovered that he entertained some doubts about the accuracy of the daily news accounts. He began to grow uneasy about the end results of the war.

Robinson's pacifism was always an intellectual attitude, an attitude which he did not support with the heat of his blood or by a cold mind. He was puzzled, worried, and unconvinced. And, though he had been acquitted of any kind of charge of subversive activity against the government, he was not to go scot-free in the opinion of the court of public judgment. Because of his position—or a lack of a position, perhaps—about the war and because he was a "liberal," he suffered. In the fulness of his strength, in the prime of his career, he was frustrated. He worried about the support of his family; he wondered whether he could sell enough drawings to buy food, clothes, and coal. His wife was mindful of his concern; she appreciated that,

had he chosen to deny his moral questions, his life could have been made easier. She gave him comfort.

. . . .

Man that is born of a woman is of few days, and full of trouble.

He cometh forth like a flower, and is cut down: he fleeth also as a shadow, and continueth not.

. . . . there is hope of a tree, if it be cut down, that it will sprout again, and that the tender branch thereof will not cease.

Though the root thereof wax old in the earth, and the stock thereof die in the ground;

Yet through the scent of water it will bud, and bring forth boughs like a plant.

But man dieth, and wasteth away: yea, man giveth up the ghost, and where is he?

The afternoon light faded into gray in the corners of the studio, and the full-bearded, redheaded man bowed slightly forward over the pages of the book. On the easel was the trial of that day—a bold, aggressive picture which failed to contain itself; the design crumbled under its weight; it was violent in disconnected values. It was another inquiry, another essay, yet another failure of a painting which would go, in its turn, with the others in the large case in the corner of the room. The smell of turpentine sharpened the air near the painting and blended in with the odor of old beams and mildewed leather.

As he removed his glasses and stared at the far wall, Robinson smiled. His blue eyes caught the flutter of the fat pigeons which kept their home in the old barn, and one, blue-gray and lousy in the puff of his feathers, staggered awkwardly as he stroked his wing with a blunt bill. A white one slapped its weight down on the board outside the window and nudged her mate sharply. Muted sounds came to the artist through the streaked window glass. "Hope for a tree, and for those damned pigeons . . . . more and more of them every year. I'll have to use Billy's air-gun."

"Job, now; there was a man with his troubles! At least, it hasn't come to the sackcloth-and-ashes stage with me; how is it?—'and took him a potsherd to scrape himself withal'—not quite—no reason yet to find myself a potsherd. And Sally, so far she hadn't insisted that I curse myself and die. Things could be worse. . . . ."

Robinson turned back to Job and resumed his reading. His interest had found numerous pictures here; he was taken with the good strong flavor of these stories: Lot's wife, King David, old Jeremiah with his fiery warning, the Prodigal Son, and the lilting Song of Solomon. There were giants in the earth in those days. They had the stature of a room-full of sea captains just returned in full sail from a journey around the Horn.

The dusk settled in the studio. The reader leaned forward, stroking his head, absorbed. He was turning another page when he heard the footsteps on the stairs. By their quick energy he knew it was his neighbor, probably back from the city. It must be about six or after.

"Hello, Mike," greeted a low, rich voice, "Ha-l-o-oo! Mike, are you there?"

"Come on up, Max," called the artist. "Finished my job for the day, anyway."

"I thought I'd see how your new things are going; still experimenting, eh?" Standing in front of the easel, Max Eastman squinted.

"Well, experimenting is a complimentary way of saying, perhaps, that I'm wasting my time," smiled Robinson.

"Oh, come! Away with such talk, Mike; you know what it's worth and so do quite a few of us," answered Eastman in his fast way.

"By the 'us,' you mean our select group of friends, I take it?"

"By 'us' I mean anyone who has an eye—and a mind. Come, let me see the drawings you've made this week. We used "Exodus XVII" in the last issue. Great, I think, and so did Art Young."

"Well, here are two things," began Robinson slowly as he moved to a bench to pick up some scattered sheets, "these are about the best of the lot, I guess."

The artist spread the drawings out, smoothed their edges, and explained the concept he had had, how this had not "come off" just as he wanted it. Eastman looked carefully at the bold brush and pen drawings, watched his friend closely as the hands of the artist indicated, in sweeping lines, what he had wanted to say.

"Let me have these two," said Eastman, "and we may use them in the next. Quite different, this, from the old cartoons—but then, these aren't cartoons."

"Go ahead," Robinson pushed them toward the editor, "take 'em along. I hope there are 'plenty more where they came from.' I'll stick at this, anyway, and maybe things will go better and better, in a better and better world. Well, it's time

for dinner, you know, why don't you come in? We always have a place for the editor."

"No," Eastman thanked him, "I'll have to get some pages done myself, this evening. Malone and Doris Stevens said they might come in tonight, anyway."

"Won't all of you come over later on, then?"

Eastman ran down the stairs. The artist went to the table, closed the book, and saw the fat blue-gray pigeon, still there, stroking himself. Robinson went down, and as he strode toward the house he saw Bart, through the window, being fed in his tall chair. He thought to himself, "how good to be alive and to have hunger and enough to satisfy it."

Eastman, turning at the door of his house, watched his friend enter the back door, saw an angle of light penetrate into the gloom for a moment, then distinguished only the silhouette of the house and the barn. He turned and entered his own studio.

He sat down, pen in hand, and chewed thoughtfully upon the end. His gray head, handsome and striking, finally bent over the paper and he scratched away, pausing now, writing, lifting himself again.

"When Boardman Robinson shows me a drawing of a painting that he loves, he always moves a big hand over the surface of it in some generous symmetrical gesture, as though to convince me that the picture is flowing as well as poised, and to make sure that I experience the balance and motion, as well as the color and the passion, which are more easily caught. Like the ancient Chinese painters, his great preoccupation, and the value that he loves most in art, is 'rhythm.'

"Boardman Robinson is composing a series of drawings out of incidents related in the Bible, choosing those incidents for their amazing concentration of dramatic feeling, and yet demanding—with some perversity—that we consider them 'designs' and not dramas. They are designs of passion as well as position. There is a relation, half spatial and half spiritual, between the mad breathless neurotic fright of this figure of Lot's wife, turning and yet trying to go, wishing to turn and yet wishing she had not, warm with infantile curiosity and yet already cooling into ageless crystal—between this tall spoiled child that might have been a wom-

1904–25

an, and the little inconsiderable round hills that pile up so plump in the background and the firm and fortified shape of nature beside her. They all relate to one another—no word can say how. But

the picture is one. It is one gesture in space, even as it is one instant in time. Sculptural and energetic and heavy with emotion. . . . .

"There is ingenious human understanding in this artist who re-persons the tempter of the idealists, not sly and sinister, not itchingly demoniac, but broad and strong and comfortable. . . . ."[14] Eastman wrote on about "The Temptation."

Finished, he leaned back in his chair and laughed

[14] Max Eastman, "Lot's Wife," *Liberator*, I, No. 3 (May, 1918), 26.

softly: "Ah, yes, ... we are in a society whose ultimate and really admired ideal *is* respectability, so how can anyone understand anything?" He closed his pen and put it gently down upon the sheet of paper.

Hendrik Willem Van Loon was in bad straits. For some reason that he could never fathom, he was considered a German sympathizer. Being a Dutchman who had the interest of his native land at heart, he was violently anti-German, especially so because he had earned a Ph.D. in Germany at the University of Munich. He knew the Germans, and he knew what they were doing to Holland. But he was misunderstood, and, consequently, he had an extremely hard time during the war. He and Robinson met frequently, and Van Loon, who was a gregarious man, poured out his troubled soul to the artist.

The writer, always a good host, decided he would let up on the work he was then doing on "A Short History of Discovery"—he had nothing else to do at the time—and asked Robinson and his wife to come to dinner at his home; he wanted them to meet a distinguished guest.

On the appointed evening the Robinsons arrived at Van Loon's apartment, where they were introduced to Sir Edgar Speyer, who had left England because, having been born in Frankfurt, he was suspected of pro-German sentiments—not to mention that he caused his family embarrassment with the liberal views he expounded. The trio fell into a light and trivial conversation while Van Loon puttered about the kitchen preparing the meal.

Speyer, carefully groomed in impeccable dinner clothes, entertained the Robinsons with interesting stories of the political scene in Britain, while the absent host threw in phrases which drifted in, now and then, from the adjoining room, where he was busy. Finally Van Loon reappeared, cheerfully announced dinner, and the guests approached the table. There, in the center, stood two steaming cans of beans which the host had heated carefully in boiling water. He carved them elegantly with a can-opener. Coffee was plentiful and very hot. The Englishman's immaculate shirt front brought a certain decorativeness and distinction to the affair. Everyone enjoyed the dinner, and Van Loon was congratulated upon having staged one of the most successful events of that season.

Idealism, that respects subjective values more than the formal qualities—which are held usually to be more sensible—has sounded a sustained note in Robinson's life. "Conscience is more than a censor," he reflects; "it prompts us to do the things we can do if we have the courage. I had to do what I did; in some ways I have been very unpliable. But then I have never been able to understand an artist who is conservative."

During the war years, most reasonably, great opportunities would have given themselves to the artist, had he reached out for them. But he had to let them pass by because he was not certain; his secret had not revealed itself to him. The devotion he gave to honesty blinded him to the fortunes which might have been his and allowed no self-pity to torment him. He and a number of his friends were in the same boat together, and they did not expect fine sailing. Caught between wind and water, they had the fortitude of good sailors.

With Ryan Walker, Robinson worked for a few months on the staff of the *Call*; and, though he spent enough time doing potboilers, as a free-lance artist, to keep his family and himself from 1916 to 1919, the artist's efforts went into the experimental paintings and the religious drawings which he made in the barn-studio.

In 1919 a series of the drawings were shown at the Knoedler Galleries. By and large, they were received with just acclaim. The force of his conceptions and the spirit of his brush and pen were too much for delicate tastes, however. Wrote Henry McBride: "In the present series of drawings the artist has taken a venture into the world of ideas, and into the Biblical world at that. He has made a drawing of 'Lot's Wife,' of the 'Prodigal Son' and of the 'Hands of Moses.' It is clear he would have been serious. Unfortunately he is only sad. Throughout the series there runs a streak of cheap thinking that is especially objectionable when spent upon sacred themes. Judging by the work, Mr. Robinson prepared himself for this effort, not by a long course of Bible study, but by a perusal of the most fetid of the Bulgarian best sellers."[15] Differently impressed was Charles Henry Meltzer, who wrote in *Arts and Decoration:* "A dreamer—an enthusiast, if you will. No worse than that. What he has done, so far, while it may class him with a few great living artists, will be

[15] "Boardman Robinson's Bible Drawings," *New York Sun,* February 17, 1919.

outdone, you may be sure, ere very long. For he has set his mind on very lofty dreams, and he has all he needs to make his dreams come true. He has tenacity and strength, and much besides; and chiefly he has what is sadly lacking in most artists of the hour, he has sincerity. You cannot meet him for an hour without perceiving that he fights for truth—his truth, of course, not yours or mine, maybe. We cannot all see life in the same way."[16] *De gustibus non disputandum est.*

There on Croton heights, with the flowing Hudson barred by the Palisades in the far distance, the Robinsons grew in stature and wisdom. They worked hard, lived leisurely, and learned that to-morrow's promises, good and bad, may not materialize. Philosophic about frustrations and rational in disappointment, Robinson was not aware of being treated badly by life. But in that house on the Hudson, on winter mornings, it shivered his timbers to find that the water in the pots under the boys' beds was frozen hard as stone.

8

Robinson continued to contribute to the *Liberator* until 1922. One of his finest characterizations, the portrait of Lincoln, was printed on the cover of the magazine for the issue of February, 1919. Also in that year he conceived his now famous drawing, a prophetic cartoon about the Versailles Treaty, entitled, "Signed, June 28th, 1919." The *New Leader,* an English labor journal under the editorship of H. N. Brailsford, reprinted many of the cartoons that he drew for the *Masses* and the *Liberator.* But, for all this activity, he earned no living wage; Eastman had no money to pay large sums to his artists.

The most entertaining and profitable venture that came to Robinson, after the years of drought, was offered him by George Harvey in 1920. The former editor of the *North American Review* and *Harper's Weekly* was a politician, the prototype of the hardheaded, practical man. Harvey met the artist in New York and asked him to come to lunch with him to discuss the possibility of Robinson's "entering his hire." The conversation went along

[16] "An Appreciation of Vigor and Imagination in Art: Boardman Robinson—'An American Daumier,'" August, 1921, pp. 228–29.

BOARDMAN ROBINSON: *Part Two*

1904–25

amicably enough, until the matter of Robinson's name came up. "Now," apologized Harvey, "you won't mind if you don't sign your cartoons, will you?" The artist saw the point without further explanation; he smiled wryly, "Oh, I know you're

ashamed of me, and God knows I'm ashamed of you. All right, I'll not sign the drawings."

Harvey, once a Democrat who had helped Woodrow Wilson win the state of New Jersey, had been repudiated by Wilson when he became president. Harvey's feelings were as hurt as they could be, and he found himself—"adding insult to injury," he said—a Republican. He was in such a state when Robinson met him.

Robinson decided to work for Harvey, though with great reluctance, because he needed money desperately. He understood, however, that many of his liberal friends, Randolph Bourne among them, would not approve of this move. But he had no choice. The only redeeming feature of the business, as he saw it, was that Harvey promised that the artist should not be interfered with; also, Harvey and Robinson saw eye to eye when they looked at Wilson, though from different angles. The cartoonist was sure that Wilson did not know enough about European politics, and he felt that the American president would be tricked by history.

At the Republican Convention, in June, 1920, the artist got acquainted with his boss; he discovered that Harvey was an amusing and instructive character, one of the unofficial but actual heads of the party, though he was always quick to deny that he had anything to do with the selection of Harding on June 12. Quite aware of Robinson's liberal views and recognizing them to be sound and reasonable, Harvey, nonetheless, would not support them. "It may be true, what you say, but it will not pay off. It's bad business," Harvey used to say with a good nature that supported his logic.

In Chicago there were innumerable parties and dinners and meetings, many of which Robinson attended with his employer. One afternoon the two, in company with a guest, were riding up the Gold Coast shore, on the way to one of these grand events which was to be staged at the Saddle and Cycle Club. Harvey, grinning slyly at Robinson, said in a low voice, as he gestured toward the residential piles, "Homes of the idle rich, eh?" and nudged the cartoonist in the ribs. "I'm the only one here who knows of your wicked past," and the third person in the cab looked puzzled and worried.

At the luncheon Robinson sat next to Marshall Field II, who then "had liberal thoughts but had not warmed up to them yet," and he and the cartoonist argued about "anarchists," between drinks.

Though it was common gossip in some New York circles that Robinson had sold out for money, he was grateful and surprised to be given a free hand in his new job; he enjoyed the most pleasant relationship, editorially, that he had ever had with a magazine. Harvey gave a finger and did not seem to mind when his hand was missing; he developed a fondness for the artist. "Every time I made a caricature of him or when I derided the political views of Harvey and his gang," says Robinson, "I'd find that drawing hanging in his office, framed with taste and elegance. His feelings were quite impervious to harm, it seems."

Some of the striking power of the cartoons that Robinson made at the convention in Chicago is revealed by a few of those which were published in the August, 1920, issue of the *Liberator*. It was at the convention that the artist wrote one of the most understanding paragraphs of his life, one that makes possible a more complete understanding of him: "I learned something at Chicago. I went feeling bright and optimistic, but the convention made a pessimist of me. I nourished the expectation of watching the politicians at their nefarious work, thought to revel in their wickedness, and tell about it with glee. But, after watching them for a week, and talking with them, in and out of the convention, the fact was slowly borne in upon me that they are not bad at all. *They're good.* That is, they are behaving just as most people would under similar circumstances. Ignorant and commonplace and out of touch with significant things, of course —but they ain't bad. This is just what discourages me—that after all they are so infernal well-meaning and decent. I shall reserve my contempt in the future for their rotten institution."[17] It goes to prove that a great caricaturist and satirist must love the sinner though he hate the sin. This psychological attitude was clearly analyzed by A. J. Nock, in the *Freeman:* "Radical artists as a rule cannot understand that their work becomes effective precisely in the degree in which they enter, impersonally, as artists, into the world of their adversaries. . . . . Who is going to be convinced by a picture in which a capitalist is pictured as a Moloch devouring babies? . . . . It is the terrible eyes of men who understand things because they have shared them, men who have transcended their private grievances or rather universalized them, that haunt the world and give the devil sleepless nights."[18]

The opportunity that Robinson received in Chicago to see the inner workings of the democratic form of government gave him an insight which, because of his large interpretation of what he witnessed, far exceeded that of many liberals who in criticizing from afar were mistaken in their attacks and therefore ineffective in their efforts.

On November 12, 1921, the Disarmament Conference assembled in Washington, D.C., under the direct management of Secretary of State Charles E. Hughes. It represented the climax and the one really memorable attempt of the Harding administration. Robinson was asked by the *Baltimore Sun* to report, in cartoons, the progress of the convention. Robinson was free to do as he wished at the conference, and the *Sun* fulfilled the spirit and the letter of the contract; every drawing but one that the cartoonist made was reproduced.

H. L. Mencken was to see it all from the writ-

[17] Boardman Robinson, "In Chicago," *Liberator*, III, No. 8 (August, 1920), 22.

[18] August 28, 1920.

er's angle. It was a marvelous spectacle, bewildering to the hopeful eyes of the world's common people and rather grotesque to the minds of the informed, who realized the enormity of the task at hand and who knew the feeble strength of man. Briand, whose eloquence won him the support of many who attended the conference, was admirable; Balfour supported the British cause; President Harding smiled and hoped for the best; Hughes worked hard. From today's viewpoint the conference may be regarded as tragic in its inconsequence. It is summed up, altogether, in a conversation between William Gropper and Michael Gold, as reported by the latter in the *Liberator:*

". . . . this sight was the fruit of my days. I shouted for joy. Gropper seemed impressed also.

" 'What's all the shootin' about, Mike?' " he asked, turning his hazy eyes upon me.

"Don't you know?" I shouted at him in amazement. "Don't you know what we've come here for?"

"I thought we came here for the ride," he muttered stupidly, staring at me with his lackluster eyes.

"No," I bellowed, "no, you poor piece of bootleggers' carrion, no; you rambling wreck of poverty, you sad-faced humorist and defiler of clean white paper, No! We came here for the Disarmament Conference! Haven't you heard that Harding has induced the world to disarm, and that there is to be no more war?"

"Well, that's all right," Gropper murmured. "I'm glad to hear it. But you don't have to get excited, you boob!" he added, with a touch of spirit. "I'm just as smart as you are!"[19]

Something of the savage disappointment of sensitive, sensible men of good will who wanted to hope but dared not is the undercurrent in Gold's comment, and it was the theme of Robinson's cartoons. It is shown, beyond the power of words to describe it, in the drawing which Robinson made of the English representative, "We grieve for the [British] dead but we don't forget." It contained the very breath of despair.

[19] Michael Gold, "On to Harding, Then Home Again," *Liberator*, V, No. 1 (January, 1922), 16.

1904–25   The convention and the conference show a man who faced two great perplexities. In one he was an *artist* who, having been charged with compromise by some friends in the leftist groups, went forth armed with conscience and with a sense of justice, searching for what he could make of truth. He was not dogmatic; he was not sure of his ability to ascertain, from the facts he uncovered, the secret of the truth. He detested complacency in himself as well as in others; he resented and rejected the confines of thoughts and actions which were given unquestioned support by conventions. Therefore, he found sympathy in his attitude toward men, as well as sternness in his opposition to ignorance; for he had attained the stature which gave him an *Überblick*: ignorance is the father of evils.

In the other dilemma the *man* stood among the crowd before the Sphinx, knowing he lacked Oedipus' answer. The riddle, he knew, would not be solved this time. But an insistent force stronger than his own confusion urged him on to make a swingeing try. Because his limits were inches on the scale of the illimitable, he dared to make a measure; yet he was apprised by what he could not reason that his effort would probably equal nothing. But by that which is the substance of things hoped for, the evidence of things not seen, that faith of Abel and Enoch and Noah, he was lent a strength which quelled despair, and he was unafraid before the Sphinx. He gave an answer. His pen and brush made savage lines across broader masses of deepest black and purest white. Why should a *man* cease trying? What are the *artist's* reasons?

Robinson's friend and co-worker on the *Masses*, Michael Gold, also believed that an attempt was worth the effort. He and the artist found themselves in full accord on the matter of the attempts an artist must make to ask questions, to find answers. In July, 1922, while recovering from a serious operation, the artist wrote a letter answering one of Gold's earlier queries:

DEAR MIKE GOLD:

"Should an artist be a propagandist?" I don't think there is any "should" about it. Everybody is a partisan and to some extent a propagandist of what he likes. If he likes what he thinks to be the truth then he is very apt to be a propagandist of it.

If an artist is moved by the iniquities of this, our Christian Civilization, to the point of making pictures about it then he's a cartoonist. Perhaps, a revolutionary cartoonist. If, however, he is thrilled by the dew-enamelled morn; or enraptured by the vision of sun-glorified bodies of men and women against the sapphire sea; then, he devotes himself to those matters.

The cartoonist who seems to be dominated by his hatreds is only pointing out the things that are inimical to his loves.

Art, as you and I are fond of saying, is about life; and that may include still-life. Art certainly can't exist until somebody gets interested in something. It doesn't make much difference what. As to this propaganda business—the artist is not merely the adorer. He is also the critic. The very conditions of his craft make him criticize whatever he looks upon. That is: he selects, re-arranges. So, when his social sense is stronger than his purely visual faculty, he not improbably becomes a cartoonist, if he can get a job.

For my part, I find it difficult to understand the man, calling himself an artist, who is satisfied with things as they are. The beauty and wonder (old, old words) of the external world forever compel and attract; but I find it impossible to be content with contemplating it in the midst of so much poverty and so many lies. I should like to see human life in more appropriate relation to its surroundings, so richly furnished by nature. Consequently, I make cartoons ridiculing the famous twins, Folly and Oppression. However, it's quite possible for an artist to devote his life to painting landscapes and still-life, or decorating china, and yet entertain a violent dislike for our political and social system.

But this is an incomparable June morning. I am profoundly enjoying my convalescence in lone possession of my back porch (what if it is mortgaged?) and of the lovely green and gold world that lies before me. I find it difficult to think of things I detest, and infinitely easy to think of the things I love. Consequently, this morning I am a landscape painter: in spirit, anyhow.

Yours,

BOARDMAN ROBINSON[20]

Always there is the lure of the journey into the land of promise, into a better country.

It was this weight of hope against the burden of ignorance which gave Robinson balance instead of cynicism.

9

A brilliant engineer whose eccentricities were widely known throughout Canada, where he had consummated a deal with the government concerning a type of firearm which he had invented, Sir Charles Ross was an unbelievable figure, whose inheritance had been multiplied by his own clever promotions. Though he had attended Oxford and

[20] "A Letter from Boardman Robinson," *Liberator*, V, No. 7 (July, 1922), 29.

though he possessed the qualities of the gentleman usually found among those of his rank, he was indifferent to the subtleties of the arts and maintained that he was illiterate.

Sir Charles was introduced to Robinson in New York by George Harvey; and, as he was laying plans at this time for the establishment of a new and liberal paper in London, he asked the artist in the spring of 1922 to join him in England.

Robinson and his wife arrived in London, where Sir Charles met them and informed them that he had arranged for the Robinsons to live in a house on Warwick Square, Pimlico, which had been built by the Kingdom of Sardinia in 1834 and purchased by Sir Charles for a town house. The Americans were bewildered when, upon arrival at the mansion, their host indicated that they were to have sole possession of the place, free from rent and the cares of this world. Sally Robinson, wise in the matter of domestic problems, was quick to see that the upkeep of such a fabulous pile would surpass any costs they might have had to pay out for the rent of an adequate apartment in the city. And so it proved to be.

As the three entered the home, Robinson's eyes fell upon a fine collection of Hogarth paintings, a dining-room set of resplendent Chippendale, and, in the center of an echoing hall, a decorative table which was a museum piece of rarest distinction. He pulled at Ross's sleeve and said: "Why, we can never bear the responsibilities of these things! I would never enjoy a moment's sleep." And Sir Charles answered: "Oh, don't bother. You know, I can have all that you don't care for sent to my home in Scotland. But I don't like them, either."

Later, when Sally and her husband were roaming from room to room, they came upon a maid, who, seeing their bewildered stares as they came to a fuller comprehension of the scope of this fabulous place, said reassuringly: "You know, this plyce was built for the quality, but the quality never cyme."

The editorial policy upon which Sir Charles's *Outlook* was to be erected was one which was designed to appease labor. Far from being liberal, the paper was impelled by fright to concede only enough to control labor; it had no social or economic ideals. Robinson thought of it as "a kind of house organ for the upper classes."

The artist evaluated the *Outlook* immediately and was completely out of sympathy with it. He

fulfilled only the letter of his contract and was relieved when, through bad management, the paper finally came to its timely end.

What stimulation was lacking, however, in the job that Robinson was asked to do was compensated for by the incidental happenings, in which, usually, a number of interesting personalities were involved. Both he and Sally enjoyed the life outside his work.

H. G. Wells was one of the first of their English friends to entertain them at dinner. He had long been interested in the cartoons that Robinson had drawn for the liberal cause in America, and his warm reception meant much to them.

While he was guest at a house party with the noted English philosopher, the artist made sketches

from which he later drew his well-known caricature of Bertrand Russell. Low, whose striking force was felt in English political life, was a fellow-guest, and he and Robinson discussed the similarities between the English and American move-

1904–25

ments of liberal thought. The American was surprised to notice that Snowden, later chancellor of the exchequer, was an ardent supporter of Low's work. "Low was rapidly becoming the most effective cartoonist in England," said Robinson.

One day while Robinson was visiting with Charles Dana Gibson, they were invited by Lady Astor to attend a tea given in honor of the prime minister, Stanley Baldwin. Lady Astor, who saw Robinson talking with Gibson in the Distinguished Strangers Gallery, scampered up the stairs and, mistaking the cartoonist for a noted American journalist, asked him if he would come to tea with her if she could get the prime minister. Robinson accepted the invitation happily. When the party got under way, Robinson looked about him to see the arriving guests, Mr. and Mrs. Cyrus Curtis of Philadelphia. The artist, who was known to the Philadelphian only as a radical cartoonist, was greeted with a cool nod. Finally, the guest of honor arrived, and Baldwin, indicating that he wanted little talk but much tea, sat in isolation near Robinson. Finally, having drained his third cup, the prime minister said: "The drawing you did of Lincoln—it reveals the man as I like to think of him. How did you do it?" For the remaining teatime, Baldwin and Robinson were deeply engrossed in the personality of the president, who was an ideal to both. Thick as thieves, the couple were unaware that the frustrated stares of the company of guests were aiming daggers at them. Finally, standing abruptly, Baldwin turned to Lady Astor: "What a figure, Lincoln! Makes any tea worth while. Thank you," and hurried away.

Later Robinson was introduced by Baldwin to the House of Commons. All this, naturally, was unprecedented for a "radical" cartoonist, and his stock went up in the office of the *Outlook*. But Robinson could not do the one thing that was expected of him: attend a political meeting of the "influential set" as the guest of Lady Astor.

"I am sorry I failed to take advantage of my opportunities to do the great faces. It was stiff-necked of me to neglect good fortune," says Robinson when he returns to these occasions. But the artist, during those years, was impatient with all who could not withstand the disintegrating analysis to which his keen eye subjected them.

When Sally returned to the United States, in the spring of 1923, she lived in the home of Mr. and Mrs. Stanley King in Boston, until her husband and Bartlett, the younger son, who was attending an English school near London, joined her in October.

Robinson made himself as comfortable as he possibly could in one end of a wing on the second story of Sir Charles's town house. He had met numerous literary people in London, and they, seeing his isolated state in the echoing halls of the "palace," as they called it, came frequently to spend week ends with him. One evening Edwin Arlington Robinson, who was given to deep gloom when his retiring nature was disturbed by drink, sat in the corner of Robinson's large studio—a converted boudoir with huge windows—and gazed thoughtfully at the strikingly beautiful features of Henry Varnum Poor's former wife, Marion. As the host glanced at the poet's features, he noted a puzzled and grieved look spread over them. When he leaned anxiously toward his guest to ask if he were ill, Edwin Arlington Robinson pointed a finger and asked the artist in a whisper of agitated suspicion: "Did I understand you to say she lives here?"

In London, Robinson found Paul de Kruif idling away his time at a bar, woebegone and in a difficult temper. "What you need to do is work," was the unfeeling advice De Kruif received from Robinson. "What are you hanging around here for?" "Oh, I'm here trying to help Sinclair Lewis write his damned book [*Arrowsmith*], and he knows so little about medicine I'm afraid to leave him alone with it; besides, I must see that he doesn't go bad at the end!" worried De Kruif, and ordered another whiskey and soda.

In the summer of 1923 Mr. and Mrs. Frazier Hunt, Sinclair Lewis, and Robinson made a motor trip through the south of England, enjoying the coast of Devon and Cornwall. It was then that the artist decided he would pay a visit to his father's grave before returning to America. So it was that, in September, 1923, Robinson visited Cardiff and Penarth and wrote his account to the Robinson family in New York.

Later, from London, the artist indicated in letters to Sally his point of development in painting, his consciousness of his needs, and yet his belief in his ultimate victory. Some of the most interesting passages are these:

I know how to do it now—work, I mean. I have a well worked out theory of method, subject to change in practice, of course, but the theory is the important thing. Old Cézanne said, "L'idéal du bonheur terrestre? ... avoir une belle formule."

I strike snags, of course, all the time. But I am getting hold of things. I've had such a terribly long road to travel. Only to have had a master! To have been taught all he knew by some great man! Everyone ought to have had that. I've never been in contact, real contact, with anyone who knew how to do his own job well.

I want to do portraits, of course, and figures against the sky and the sea and the hills. I've always wanted to do just that, as you know. And I've never got Giorgione's Fête Champêtre out of my system and never shall. . . . .

It's good of you to have so much confidence in my painting, darling. I wish you were here to check it up a bit. Nothing can stop me from keeping on with it. It's opening up the world for me. I can't understand how drawing alone has been able to occupy me for so long. This is a colored world and without color there is no real expression. . . . .

Isn't it hell that just when one begins to find some solution to life, when you begin to understand a little—yourself and others; when you can see a glimmer of light ahead, just then your capacity for enjoyment begins to slacken, the rest of your hair comes out and you want to go to bed early—and sleep!

I saw Brailsford this morning. He tells me, with evident regret, that the stuff of mine which the *New Leader* used proved to be too "subtle" for their readers. So, if I'm not too vulgar for England I'm too subtle and refined. My chances for a living here seem rather poor.

Bartlett and his father left England for Boston in November. They went to the King home; and, after a discussion of plans for the immediate future, the artist went down to New York, where he took a studio in the residence of Wolcott H. Pitkin, an old friend.

Here the artist devoted himself, with intense effort, to painting. The long career of Boardman Robinson as a cartoonist who turned his eye and mind upon contemporary political and social scenes had now come to an end. Upon occasion he made a drawing or so for the *New Yorker*, but not many. His interest centered definitely upon the problems of the techniques of painting and the construction of easel pictures.

Now there was a maturity in the artist's concepts and a vision of what he might accomplish in color. He had attained a mastery of drawing, which had won wide recognition for him. His comprehension of the scope of the cartoon, his power of draftsmanship and daringly brilliant use of val-

ues already stood as a monument in the history of the cartoon.

"More than anyone I know," says Daniel Fitzpatrick of the *St. Louis Post Dispatch*, "Boardman Robinson has contributed art, with a capital 'A,' to American cartooning. His work is in the great tradition of the painter-cartoonists such as Goya, Daumier, and Forain. The great, broad sweep of his brushes and crayons is only a revelation of the breadth of his ideas and the depth of his understanding."

The artist himself regards his cartooning period, in his estimate of his three phases of development, as one of journalism primarily, in which the cartoon-drawing and the illustration were the objects of his paramount consideration. And this period is divided into two phases: first, the early and formative years, when he passed from under the French influences, mostly that of Forain, to concepts of his own; second, the gradual evolution of his own mode, begun about 1907, when he grew naturally into a self-realized and individualistic manner of expression. The finest examples of the latter phase, of course, were published in the *Masses* and the *Liberator*.

"These masterly drawings," in the opinion of Reginald Marsh, "unique in twentieth century newspapers, had the breathlike delicacy as well as the power and magnificence of the old masters. Like all good drawings, they were made in terms of the materials worked upon; the very newspaper stock turned into glowing, beautiful color. The drawings were probably too characterful and grave to be popular. Here was expression, thought and warmth, for once, in a world that prefers work cold, mechanical and flat."

"Those years of cartooning for *The Masses* and *The Liberator*," adds Allen Weller in a summary of the artist's drawings which appeared in the *Magazine of Art* in June, 1941, "gave Robinson an extraordinarily large view of humankind as a whole: how large, we are only beginning to realize today when we look back, for instance, to the war cartoons, or to the peace conference cartoons, and see with what unerring comprehension he saw through the thin hypocritical shell of things to the

1904–25 essential core. The cartoons are prophetic: their content grows more significant with the years."

10

When Robinson returned to New York in the winter of 1923, working in a studio in the home of Wolcott H. Pitkin, he began a new career. As sharply marked as it is possible to distinguish one period from another in an artist's life, the time of his contribution to the history of the cartoon ended, and a new interest in painting urged Robinson into a period of searching and experimentation. This quest had two aspects. First, there was the problem of the painter's skills and techniques, which made him, in company with fellow-artists, try numerous media in diverse manners. Next he became a student of design, of composition and construction; he made analytical studies of the works of the masters and attempted a variety of forms, on his own, which would contain the ideas he wished to express.

"There was a slowly rising inquiry among artists in New York during the nineteen-twenties," Robinson says, "which had to do with the basic skills and techniques of that which is pure workmanship in the business of the artist." The part of the artist's profession which is related to the work of the artisan—the skill of preparing a painting surface; of grinding pigment; of binding pigment; of protecting a painted surface; of the many workmanlike things that the apprentice in the atelier of a Renaissance master learned thoroughly to know before he began to work with compositional problems in the making of a picture—these skills had been gradually slipping from the artist's store of professional equipment since the beginning of the Romantic movement in France in the nineteenth century. In open rebellion against the contemptible influences of the Industrial Revolution upon the manufacture of badly designed articles of utility and other articles of "decoration," Whistler had given out the battle cry: "Art for art's sake." He did not stoop to stretch a canvas; he would have nothing to do with common claims upon him. He demanded freedom. And in the light of what he opposed, his often misconstrued statement makes some sense.

But this scorn of the artist for the artisan became serious. "In Paris, in 1900, I never heard a whisper about craftsmanship; in fact, it was held in utter contempt," recalls Robinson. "There was no concern at all for the most elementary skills of painting; the color was daubed on the canvas—color which was purchased in tubes while the canvas was prepared by the manufacturer—and the artist took the result for granted." Straight oil on canvas was the usual manner of painting.

During the years that Robinson devoted his efforts mainly to drawing with pen, brush, and ink, this neglect of techniques grew among American artists. The flash of the brush, in the manner of Sargent, occupied the hands of a majority of minor artists and even tinged the work of such men as Henri. The Manet influence of solid painting did impress a number of the members of the "Black Gang." But most of the painters, under the influence of the upsurge of postimpressionism, were talking about color relations and working with broken hues upon their canvases. A few understood the importance of Cézanne and the inventions of cubism.

So, in 1923, Robinson began to ask the question: How did the Renaissance painters obtain their effects? And he found no answers. He and Thomas Hart Benton worked to discover what the answers might be.

Now that the years of experimentation which the artists of New York gave to this search can be added up, it is plainly a tragedy that there was no direct and effective communication between them and various centers where a study of these skills was going on, such as Munich, Vienna, and Budapest. Even in Paris the scorned Academicians had, to their own small profit, preserved not only the outmoded forms but also the sound and historically proved skills and techniques of the Renaissance.

"For years some of us worked," said Benton, "and we wasted precious effort, as well, in a hunt for the basic techniques which were the stock-in-trade of any second- or third-rate craftsman in a sixteenth-century Florentine studio." Other artists who spent time and energy in this quest, twenty years ago, have said that they tried everything from molasses to floor-varnish for binding pigments.

Max Doerner was working in Munich in a studio-laboratory with the imagination of an artist and the craftiness of a trained scientist. As a result of years of research and trials, he published in 1921 a bulky and confused book upon the subject of the artist's materials. No artist in this country, apparently, was aware of it. Doerner knew that "art has abandoned the sound principles of craftsmanship and it is therefore lacking in a dependable foundation"; and his work of definitive quality did much to re-establish the principles and give a sound foundation to the painter's work. When the fourth edition of his splendid volume, *The Materials of the Artist*, was finally translated into English by Eugen Neuhaus and published by Harcourt, Brace and Company, in 1934, a treasure was opened up to thousands of artists; no book with more significant results has been written in modern times.

But Doerner's work did not help the artists in New York after World War I. It could have, probably, had it not been for the fact that, as Robinson said, "all the artists despised the Yale Prix de Rome factory," and most of them were uninformed about the work that was being done in the Fogg Museum at Harvard. In 1922 Daniel V. Thompson, Jr., an instructor in skills and techniques of painting in the Yale School of Art, studied the *Malmaterial* under Doerner in Munich. Thompson returned to New Haven and trained many students in the sound principles of tempera painting. At Harvard, Edward Waldo Forbes was making scholarly experiments, and, finally, in the 1930's, he succeeded in bringing into prominence the remarkable scientific equipment of the Fogg Museum as an aid in the study of materials and their use in painting, as well as in adequate and safe methods of picture restoration.

Robinson and Benton tried to develop these crafts, and they worked hard at the job. Benton, especially, painted hundreds of panels with the sole aim of obtaining a more satisfactory method of paint application. "He did the first experimentation that I knew anything about," remembers Robinson.

The concern with the painter's craft did not end there, however. Many artists were working for new terms of organization, also; they were concerned with design—to use the word in its broadest sense. George Bellows tried to remove the accidental quality from his pictures by devoting himself to "Dynamic Symmetry"; others worked with the "Golden Sector." But few, when they attacked the problem of filling a large area in their

mural experiments, were able to sustain a theme and develop a consistency throughout their work.

Robinson began to look for system, an order of procedure, in the making of pictures. "I had never known *method*. The great masters had it. And though Benton's technique was not flawless he did work intelligently and I profited by his keen reasoning."

"Benton and I often spent afternoons analyzing the old masters' compositions: El Greco, Rubens, Titian, Tintoretto and Rembrandt," says Robinson. "Rubens appealed greatly to Benton; Rembrandt to me. It was then that I found there is much in the Dutchman which is not to be analyzed!" Later Robinson's interest turned to Grünewald, and he made many studies of that artist's compositions.

Gradually, as a result of such consideration of space and form, Robinson became interested in monumental design. It was a result of this interest which prompted him to complete the large fresco, "The Sermon on the Mount," which is now on exhibition at the Colorado Springs Fine Arts Center. The gist of the type of analysis which he and Benton made of the work of the early masters is clearly elucidated in articles which Benton wrote for the *Arts* magazine. In 1924 he wrote "Form and Subject"; in 1926 he discussed "Mechanics of Form Organization in Painting."

This experience, with its searching study into the history of art, was the foundation upon which Robinson built his new career. Since the time of his training at the Massachusetts Normal Art School and the days when he had worked in his studio in Paris, he had not worked intensively at painting. It was necessary for the artist to supply a thorough foundation in the skills and techniques, because, during the two decades in which he had devoted himself to drawing cartoons and making illustrations, he had not had the opportunity to develop extensively this early beginning.

He did continue to work at painting, however, in the time he could afford to take away from his business as cartoonist. When he first began to work in his Croton studio-barn, he painted and he experimented. Among these first paintings were a head of his friend, Carl Ruggles, the composer, and some bold and imaginative studies—figure

1904–25

compositions. He was shy about these efforts, though, realizing at that time that not all black-and-white artists had successfully translated their thoughts into color. He tried; he studied Giotto; "I want to go back to the primitives," he remarked to his friend, Charles Meltzer. These hours of painting, one might say, tied his new period to the phase of his training when he was a student in Paris, and they also prepared him for the challenge which he would meet when, from 1924 on, he worked with the painter's problems.

The mastery of drawing which was his made the painting problem easier, and it enabled the artist to grow rapidly. An examination of the works of this period, from about 1924 to 1928, shows that he was not at a loss to know how to use the brush and pigment. The dancers, the figure studies, the landscapes—many of them have a maturity, they reveal a wisdom in the use of the medium, which shows how readily Robinson stepped from his first career into the early stages of his second.

Early in 1924 Robinson showed some of his new work, along with his well-known drawings, in an exhibition at the Dunster House Gallery in Cambridge. Though the force of the compositions evoked a frightened sound from the critics, in it was a note of approval which could not be suppressed. The sculpturesque quality of the figures in the "mystic compositions" were said to be "quite elemental" in their effect. "You may not like some of these things," warned one Bostonian, "but they will stick with you!"

These new compositions, to be sure, were not profound, nor were many of them well executed. Their one splendid feature was the boldness of their strength. Robinson had no purpose other than this: he wanted to grope his way to a new level of understanding of the art of painting. And in this struggle, because he was a consummate draftsman, the emotional content was often a flame which lighted up the way. The man, because he was an artist, put his force and his vision into his efforts.

11

After the discomfort of the winter months on Croton heights, the Robinsons looked with eager anticipation toward the summer months when they would live in the carefree days of June, July, and August on the island. At Martha's Vineyard, between Vineyard Haven and Gay Head, the children, Bart and Jack, would play on the South Beach. Sally, free from the confines of the duties in the home in New York, enjoyed the vacation probably more than the children did. The Martha's Vineyard group was not a colony, the place was not an art resort; rather, it was a co-operative community, an informal group of people who enjoyed sharing the experience of living in that excellent summer climate.

Stanley King, now president of Amherst College, had met Robinson in Russia, at the time that King was eastern manager of the International Shoe Company. During Reed's and Robinson's stay in Russia, King's well-related experiences of obtaining contracts with the heads of the various depart-

OH, MAMA! SEE THE POOR LITTLE BIRD.
IT HASN'T GOT ANY CAGE!

ments of the Russian government were helpful in clarifying for them some of their puzzlement about the Russian temperament. Robinson liked the man, and when he returned to America he asked King to help him and Sally found the place at the Vineyard.

Soon after 1917 a number of congenial people had become interested, and the community came to own about fifty acres of land; a barn or two, which had been converted into living quarters; and a good many chicken coops—a literal, not a figurative, name for the structures in which the families lived. The Robinsons were members of this group for about fifteen years, and they count that time now as one of the stimulating experiences of their lives. The beauty of the island, the warmth of the sunlit beaches, the Yankee islanders they saw, the unspoiled charm of a place which "society" had not then discovered, held an undeniable appeal for city dwellers.

Among the members of this community were Adam and Natalie Haskell, Stanley and Gertrude King, Wolcott H. Pitkin, Valentine and Ethel Pulsifer, and Boardman and Sally Robinson. Intimate friends of the members of the group who came to spend a part of their summer at Martha's Vineyard were Van Wyck Brooks, Raymond Fosdick, Manley Hudson, Julian Huxley, Walter Lippmann, Lewis Mumford, Louise Seamon, Graham Wallas, and Hans Zinsser. It was a congregation of people who enjoyed the benefits of good weather, good food, and good company.

Thomas Hart Benton and his wife, Rita, though not actually members of the group, owned a barn near that of the Robinsons. The Missourian invited many artists from New York to spend their vacations with him and Rita and thus added considerably to the interest that the island resort held for the whole group. One of Benton's most intimate friends, Thomas Craven, was a constant visitor. Craven, a writer on art who had won Robinson's admiring comment when the artist had read Craven's work in 1923, was deeply engrossed with Benton in a study of aesthetics and wrote, during these years, his most penetrating articles, which appeared in such magazines as *Harper's* and *Scribner's*. Robinson, in a letter to his wife written from London in 1924, remarked: "Some of the best thinking about painting has been done by

Tom Craven whose articles I have enjoyed seeing here."

Serious work was done on the island. Robinson completed a series of paintings during the summers in the twenties, some of them excellent compositions. He and Benton continued here their discussions of Renaissance painting.

During the years 1924–30, Robinson resumed his teaching at the Art Students League; the occupation was one that he came to enjoy, and a fortunate one for him, since it brought approximately three hundred dollars a month into the family exchequer. Aside from his teaching, he made occasional drawings and worked on the problems of his own painting. Like most American artists who were in New York at the time, he experimented. In the summers he saw much of Benton, who was everlastingly working on the same problems.

The medium of lithography appealed to him during those years, and he turned out thirteen or fourteen lithographs which were sold by Weyhe. Both he and George Bellows gave George Miller, the printer, a great deal of business at that period by directing many artists to his shop.

In 1925 the Robinsons bought a house situated at the corner of Tenth Avenue and West Twenty-fourth Street. Sally was delighted to discover that the residence had exposure on four sides. It was in this home that Robinson and his wife celebrated their twenty-fourth wedding anniversary.

Although occasionally Robinson drew a few things for the *Dial* and the *New Yorker* magazines, yet he had very little to do with the art world during that period. Professionally, it was a quiet time, a time for building for the future.

PART THREE

O joy! that in our embers
Is something that doth live,
That nature yet remembers
What was so fugitive!

. . . .

The innocent brightness of a new-born Day
Is lovely yet;
The Clouds that gather round the setting sun
Do take a sober coloring from an eye
That hath kept watch o'er man's mortality;
Another race hath been, and other palms are won.
Thanks to the human heart by which we live,
Thanks to its tenderness, its joys, and fears,
To me the meanest flower that blows can give
Thoughts that do often lie too deep for tears.

1

"I T IS extraordinary. You alone of all men of genius I have ever met seem totally to have conquered pride," wrote John Cowper Powys to A. R. Orage. This tribute was paid to the great English editor and philosopher after he had reason to be proud. As the founder and editor of the *New Age*, a magazine of broad scope and discerning standards, Orage had received the support of writers of such eminence as Hilaire Belloc, A. E. Housman, George Bernard Shaw, G. K. Chesterton, and H. G. Wells, all of whom contributed their work freely to the magazine because they believed in the ideals of the editor. Among the younger writers who received recognition on the pages of the *New Age* and who were encouraged by Orage were Katherine Mansfield, Richard Aldington, Ezra Pound, Edwin Muir, G. D. H. Cole, Ivor Brown, John Middleton Murry, Michael Arlen, and Herbert Read. The magazine, as a re-

sult of the editor's discriminating leadership, became one of the most comprehensive and profound influences among the intellectual groups of England.

Orage was especially qualified to interpret philosophy, specifically the philosophy of economics; literature; aesthetics, not directly concerned with systematic arrangements of evaluation and description but rather more helpful than such methods usually prove themselves to be; and religion. Above all, he was enthusiastic about things which are commonly considered too simple to be worthy of notice or too elevated to be profitable for the practical needs of man. He was a critic of the things which are thought to be highly respectable and therefore inoffensive to the regular comfort of the average.

The magazine which he edited for nearly two decades had a varied but interesting history. It was a liberal magazine, of course, which expounded broadly the views of socialism. Although the editor was confronted frequently by bickerings and it was not always clear just what directions the socialistic program that the magazine promoted would take, there was a common agreement on the part of all contributors, at least, that the aim of the magazine was one which had to do with the betterment of the lot of men in a noticeably imperfect world.

Orage, whose creative work was preserved in the *Selected Essays and Critical Writings*, which was edited by Herbert Read and Denis Saurat and published by Stanley Nott in 1935, was a sensitive analyst of the arts, which he approached through "divination rather than by description." His appreciation of the rich implications of the inner qualities of objects of art made him stress the virtues of what he called "contemplation," which may be described as a modest manner of absorbing, with understanding, the creative process itself, to the end that, as he states in his essay on *Art*, "all art thus plunges the beholder into a high state of reverie or wonder or contemplation or meditation; and that is both its nature and its purpose. We should suspect a work professing to be art when it arouses either caution or thought. Unless it can still both of these inferior states, and arouse us to contemplation, it is human, all too human."[1]

His was not a dull mechanism which assumed that the sum of the parts equals the whole. Orage wrote of his understanding of the subtleties of what composes the whole with a feeling and a skill which is refreshing. "I know few who have such a sense for the Essential behind and within the transient things of this world, and I know few who are so honest without being pedantic," says Robert Ulich, of Harvard, about Orage's chapters on the arts.

There are those like Robinson, however, who feel that the genius that Powys attributed to Orage lay not only in the power the Englishman possessed to see through the foibles of living and to detect the frailty of the supports upon which men dare to build their structures of "security" but also in his ability to impart the right kind of questions to others, who, like him, may have carried esoteric doubts about the customs, the institutions, and the destinies of men. "Orage is the most vigorous and

[1] A. R. Orage, *Selected Essays and Critical Writings* (London, 1935), pp. 152–53.

lucid interrogator of our time," G. K. Chesterton noted, in speaking of this quality in the editor. His conversational method was Socratic; he used it in such a way that his associates—those friends who visited with him informally for an exchange of ideas—came to a knowledge which they had not known before, one which made them more at home with themselves.

Briefly, Orage was what one might call a practical psychologist, one who interpreted so broadly the word "psychology" that one recalls the eighteenth-century scope of the word "anthropology." He believed in the biblical statement, "the tree is known by his fruit"; he saw that, after all, a man

is judged by his acts. Therefore, he must find harmony between himself and his world through clear self-realization; but, rather than judge himself, he should learn to observe himself accurately. This objectivity, said Orage, can be developed through a profound study of what he termed man's "consciousness." Coming to know more about himself, man comes to a realization of what he is and what he may be; he may achieve more of what he may be if he knows the power of the *wish*; the eventual goal, then, is the worthy object of the wish: a *self-realization*, a fulfilment of the self.

Such a summary is inadequate to present more than the gist of Orage's thought, but this progression of ideas was the basis of his philosophy. It was a design which, adapted to specific need by a

1925—

sympathetic and desiring individual, could prove itself in helpfulness.

Robinson found it to be that. He had, in his work in the studio, come upon questions deep inside him which denied him answers. It was not that he was acutely unhappy in a state of complete confusion. He was not more aware of perplexities, probably, than the thinking man usually is. But in the new search for painting skills and modes he found his mind quite naturally making inquiries which extended beyond the walls of his studio. His art is and always was concerned with life.

Sally met Orage in 1924, when the Englishman first came to New York. She saw something in his striking personality, and she was impressed by his questions, his reasoning about the questions, and finally his assurance. She urged her husband to meet Orage. After Robinson's first meeting with the philosopher, the artist was unimpressed. He was in the habit of caring for himself and his problems, and he thought it best to continue to do so. Yet he was aware that, with the limited time he could give to any systematic reading and to quiet thinking, he was lacking in a unified and inclusive philosophy of life. Since 1917 he had pondered the meaning behind the events and conditions of life that he had seen, and he realized that fortitude, an essential quality of character in the strong individual, does not solve many problems. He had done his share of thinking, with balanced humor, about the seriousness of life; and his heart was honest enough, his mind keen enough, to realize the dichotomies which exist in a man's days. He could not remember that he was ever bitter in his realization, but it did sober his thoughts when he contemplated the stirring things he had experienced: the state of the poor; the war; the dilemma of the innocent in times of war; the force of idealism; the suppressing power of conservatism; and the subtle difficulties of those who aspired to standards higher than the common norm.

As Robinson became more conscious of his inability to co-ordinate his thoughts about such conflicting aspects of life, he was more receptive to the ideas which Orage discussed. And gradually he came to feel that the methods that Orage used were sound studies in practical psychology; so he em-

ployed them in his own thinking. No doubt the English philosopher would be the first to say that Robinson's motivation came from within himself and from his recognition of his need; the aid which the artist found in the ideas of his friend was the reward he received for his own seeking. Long a student of Emerson, he was not newly acquainted with the thought that he "must attain and maintain that lofty sight where facts yield their secret sense." Orage furnished the vehicle which brought Robinson to a better view of that high peak.

The Robinsons, in company with Meredith and Betty Hare, Carl Zigrosser, Mrs. Blanch Rosett, Amos and Ruth Pinchot, Gorham Munson, and Mr. and Mrs. Larry Morris and many others, saw Orage once or twice a week for discussions during the years from 1924 to 1930. The meetings took place most often at the home of Muriel Draper, author of *Music at Midnight*.

The conversations, naturally, ranged from questions of religion to current happenings which headlined the daily news. For his part, Orage, a brilliant conversationalist, guided and amalgamated the trends of the topics of discussion.

Orage's contribution to the philosophies of Robinson and his friends may be summed up to be an orientation, a direction toward a purposive life. Orage, a teleologist—a Christian—believed it wise that a man discover as much as he can about the plan of life. In such an effort he develops a personal conscience. This conscience leads him to self-discovery and hence to self-confidence. In this confident state a man may find his happiness in the plan of life.

From these discussions the artist found aid in what might be called his "rules of objective morality": to keep the body in health; to increase his potentialities through a greater knowledge of his own being; to discover what he may know of existence; to repay the debt to nature for his *arising* —his coming to self-realization—through the application of the idea that waste, in the form of regrets, remorse, and wishful thinking, is bad and that action, following an idea for direction, is good; to be of service to his fellow-man in the best ways that are dictated by a clear head and a full heart.

"What I learned from Orage," says Robinson, "was most valuable to me. In many ways he had a greater influence upon me than anyone else has had. I began to attain an objective attitude toward myself and my work, while before, I realized, I had been a pure romantic."

Robinson developed a new discipline, something more sturdy than that which had frequently crumbled beneath him in his impatient moments; he won new confidence from doing the job well, any job, even though it might not be the ideal one. He began to prepare himself, unknowingly, for what was to be his biggest work before he was to leave New York City.

From the dog-eared pages of the well-worn book which had traveled a long way with him, Robinson refreshed his memory, with a glance now and then at the underscored phrases to give him a cue, his lips shaped the words of the keenly tempered lines. For him this reading was like visiting with an honest friend who kept a full and accurate record of the past but who did not account the future with the errors; a friend always forethoughtful but never forespeaking with idle promise; a friend whose vigor stimulated the idle hour with scintillating, pointed sharpness. A friend that Thoreau was thinking of, no doubt, when he compared his contemporaries to him: "Much of our poetry has the very best manners, but no character." Character! Emerson was a man who spelled character in every sentence.

He read aloud the robust, resounding, trenchant phrases, each like a nail driven into good, hard oak: ". . . . deal with Cause and Effect, the chancellors of God." "In the Will work and acquire, and thou hast chained the wheel of Chance, and shalt always drag her after thee." ". . . . you think good days are preparing for you. Do not believe it. It can never be so. Nothing can bring you peace but the triumph of principles."

Robinson felt a full laugh in his throat, a vital laugh of approval for the old preacher, who stormed high above the trivial issues of the petty apology and polemic of his day—of any day. The blunt, tough-minded New Englander thundered his sermons in furious indignation at the dolorous stupidities of little minds, almost as if he knew before he wrote them that his words would fall to the ground, their force too feeble to penetrate the sodden indifference, the apathy of opinionated humanity which these words were designed to lift, to spur on, to help, to drive.

Now, what is the prescription? How may a man grow to full stature? Why, be full of con-

fidence, my friend, be worthy of yourself! "To believe your own thought, to believe that what is true for you in your private heart is true for all men,—that is genius." ". . . . the highest merit we ascribe to Moses, Plato, and Milton is that they set at naught books and traditions, and spoke not what men, but what they thought." "A man should learn to detect and watch that gleam of light which flashes across his mind from within, more than the lustre of the firmament of bards and sages." And after that the scornful charge: "Yet he dismisses without notice his thought, because it is his." Sad, now, to think of what might have been, had you had more courage, more strength, more self-reliance. Ah, you groveling slave to tradition, you weakling, you spiritual crawler: "In every work of genius we recognize our own rejected thoughts: they come back to us with a certain alienated majesty." How will you arrive at your potentiality? What should be indicated, that you see finally what is needful? What man, what race, what nation, will bring the force of will, the reason and the direction, the light of vision, to other men and other races and nations? Only the artists and the poets have told about these visions and reasons and forces, but they are not the men at the wheel, they are not practical men. They are dreamers. Yet, "great works of art have no more affecting lesson for us than this. They teach us to abide by our spontaneous impression with good humored inflexibility . . . . when the whole cry of voices is on the other side." Else, alas! perhaps tomorrow a masterful voice will say what you should have said, a stranger will tell you what you knew intimately as yours.

Robinson arose from his chair, took from his bench a brush and ink, and wrote another card, a motto for himself, to be pinned up on the studio wall with the others. This one, surely, he had written before, but somehow the card was lost. The best thought of Emerson: "There is a time in every man's education when he arrives at the conviction that envy is ignorance; that imitation is suicide; that he must take himself for better, for worse, as his portion; that though the wide universe is full of good, no kernel of nourishing corn can come to him but through his toil bestowed on that plot of ground which is given to him to till."

BOARDMAN ROBINSON: *Part Three*

1925—

With the ink still wet and glistening upon it, the artist placed the card in the very center of the studio wall, between the two large supporting beams. He tacked it firmly on the boards with four nails. Then he stood back and studied it. He knew then, finally; he understood what Emerson had been talking about to him all these fifty-one years.

Therefore, on January 1, 1927, Robinson made a resolution.

2

Orage said: "It is the strength of the *wish* that gets things done." From the time that he and Benton had discussed the methods of the masters and had studied their designs, Robinson had had a desire to try his hand at mural and fresco painting. He began a series of studies for a fresco, "The Sermon on the Mount," the best of which is now in the Fogg Art Museum in Cambridge. The framework upon which he built the fresco was, like Benton's larger panels of scenes from American history, not assigned to any particular space. There was but small demand for wall decorations of this type during the 1920's; the tremendous upsurge of interest in mural painting which came in the next decade was anticipated by the movement which was under way in Mexico; but at the time that Robinson and Benton worked at their experimentation, that influence had not yet spread to the United States.

That great development in Mexico had its beginning, of course, in the herculean efforts which Diego Rivera and José Clemente Orozco put forth in the wall paintings—frescoes which covered fabulous expanses of space—in Mexico and in Russia. In 1923 Rivera began a series of one hundred and twenty-four frescoes in the building of the Ministry of Public Education in Mexico City; this incredible work inaugurated a revival of mural painting, decadent in the Western world since the late Renaissance, which was to presage the time when vast areas of wall space were to be covered, with mediocre, good, and excellent results. But, as neither Orozco nor Rivera had an opportunity to work in the United States until 1930, when the former completed his work at Pomona College, in Claremont, California, and Rivera did a small fresco in San Francisco, their influence was not of much material aid to Americans like Robinson and Benton who were interested in this field of painting in the early and middle twenties.

Robinson realized, after he began to examine the history of murals in the United States, that, though mural painting had been practiced in various forms since the early eighteenth century, it was not a chapter of art which read with any interest. Perhaps the best work in the nineteenth century was executed by John La Farge and his associates in the Church of the Ascension in New York, but, unfortunately, it produced unhappy results in its influence upon subsequent mural painting. The work which was presented at the World's Fair of 1893 was, by and large, of no distinctive quality. What hopes were aroused for mural and fresco

decoration in America were but faintly realized by the artists who attempted to further this movement; the Sargent and Abbey misapprehensions in the Public Library in Boston, as Robinson had already evaluated them earlier, were illustrations of a kind which hindered the healthy progress of mural painting.

Throughout the spring and summer of 1927 Robinson continued to think of the mural problem, his absorption with the aspects of shape relationships showing even in his easel pictures. He made a number of nude studies, broad and simple in their construction, which are quite different in character from the manner in which he had drawn figures in previous years. The influence of his research in Renaissance history made its mark now; he began to get the feeling of the painterly manner.

Eugene Schoen owned the building in which Robinson's studio was located at this time. He was interested in Robinson's work, and, when he was asked by Edgar Kaufmann, of Pittsburgh, to recommend an artist who was competent to paint the murals which were to decorate the first floor of the Kaufmann Department Store, Robinson's friend took the department-store owner to the artist's studio. Robinson was not in New York at the time; but Schoen, an intimate friend of the artist, showed Kaufmann the studies, the fresco, and the easel pictures which were displayed in the room. Kaufmann was enthusiastic about the things he saw and promised Schoen, who was the consultant architect for the remodeling of the store, that he would invite Robinson to Pittsburgh to discuss the possibility of having the artist execute the large commission.

In the early winter of 1927 Robinson visited the Kaufmanns at Pittsburgh and received a substantial sum of money for the preliminary work, the research, and the sketches that he was to make for the series of ten mural panels which were to depict a history of commerce through the centuries. As the task unfolded itself to the artist, he conceived the idea of presenting this history in a chronological progression: "The Arabs and the Persians—before the Christian Era"; "The Carthaginians in the Mediterranean—Dawn of the Christian Era"; "The Venetians in the Levant—End of the Middle Ages"; "The Portuguese in India—the Fifteenth Century"; "The Dutch in the Baltic—the Sixteenth Century"; "The English in China—the Seventeenth Century"; "Slave Traders in America—the Eighteenth Century"; "The Clipper Ship Era—the Middle of the Nineteenth Century"; "Commerce on the Mississippi—the Nineteenth Century"; and "Commerce and Industry in the United States—the Twentieth Century." Robinson thought of the whole architectual scheme of the interior of the main floor of the Kaufmann store rather than the isolated decorative problem; the conception, as he brought it to being, required all the background of design that he had studied during the three previous years.

The historical research, of course, required no end of time. In the process of completing the sixth composition, depicting the English in China, the artist found it necessary to go to the Brooklyn Museum for information. He entered the rooms in which the oriental displays were presented and, to his surprise, found no one about. Searching in the labyrinth of galleries, he stumbled into a gloomy interior, and, in the corner at the top of a ladder, he faintly distinguished a seated figure. Irresolute and

hesitant, fearing that he might disturb the studious one and cause him to fall from his lofty perch, Robinson announced himself in a low voice. The figure did not stir. Moving closer to the ladder, the artist raised his tone, "Is this the Oriental department?" There was no answer. "I say," with a note of impatience—and louder, "are you there?" The man lifted his head from the book and peered down upon the visitor, "Hah?" Robinson shouted, "I hate to bother you, but can you help me?" "Hah?" answered the figure; but before Robinson could give vent to his rage and pull the ladder out from under him, the man descended slowly.

Robinson received much help from Stewart Culin, curator of Oriental art, of the Brooklyn Museum. The talented but seclusive curator had all the information the artist required concerning the Chinese in the seventeenth century. As they were walking through the museum, after one of their meetings, Robinson noticed an arresting piece of sculpture. He laid his hand on Culin's arm and pointed to the stone, "That's an excellent thing, don't you agree?" The curator was curt, "That's art; I don't know anything about it."

Culin had a remarkable gift for discovering, in Brooklyn homes, objects of outstanding value. He was suspected, by his fellow-curators, of having a fund of purchase money the size of Croesus' fortune. When he was prodded to reveal the amount he had paid for some excellent acquisition, he would snarl, "Didn't pay a thing for it"; and no one was ever the wiser because no one pressed him for an answer of greater length.

In the first stages of the painting, Edgar Kaufmann used to make frequent inspections of the artist's work and study the progress of the murals. The artist was conscious of his patron's unexpressed disapproval as the large masses of the work were laid in without a special regard for detailed and finished drawing. Finally Robinson, unable to bear the suspense of Kaufmann's silent questioning, said, "Don't come in again until the job is finished!" and with such emphasis that Kaufmann did not return until the last mural had been completed. The department-store owner was considerate and generous in all his dealings with the artist, even making expensive adjustments of the ceiling heights, which increased considerably the

1925— cost of the remodeling of the floor of the building in which the murals were to be placed.

In the ten murals, Robinson divorced himself completely from literary conventions; he attempted to work with symbols, a process which in many murals requires laborious elucidation of details. The various centuries and the different lands are given distinction by the use of a variety of costumes and appropriate activities, in which the figures of each panel are engaged. Compositional devices of arrangement, value, and color hold the ten pictures together in a unified spirit.

Many models were made in three dimensions to obtain clearly the estimates of perspective and value content. This method, used frequently by Renaissance painters, helped the artist to achieve the effects he wanted: a clear presentation of his subject which might readily be comprehended because of its technical clarity. Valentine Pulsifer, then the president of a large paint-and-varnish manufacturing concern, furnished him with a special oil-bound pigment when the artist asked him for a "paint without varnish that will stand the rigors of Pittsburgh's climate."

Robinson himself feels satisfied that he produced a meritorious work; but, as he at one time remarked, "I have never noticed that my paintings improve because I blow them up to the size where they will cover a wall!"

In the history of mural painting, this Kaufmann group will be listed as among the first of any significance to appear in the United States. Robinson completed them in the last weeks of 1929, a short time before Benton put the finishing brush strokes on his work at the New School for Social Research, and a full year and a half before Diego Rivera was asked, by the Detroit Institute of Arts, to paint his mural for that institution. Later, under the supervision of the United States Treasury Department Section of Painting and Sculpture in 1934, the Works Progress Administration Federal Arts Project in 1935, and the Public Works Administration, thousands of square yards of wall were covered, and, to the average citizen who noticed a mural or two in his post office, it must have seemed that mural painting was indeed a national activity to which uncounted numbers of artists had devoted themselves since time immemorial. The fact of the matter is, as Martha Cheney wrote in *Modern Art in America*, "The painting of Boardman Robinson and the propagandizing of Thomas Hart Benton were outstanding in keeping the subject forward until the Federal Government produced its program."[2]

Nine of the commerce murals were presented at an exhibition in the Art Students League Gallery, in New York. After this showing they were sent to Pittsburgh and installed in the Kaufmann Department Store, where the artist made final adjustments and completed the last panel of the commission which had taken over two years to fulfil.

In 1930 Robinson was awarded the Gold Medal of Honor by the Architectural League of New York, a distinction which was well deserved in the light of the correlation that the artist maintained between the aspects of the interior design of that portion of the structure in which the murals were installed and the quality of the pictures themselves. It was a thoughtful piece of work, and Edward Alden Jewell evaluated it thus in his column in the *New York Times* for December 8, 1929: "In the execution of this formidable task Mr. Robinson's power of illustration never loses its edge. It is one thing to take an elaborate historical theme; quite another to make it, throughout, vibrant with life. Archives, however ancient, have been asked to keep their dust at home. So the artist's vitalizing enthusiasm for man's labor, of whatever period, remote or close at hand, is never obscured. That is primarily why the murals are so excellent."

However, as the murals at Pittsburgh are viewed from the vantage-point of a decade and a half of time, the honesty and perception which prompted Jewell to conclude his article with the following thoughts becomes more apparent: "Particularly in the work of Orozco one is impressed

[2] Martha Cheney, *Modern Art in America* (New York, 1939), p. 165.

with a dramatic economy that does not figure in that of Boardman Robinson . . . . his art does not yet transcend illustration. But this is only the beginning and, anyway, good illustration is not to be despised."

Indeed, it would be incredible altogether if Robinson, with four years of self-discipline in painting and in scholarly study of the works of the masters which prepared him for this huge task, had been able to contribute one of the great mural paintings to the history of art. The remarkable thing, no doubt, is this: that he was capable, through hard work and honest contemplation, of making the transition from draftsman, per se, to painter. There are few artists who have done it, and those who were successful, like Daumier, worked for years and struggled desperately to make pigments and brush do what they had done as draftsmen with pen, crayon, and ink. Perhaps only a fellow-artist, faced with such a problem, would be in a position to appreciate fully what this stage of development meant to Robinson. It is difficult, if not impossible, to talk about it; it is the painter's problem.

Because he believes that "there is no such thing as painting—by and in itself; drawing and painting are most obviously, yet subtly, intervolved," Robinson had never ceased to paint. During the years that he worked as a cartoonist, he occupied himself, nearly every week end, with a picture that was not meant to be reproduced or commercialized. Always he tried to think of himself as a painter, and he discussed his problems frequently with interested friends.

"One of the blessings of these years," the artist says, "was that I associated with few artists; I did not become involved with talk about rarefactive theory. My errant bourgeois friends, before whom I could appear superior, forced me to explain and therefore to clarify my process."

Thus, though his hand would often do a clever thing which he had learned as a cartoonist, he did not sit back and assure himself that this was sufficient; Robinson turned his attention to the basic matters of painting, and it was this attention which enabled him to control the large areas which challenged him on the walls of the Pittsburgh store. It was an enterprise of ambitious scope.

3

Mrs. Meredith Hare, formerly Elizabeth Sage, an intimate friend of Arthur B. Davies and Walt

Kuhn, who had given her support to the Armory show and who was responsible for the publication in 1924 of the catalogue of the John Quinn collection—a woman with social vision and political courage who had transcended the conservative influence in which she was reared—was one of the group that met with Orage.

Interested in boys and their education, Mrs. Hare had with skill and determination raised the money and helped to build the Fountain Valley School for Boys, which is located at the base of the mountains in Colorado Springs. Mrs. Hare persuaded Francis Mitchell Froelicher, a school administrator who had successfully directed the Avon Old Farms preparatory school in New England, to accept the position of headmaster at the western institution.

In 1930, having enlisted the co-operation of a number of his colleagues at the New England preparatory school, Froelicher sought for the man who could give to the students of the Fountain Valley School an appreciation of character and its nature as revealed in the work and in the personality of the worker.

"I consulted Mr. Boardman Robinson on a hot summer day in New York City," Froelicher recalls. "It was, in fact, one of those sweltering days when city people dream hopefully about higher altitudes and cool, dry air. Happily for the school and for Colorado Springs, Mr. Robinson decided to go west."

"We had no particular ties in New York at this time," the artist says, "and, besides, we had had a good deal of trouble there; it seemed to be the end of a chapter when I completed the mural job at Pittsburgh." Robinson and his wife had thought frequently about going west, perhaps to California; Sally had returned there only occasionally since her student days, but the West Coast never lost its attraction for her. The two boys, John and Bartlett, naturally, were more than pleased at the prospect of going to the mountains; the elder, especially, was "a westerner by temperament." Thus, in the late summer of 1930, the Robinsons left New York City to live at the Fountain Valley School, in one of the apartments of a dormitory. The artist began his work as director of the art department, a position he held until the spring of

1925—

1944. In addition to the work which Robinson supervised in the studio, he co-operated with Alexander S. Campbell, director of the plays which were presented by the students, in creating costumes and making scene designs and drawings for the posters which advertised the performances.

"I confess," wrote Robinson in summing up this experience when he had completed his years of teaching in the Valley School, "that at the time of my first interview with Mr. Froelicher I had rather an exalted notion of what *I* as a painter could do at a boys' school . . . . after fourteen years' experience I am still very much in the dark as to a good method for developing in the younger boys an independent desire to make designs or to study from nature. I have never conceived it as my function to produce *artists* from among these boys. Many parents would shudder at the thought of their sons becoming artists. . . . . But I wanted to instil in the boys a love of work for its own sake, and a consequent integrity in its performance.

"It has been my hope to exceed the teaching of technique in its narrow sense and to identify the arts with important human activity," concludes Robinson. In part, he fulfilled his aspiration; some of the boys who studied with him came to occupy the vacant hours with handicraft and with drawing; they went away with an intuition of what goes into the making of a man. For which of them can forget, as he goes on his way, the quotation, greatly admired by his teacher, which used to stare at him from the wall of the studio in which he worked in the company of an artist: "Not in that he leaves something behind him, but in that he works and enjoys and stirs others to work and enjoyment, does man's importance lie."—GOETHE.

After his first year at the Fountain Valley School, he was selected by the Broadmoor Art Academy in Colorado Springs to become instructor in figure painting. Though the Robinsons, when they arrived in Colorado, had thought of remaining but a year, the prospects for the future convinced them that there was an excellent opportunity for development in the Valley School and in Colorado Springs. So Robinson spent his time, when he was not teaching either at the Academy or at the boys' preparatory institution, in painting landscapes, drawing illustrations, and working at the mural commissions which he was, from time to time, to execute.

Forward-looking people in Colorado Springs, who were interested in the progress of the program which was offered by the Broadmoor Academy, saw that for various reasons their city could be a center of the arts in that section of the Rocky Mountain area. Eventually, by 1934, architect John Meem's plans were created for the construction of a new building of modern design, which was to serve the community and the students of Colorado College.

Mr. and Mrs. Spencer Penrose had given their large home to the Broadmoor Art Academy, and, until 1935, this was the center of the fine arts in Colorado Springs. Through the generosity of Mrs. F. M. P. Taylor, a member of the Bemis family, who contributed the money for the new home of the Museum of Southwestern Art, the art school, the galleries, and a well-equipped stage, John Meem's distinguished design was carried out in simple expanses of concrete and stone. Upon the site of the old Penrose home, an elevated and attractive location, the new structure was erected to house not only the school, the museum, and the stage but also the community activities which were devoted to the arts. Robinson, as an active member of the building committee, was happy to see all the arts combined and practically unified. Mrs. Hare, president of the board of the institution, worked incessantly to interest the community in the project; she visualized, with Mrs. Taylor, the extent to which such a center would contribute to the cultural wealth of Colorado. By 1936 the splendidly designed building, with its richly blooming gardens and its deep border foliage, was complete.

"It is Mr. Robinson's dream," wrote Archie Musick in the *Magazine of Art* in an article commemorating the gala opening of the Center in April, 1936, "to resuscitate that high standard of excellence in Renaissance craftsmanship." The artist, as director of the art school, brought to the Fine Arts Center as visiting teachers and guest artists from distant parts of the country: Kenneth Adams, Thomas Hart Benton, George Biddle, Edgar Britton, Arnold Blanch, Paul Burlin, Warren Chappell, Andrew Dasberg, Adolf Dehn, Lamar Dodd, Ernest Fiene, Doris Lee, Charles Locke, Ward Lockwood, Peppino Mangravite,

Frank Mechau, Willard Nash, Oscar Ogg, Henry Varnum Poor, and Frederick Shane.

Exceptional opportunities were arranged for the students, especially during the summer sessions. As a consequence of such a wealth of teaching ability among the instructors, the school enrolled such promising artists as Lawrence Barrett and Otis Dozier, who became members of the staff at the school, Lawrence Adams, Manuel Bromberg, Edward Chavez, Nadine Drummond, James Fitz-

gerald, David Fredenthal, Archie Musick, George Vander Sluis, and Lois Wilcox. The Fine Arts Center, with its collection of treasures of the American Southwest and its musical programs, has made Colorado Springs an important center of the arts.

The Robinsons have come home, finally, and the artist and his wife think at times how far it is from the New York barn-loft, where the pots and pans caught the water which dripped down upon them from the rough ceiling and they knew that the fair days of youth were behind them.

4

Across the top of the doorway which admits the students at the Colorado Springs Fine Arts Center to the studios, where they meet the teacher, Boardman Robinson, and where he, the moving and central spirit of this school, gives of his knowledge with an energy which stimulates the members

of his classes, these words are clearly outlined for each student's contemplative eye: "The business of art is with the difficult and the good."

Robinson is profoundly impressed by the author of that sentence. "Goethe, unlike so many German philosophers," he says, "did not commit the error of elevating pure mind to an unnatural and isolated position."

To the alert and prepared student the opportunity to learn about drawing and painting from the depth of Robinson's store of knowledge is appreciated as one which is richly rewarding. He realizes, after the first meeting of the class, that Robinson has something specific and actual in mind when he says: "Try to understand what Orage meant when he said, 'An object is a blend of the reality which affords the stimulus and the subjective extension of the impression received.'" The student knows, when Robinson has examined a few of his drawings, that he must see into, around, and through an object and that he must give something of himself to the expression he gives to the object.

The student must have something to give, must comprehend a proverb and its interpretation, must know the wisdom in the sayings of the wise. Good teachers have not altered their methods of speaking since Solomon wrote the Proverbs.

In recent years the teaching of Robinson has, sure in that understanding which is born of long experience, urged the student to see with a penetrating eye, to analyze with a critical mind, and to plumb a meaning with the sounding rod of insight. As he points out frequently, details are often impediments which prevent the student from obtaining a total insight.

This total view, this going to the core of the subject, was known by the artist to be an indispensable factor in the business of making pictures when he met his first student at the Art Students League in New York in 1919. For a period of approximately a year, before the cartoonist was called away from his classroom by Harvey and the *Baltimore Sun* and then by the work which he did for the English paper, the *Outlook*, he instructed his first classes in drawing. Edmund Duffy, cartoonist for the *Baltimore Sun* and a member of the board of the League, obtained the position for his friend.

1925—
Robinson agreed to teach drawing and "composition in illustration." As Guy Pène du Bois wrote in his autobiography, it was at this time in the history of the League that "Robert Henri forbade his students the use of small brushes; . . . . Boardman Robinson ordered one of his students to be honest and paint an onion."[3]

After Robinson returned from England in 1924, he resumed his work at the school in New York, where he remained as a member of the teaching staff until 1930. A teacher is known by the students he keeps. Judging from a standard which assumes that an instructor should stir and stimulate the eager and willing and give them skills and techniques with which to express their ideas, Robinson was, even in those first years, a teacher of exceptional ability. "One of the reasons why Mike Robinson was so effective as a teacher," said Thomas Hart Benton about this period of the artist's classroom work, "was that he had a rare kind of ability to keep his students enthusiastic, and he could help them strengthen their will to use this enthusiasm."

Among those who were members of his classes were Lucille Blanch, Arnold Blanch, Lamar Dodd, Stuart Edie, Jerry French, Frances Kent Lamont, Donald McKay, Carl Rose, and Concetta Scaravaglione. Arnold Blanch, a member of the first class and "obviously a most talented youth," as Robinson remembers him, was a highly individualistic draftsman who received his first criticism from the cartoonist in the manner which Blanch describes in his essay. Adolf Dehn, though he had gone to Europe shortly after the war and therefore was not one of the students who attended Robinson's classes, received constant guidance from him. Dehn attributes much of his understanding of drawing to this friendly assistance which he received from Robinson. At one time Dehn used a trick or two to attain what seemed to him to be a desirable effect in black and white. Robinson, examining this work, advised him to "take a hard pencil and some smooth drawing paper and sit in the most uninteresting corner you can find—and draw! Cézanne could sit in front of anything and find interest in it." Later, when Adolf Dehn was

in Vienna, he kept up a fruitful correspondence with Robinson, and, because of this relationship, according to the Minnesotan's letters of that time, he avoided the extremes of expressionism which were, in various manners, the vogue in most of the studios he visited.

At the Colorado Springs Fine Arts Center, Robinson perfected his manner of presenting his ideas to his students. Those who are incapable of receiving instruction are baffled; but the alert grow strong as they digest the ideas which are offered to them, often in the form of allegories and parables. Ironical, allusive, and full of wit, the teacher's suggestions never hide the qualities which Francis Froelicher enumerated when Robinson had completed his fourteenth year of work at the Fountain Valley School and in Colorado Springs: "With the effortlessness of the perfectly generous nature Robinson practices a kindliness to all in adversity. He has that strength and breadth of character which will not permit the isolated disappointment, no matter how keen it is, to discolor his attitude toward the goodness of life. His extraordinary and spontaneous energy allows him to follow his ideal—never to pass even the small opportunity without putting into it all his strength."

During a summer session held at the school of the Colorado Springs Fine Arts Center, a respectable number of experienced students mingled with teachers of high-school art who had come west "just to freshen up a bit" and dilettantes who were comfortable in a sublime climate. After the model's rest-period, the students in Robinson's class in drawing left the comfortable chairs which bordered the patio to reoccupy their places at their drawing boards. The voices blended into a hum and murmur and subsided as the students returned to the problems on canvas and paper.

Busily, with deft performance, a skilful young man furthered his drawing, favored the lights and speeded the darks with dramatic effect, crosshatched with adroitly form-following lines, dexterously applied the kneaded eraser like a drawing instrument. His neighbors turned envious and admiring eyes at this cunning contrivance. The expert felt a proud flush creeping up his neck, as he saw the door open; Robinson entered the room quietly and walked to the back. He looked about briefly, measuring the scope of his job for the day.

[3] Guy Pène du Bois, *Artists Say the Silliest Things* (New York, 1940), p. 83.

The teacher's eye fell on the artful drawing. He turned from it and began his criticisms, one by one, at the other end of the studio. At the end of the period he walked over to the young man, placed an encouraging hand on his shoulder, and spoke to him in a kindly tone: "A clever man must have an awful lot of character."

A student's father had made a great deal of money as a portrait painter. The father, realizing that he had spent more than his money, had lifted his experienced voice and advised his son to study drawing which was not bare description. The son found himself one day in Robinson's painting class because he found it convenient to attend it in the afternoon hours. He did not understand his father's advice; he had seen only his father's paintings.

For two weeks he worked at a still life. Robinson came in and went out, speaking not a word to the student. The still life, gradually, transferred itself from the table to the canvas; the similarity of shape, form, texture, value, and color between the real and the paint became a perfect wonder.

Finally, the student became irritated at the neglect he was shown by the teacher. The next time Robinson made his appearance, the painter approached him and asked: "What do you think of that work? You haven't said a word about it."

Robinson grew embarrassed as he studied the sure representation. Back and forth, his eyes traveled from the fruit to the painting of the fruit. Finally, in weak frustration, he blurted out: "What the hell are you doing? What's the matter; aren't you interested in this thing?" and dashed from the studio.

The views of an artist who considers "drawing an act of devotion," as Robinson does, are doubly interesting when they are turned upon the work of artists who have made up a great span of the history of drawing; not only do these views reveal the quality which is seen in the great draftsmen by a man who may be listed as one of them but they may also give the audience which hears these views a new ability to see qualities which before were passed by unseen.

Pisanello.—A delicate and truthful draftsman who was aware of the fact that art cannot be divorced from its subject.

Mantegna.—His scientific preoccupations are wearisome, based as they are upon the sculptural discoveries

of the Renaissance. He seems to be more aroused by archeology than by nature.

Botticelli.—His emotionalism and mysticisms obscure, to the unknowing eye, the strength of his drawing.

Dürer.—Sometimes there is a "dandyism" in his work because of his overconcern with detail. But he can't be damned by such faint praise! He is the illustration of the bridge between Gothic and Renaissance representation.

Holbein.—A comparison between Clouet and Holbein, for example, will reveal the lesser excellence when displayed with the greater. Holbein is a man with incredible skill—but he has more. He commands a line of brilliant strength, supporting tasteful simplification of masses.

Tiepolo.—Here is an expert who stresses virtuosity.

Rembrandt.—There is much in Rembrandt that is not to be analyzed. He is the sublime figure in the history of art, revealing something of both its beginning and its end. Rembrandt and Michelangelo have always seemed to me to be the most complete in their drawings. Between them they cover the whole gamut of expression in draftsmanship.

Goya.—He was one of the first, if not the first, who released draftsmanship to modern expressionism. I should not call Goya, however, the great draftsman; he did not draw structurally. Compare his drawings with those of Signorelli, Rubens, and Veronese. Goya *sketched*, you see. At the base of expression one must find the knowledge of structure. Finally, Goya's drawings are not large, in the sense that Daumier's are large.

Ingres.—A good and clever draftsman, but his recent popularity can hardly be deserved. He lacks imagination.

Delacroix.—Had it not been for the infernal sentimentality of his time about North Africa and the Orient, Delacroix could have shown us more of his great ability. He did not understand, seemingly, the dangers of romanticism. Always he drew, he drew everything that came under his eye, and he drew these things with studiousness.

Blake.—He is the revelation: you may be literary, you may lack technical training, and yet do great drawing. He is one of the few great English artists—but then, he was not of this world.

Daumier.—There was no false thing in him. He was a romantic, true; but he dealt structurally with that which he knew. There was a man! He went right at form, working as one does in modeling. His drawing came, daily, directly, and hot off his mind. Here is another example where one cannot separate the man from

1925— the craft; Daumier was a great man. His drawing is frequently calligraphic; he seems to achieve the form and the symbol at the same time. He painted as a draftsman. There was no hiatus between his thought and his stone or canvas. (Had the photographic process of reproduction not been developed to such an extent between the time of the death of Daumier and my early years as a newspaper cartoonist, it might have been better for me. I feel sorry that I did not make more lithographs.)

Toulouse-Lautrec.—Lautrec had a dark and pessimistic view, which Daumier did not entertain. Therefore, it seems to me, Daumier was the bigger man and the greater artist. Lautrec did something which always sets my teeth on edge; he saturated his pigments with turpentine. Of course, he is essentially a draftsman, and one of highest excellence.

Degas.—Here is an artist who stands by himself, in temperament and in the quality of his work. Degas was a reserved person with narrow interests, but within these reservations he was superb. He was a scholarly draftsman; he had a watchful way. It was character, the character of his object of study, which fascinated Degas.

Pissarro.—He made beautiful drawings, all of a piece, solid, simple, and beautifully searched. His quality is often neglected.

Seurat.—I love all kinds of drawing—even the smudgings of Seurat!

Cézanne.—Fragmentary as they are, the drawings of Cézanne interest me but little. Except in his landscapes he was not primarily interested in drawing; he was the painter, par excellence. How to draw a contour which would incase a volume was the constant concern of Cézanne. His is the honest foundation upon which the modern student ought to build; here color and composition meet in structural unity.

Van Gogh.—He copied all qualities, from Rembrandt to Jules Breton. His development came from self-correction. A man like this does not need "taste," as we commonly speak of it; with him taste takes care of itself.

Rodin.—A sophisticated draftsman who, to the experienced eye, shows what can be revealed through purpose.

Forain.—Forain is greatly indebted to the Chinese, though obviously Degas was his master. The glimpse is what is so attractive in Forain; he could catch the essence at a glance. His painting is superficial, compared with his drawing. He is a brilliant journalist.

Matisse.—One of his great weaknesses is his inventiveness. This may betray an artist, for a basic idea and emotion must impel him. Matisse's fear of repetition is not worthy of him. In no case is he so concerned with the thing as he is with his way of expressing the thing. The object, and all the artist's connection with it, should bring forth a spontaneous way of dealing with it. The draftsman never stops to ask himself, "What manner shall I employ to express this object?"

Picasso.—There is a nobility about Picasso, though I often feel that he is trying to "do something" with consciously used techniques. Expression, for its own sake, is hardly enough. Picasso's eclecticism has added up to some unique and great contributions. The great drawing of the Guernica cartoons reveals the magnificence of Picasso's ultimate possibility.

Rouault.—Here is a soul who interests me profoundly. He goes straight to the heart of the matter, though, in his search for symbols, he reaches into highly personal expressions. There is, to me, a sense of compulsion about him. Here is a powerful draftsman who uses none of the draftsman's tricks, old or new, to achieve his purpose. He eschews the pretty, yet he avoids the ugly by the quality of his spirit.

"These artists are established," says Robinson, "their work is monumental. We may talk of these. But I distrust myself when I approach the work of most of my contemporaries."

Through the years of trying to put into words some thoughts about art which may create a new meaning for the student, Robinson has collected in his mind a series of ideas which, when he is speaking to his classes, take forms which may be written down in trenchant sentences. The energetic, spoken phrase too often lies down, sick and wan, when it is captured and groomed by syntax. These sentences, however, did not suffer when they were placed between the covers of a notebook:

A work of art should relax you physically, delight you emotionally, enlighten you mentally.

Too great a harmony is soothing—it lulls you to sleep. Art should not do that. It should jolt you. Therefore it is best to get your harmony first and then throw it out.

The spectator should receive a stimulant, not a soporific.

An artist should be always stretching, trying to achieve the impossible.

An academic work has everything that is necessary —except that which the artist can give it.

As the artist works, a new experience should be born of the original experience. A full realization of this fact should strike the observer of the completed work.

What we see is qualified by what we think. Knowledge must qualify our vision, and vision must enrich our knowledge.

You cannot imagine anything you have not experienced yourself. You have to have some memory for your imagination to work with, otherwise it is only fancy.

Perception is a three-cornered activity which involves the retina, what you feel about the thing, what you know about it. Association with the facts accounts for this feeling.

Develop form, for form is to the plastic arts what idea is to the Platonic concept of the world.

Memory is the material of imagination. When it is absent, only fantasy results.

Let theory work for the emotions.

Find out why you like or dislike things.

Be sensitive, but not dainty.

Don't always keep your end in view. Recognize it, do your work, and forget about it.

The relation between what you leave out and what you put in is what makes a work of art.

Expertness often confuses the worth of the content.

Symbols cannot be invented; they must be found.

Many mistake mannerism for style.

Mannerisms become mechanical.

Artists, to be whole, should fight eccentricity.

It is not enough for the painter to fall back upon eccentricity to obtain effectiveness.

Normalcy: the fulfilling of our natural potentialities to do what we are equipped to do.

No artist should ask for special permissions.

You accept other people. Accept yourself. You are only so much, but capable of development.

Artists are not better than other people.

Try not to imitate yourself; it is a low form of flattery.

Imitate not only your favorite artist; learn from your betters though they may not please your personal tendencies.

It is very much more important to ask the right questions than it is to answer them. We cannot expect answers to all our questions, but there must be questions.

The sense of power in our potentialities that makes us dissatisfied with everything we do should be cultivated.

Among great men the search is for something eternal.

Know yourself. Study yourself by placing yourself in another person's place. This develops the imagination.

Try to do things that go against the grain to help yourself to find your grain.

Exercise preference, will, and judgment.

Don't take the exception first.

When you get stuck, try deliberately to change your attitude toward everything.

Nothing is so deadly as accuracy.

Avoid anything that is glib or easy.

I am born to meet difficulties and overcome them. If I don't meet them, I must create them.

When you find yourself slack, demand more of yourself.

Do not be half-hearted, perfunctory.

We unwind as we are wound.

Now think of this class as a kind of laboratory where you make experiments with your conscience.

A school is not a place in which to make pictures. It is a place in which to collect data.

Strive to get the hand, the mind, and the feelings to work together.

Don't try to finish up. Try to carry on.

Style is the expression of true personality in the artist.

When I think of drawing I think of *drawing*. I do not think in verbal terms. For this reason I often get bogged down when I try to speak of drawing.

Drawing implies so much that I have never tried to define it.

A good drawing is a balanced composite of what you know, what you see, and what you feel.

A good drawing may be calligraphic. Lines must symbolize form.

The motive of drawing must have no taint of a desire for virtuosity or of exhibitionism.

Get what you do get down right.

The subject should not assume an undue importance in a picture.

Get the kind of reality a camera can't get.

Imagine yourself on the other side of the scene you are drawing. Notice how often Rembrandt drew the same group from different angles.

Start to build forward from one point, and dig back behind it.

The relation between depth, thickness, as well as length, is proportion.

Only brains and ability make a good drawing.

Don't try to be an illustrator. Try to be yourself in observing nature.

There is a woman on the model's stand; get at that idea as soon as possible.

1925— Keep your eye on the model and work with long sweeps, slowly describing the action.

Think with the pose of the figure; think with the volume.

Get the angle of the spine and then the counter angles.

You may not have a picture, but you know something about the pose if you get the essential forms and angles.

Think of the pose as a distribution of weights. Think of it as so much shape, and reason about what that shape is doing.

Exaggerate and suppress within the character of the model so as to get the character more vividly.

Get yourself mentally into the pose.

You get an arrested movement in the pose. Try to get something of the action that went before and what comes next in your drawing. Exaggerate the movement.

Justify distortion.

This model is much heavier than she looks because her proportions are so beautiful. She is in scale. She might be fifteen feet high.

Unless you have got the spine in the right relation to the supporting leg, you have got nothing.

The understanding of the shoulder may be just revealed in the way you end some line. If you have understood it, it doesn't make any difference how you get it down.

Keep your eye on the whole pose.

If the head is up instead of down, the whole spinal relationship is changed.

Head rests on spine, spine on pelvis, pelvis on knees, knees on ankles, ankles on feet. The whole figure is suspended.

Learn to know how the skeleton works.

If you know animal skeletons, you know the human skeleton. They work on the same principles.

You can put features on a head, but you can't put a head on features.

Get to know how an ear works until you could run your thumb along the form with your eyes shut. It has a beautiful design, a reason for each curve.

Draw from memory. It is the best thing in the world for you. Draw a foot from memory, but be careful to get a particular foot you remember, and not just any old foot.

Get that model in that gesture, not just a mannikin. Sometimes you can get it in just one line.

Solve the gesture, and the drawing will often need little more to make it complete.

Get the gesture. It is what the core of the thing is doing that counts.

Avoid waste gesture.

Go back to the box plan of drawing once in a while.

Don't draw too much by silhouette.

A contour can be three-dimensional; an outline is merely diagrammatic.

A contour is strongest on the curve, not in the hollow.

Draw differently over bones than over tissue.

A good drawing reveals the hollows and the humps of form.

Make an hour's study of some part of the body from time to time.

Overaccentuation is the enemy of good drawing; it clutters drawing as adjectives do writing.

Make it simpler than it is at first; then when it can stand some detail, put it in. Leave out the accents at the beginning.

Don't let your drawing get soft; keep it stiff.

Make line drawings. Try tracing studies over and over again.

A line is dynamic. If there isn't a countermovement, it keeps right on going.

When you double a line, be sure you need to. Don't just scratch.

Try silverpoint for studies. You can't erase, so you have to be accurate. It gives a beautiful texture.

Be precise about the character of planes.

Achieve your roundness by starting with planes.

Let your textures be deliberate.

Give a sense of the material the object is made of.

One who does not come to drawing through the material can understand it only incompletely.

Wrinkles are conditioned, first of all, by the form under them, and, second, by the nature of the material.

Find the system of the wrinkles' relation to each other. They have just as much system as an arm.

Drawing is largely a question of mechanics. Find out how the thing works.

Perspective is just a scientific fact. If it disturbs you, design and change it. If you want a man a mile away. in the foreground, put him there. Most of the great art was made before perspective was discovered, anyhow. You have to know about it so you can use it and disobey it.

It is strange how anyone but a mechanical draftsman will change every line and curve just a little bit, even when making a copy.

In drawing or painting the human figure you have to run the whole gamut from light to dark.

You have to look through the light and dark.

Don't get too monotonous with either too many lights or too many darks.

Study the nature of gradations from light to dark.

Distinguish between a reflected light on a polished surface and the form itself.

When you are modeling in the shadow, you are influencing the modeling of the part of that same form in the light.

Keep your rhythm sequences closely knit. Get your organization.

Let your forms grow out of your rhythms.

Get rhythms that do not destroy the anatomical features but which merely exaggerate some of them.

If your rhythms are working, you will get movement.

Don't come to any definite conclusions until you have a mass of form. Then the proper relationship of the details to the whole. Don't refine any one place first.

Work in: build up your form. Make it heavy and full.

Avoid accents until the form is built.

Exaggerate the big forms, not the little ones.

Get distinct, cylindrical forms when you study the model.

Consider the model as just so much form against so much space.

Don't let your form get puffy and characterless in your effort to make it rugged and heavy.

Keep it working until you get the balance of the forms.

Get behind the form and push out when you model your drawing.

Have a reason for every change of form.

One form demands another.

First you must learn to imitate form; then you can go on to suggest form. Then you can draw calligraphically, like the Chinese or like Rembrandt.

Look out for thin form.

Primarily, keep the form solid.

If you are using the wrong forms to express your idea, people won't react right, no matter how hard you tried to get it.

Every artist has his own interpretation of the emotional content of forms.

Caricature the form.

Find the forms under clothes.

You missed your man, his character. Always strive for the very character of the forms.

When you design, consider the total page.

Line and form equal pattern.

Invisible structures exist in the design, like the timbers of a house.

If you get many lines that are parallel to the vertical or horizontal, your design will be static.

Emphasize your composition with telling line, or values and texture. They will strengthen it.

Charcoal and ink are good tools for use in the beginning of a composition.

First impressions are almost never good enough. You can imagine your composition only vaguely, for its end cannot be wholly anticipated. As soon as you put down a line, things begin to happen.

Avoid the preconceived idea in a composition. You have to know how to draw from memory. "After thinking about that Fighting Cock for three years," the Chinese artist said, "I drew it in five minutes." The more you study design, the more you will find it interesting.

A good composition requires contrast of color and variety of form.

Don't let the figures scatter the composition.

A composition looked at upside-down eliminates the psychological element.

The effort to find good structure produces emotion in itself.

Let the composition evolve, and watch it.

Think less of art and more of physics in design.

In a sense, you could prove a composition.

Start your composition primarily with structural, not with psychological, intent.

Composition is something engineers sometimes know a great deal more about than painters.

Composition is the organization of disorganized things. Everything around us seems disorganized, but we know that there is some underlying harmony. We introduce our method of organization.

Color means form. It has formal qualities.

A neutral green is a very good underpainting for reds and violets. It is a good underpainting for almost any tone. You can work over it, a little more warmly by degrees. There is some green in every red shadow; some blue in orange, orange in blue.

Experiment with going the limit of your medium. Saturate the color. Make the orange *orange*.

Learn what colors will model form and what will not. Learn to know how colors act on each other.

1925—

Start with the general color of each area. Know what color scale you are going to use. The point is to scheme it before you begin.

Colors have objective quality, psychologically and physiologically.

Experiment with colors in relation to each other, on white.

Work out your color scheme on a small scale before you begin a large composition.

When glazing, avoid a cabinetmaker's finish.

Painting, it seems to me, is color drawing.

You can see any color you want in the human body.

If you have no hint of the foreground color in the sky, the sky has a habit of detaching itself from your composition.

I sometimes paint in the underpainting with the complementary color of the hue I want to predominate.

Work out the color scheme with the colors of the body color in the light. You can't take the colors of the shadows from nature.

An organization must have purposeful interrelationships. Making a picture isn't just assembling parts from nature.

Your work looks like sculpture. Do some modeling and find out the difference between painting and sculpture.

The most difficult thing to reveal to a student is that he must find a way of life.

5

When the hours that Robinson devoted to teaching during the last fifteen years are added up, it is surprising that he was able to complete five fresco and mural commissions and to illustrate an even half-dozen books. Not only this, but, in addition, he painted many easel pictures, which include portraits and landscapes and genre pictures.

After his first year at the Fountain Valley School, the artist began three frescoes—dry pigment in wet plaster—for the portal and the reception hall of First House. The largest of these, the two on either side of the fireplace in the hall of the school administration and classroom building, depict mountain scenes of Colorado, which the artist designed in almost abstract shapes. The smallest, and in some ways the best, of the series is in the portal of the building; it shows a number of workers in the mountain area, well related to the background of trees and distant hills. These composi-

tions possess a pleasant and decorative quality which is well suited to their location.

In 1932 Robinson began his murals for the R.K.O. building, at Radio City, New York. The location was not a happy one, and the artist could not control his design as he wanted; he lost interest and, as Thomas Craven put it, "he did it with his tongue in his beard." It is one of the few things the artist did which gave him no satisfaction.

The frescoes on the façade of the Colorado Springs Fine Arts Center were executed by Robinson in 1936. Low in intensities and with no great value ranges, they fit unobtrusively into their pan-

els and lend a quiet variety to the expanse of simple design in this striking structure.

In the Department of Justice building, in Washington, D.C., the artist completed his "Great Figures in the History of the Law." When the final panel was finished, in 1937, the *New York Times* reviewer ventured to write on November 14 that "without waiting for the test of time it is safe to say that Robinson's series of great figures in the history of the law will rank among the most notable achievements of modern mural painting."

Whether or not this statement contained an accurate prophecy must be determined later. The murals are impressive, dignified, and well suited to their positions. In the opinion of the artist, however, only two of the panels turned out successfully: the figure of Christ and that of Socrates. It remains for a later time to give this work its fair evaluation.

In "Topics of the Times," on November 21, 1931, one of the editors of this same New York newspaper speculated on why "Queen Victoria is included; she is the only head of state on the list since ancient Egypt and Babylonia." Robinson corrected the editor's impression:

May I call your attention to a slight error of identification in "Topics of the Times"? Victoria in my mural is not a portrait of the late Regina, but of Francisco de Vittoria (1480–1546), a Dominican monk of Salamanca, one of the "fathers" of international law. Though he wore skirts, he resembled the Queen in no other way. I used the English spelling—perhaps inadvisedly—in conformity with the general custom.

BOARDMAN ROBINSON

NEW YORK
November 29, 1937

The Englewood, Colorado, post-office mural, "The Horse-Sale," done with a tempera base and oil glazes on canvas, is the last mural designed by the artist. In this design the proportions of the subject matter have been scaled down to suit the situation; it is the most like an easel picture of any of the mural compositions which Robinson has painted.

Because, as the artist has many times remarked, the method of working which he finds most suitable is one in which "everything keeps moving under the hand," it is possible that Robinson did not find an opportunity for his highest expression in these mural commissions. He is most happy when he can control the total area of his consideration with ease, when he may alter the whole of the composition at will, to add or subtract, to change and improvise. And for that reason the problem of illustration has appealed greatly to him; here he has found, in a way, the summing-up of his skill in drawing and in painting together.

There is an admirable degree of perception in the idea which Jerome Mellquist is getting at in *The Emergence of an American Art*,[4] when he asks, "Who would not exchange the oils of Winslow Homer for his watercolors? Who would not gladly forego the murals of Boardman Robinson for some of his earlier cartoons?" But had Mellquist looked further into the career of Robinson, he would not have concluded so disconsolately that "man neglects himself"; for it is not difficult to see that, in the illustrations which Robinson made during the past decade, he wedded his talents as a draftsman and his abilities as a painter.

[4] (New York, 1942), p. 316.

This is the mature period of Robinson's life as an artist. It is the gathering of the sum total of his experiences: the first phase, which is composed of his journalistic work; the second, which is the time of the development of his philosophy and technical experimentation with form and color. Robinson feels that, since about 1940, he has entered upon a spontaneous stage of subjective painting, in which composition "flows from the hand" and in which he has eliminated much of the earlier predesigning of the picture. He formulates the main concept in his mind and proceeds to paint, the plan being created in detail as the picture comes on in development. "This is quite opposed to my earlier conviction about composition," he says, "and it is not a way that I encourage my students to follow." Such a concept is not difficult to understand, when one studies the lifelong experience behind the process which Robinson now employs. The "functioning-friction" in this work is the inner working of material which the artist has garnered and stored away in himself through the years he has worked as an artist—over forty years.

Now the question arises: What is an illustration? In the popular sense, illustration may be good red herring drawn across the path of the reader with the aim of dulling the olfactory sense when the odor of the story becomes intolerable. Or it is a parody on the story, done in a manner which is detested by the author and neglected by the reader.

Illustration, like Boone County ham, violins, and race horses, has a range of quality from here to the moon. Illustration, in the broadest sense, is many things. It may be the Sistine ceiling decoration, where the Florentine artist illustrated some of the Bible stories. It might be a Matisse line etching, designed to accompany the deepest stream-of-consciousness novel. But it certainly need not be the kind of stuff which embellishes the stories printed in our popular magazines.

Upon occasion, then, Robinson is an illustrator. Along with painting murals, easel pictures, and frescoes, in addition to the thousands of cartoons he has drawn with acid-filled pen, he has found the time and produced the energy to interpret what he knows of the meaning of this book or that. No doubt his illustrations are not superior to some of

1925—

the literature which they accompany, but he chose Samson and Delilah instead of Paul and Virginia as the subjects of his inspiration; he painted scenes from *King Lear* rather than from *The Second Mrs. Tanqueray*; and he depicted his imaginative concepts of the life and time of Captain Ahab in *Moby Dick* in place of the adventures of Sherlock Holmes.

The sincerity and the profound perception which the artist reveals in these—his paintings and drawings which increase the stature of the characters with whom he deals—come as a result of personal experience which he has had with them. In studying the books which Robinson has illustrated, one can see that in no instance has he depicted personalities with whom he has not had long acquaintance. Such a familiarity with his subject is, to be sure, in accord with his ideas concerning the requirements which a work of art demands of its creator. "I use my imagination" he states, "and this, of course, is very subjective. But this imagination is the organization of ideas and emotional impressions—and these must be based on experience. It is not fantasy that I speak of; I mean to deal with that which is our knowledge of human experience and behavior. I aim at an understanding of the whole."

To clarify this statement for the observer who has casually turned the pages of the books which Robinson has illustrated, a few examples can be selected which will establish the fact that he had the "experience" he speaks of when he organized his ideas and emotional impressions through his imagination. From the sketchbook which he had filled during his trip to Russia, the artist gathered materials which he later used in illustrating Dostoevski's psychological works; his notable achievement in catching the spirit of the great Russian novelist's creations can be appreciated by a comparison of the character, as conceived by the author, to the pictorial revelation of this personality, as created by the painter. It is doubtful, to be sure, if Robinson would have chosen the Russian novel as the inspiration for his work, had he not himself been stirred by an experience which made a deep impression upon him, one which has colored his life.

In illustrating Walt Whitman's poems, Robinson was gratified to make his translations, in plastic form, of the lines which had stirred him since his student days in Paris. He loves Whitman, and he knows him; one can sense that his fellow-spirit recognizes and understands the American poet. He knows the same country, he has read the same history, and he has lived among the same people, from

the Atlantic Coast to the Pacific, whom Whitman glorified, praised, and admonished. Who fails to see and comprehend the artist's oneness with Whitman when he reads a song of the rolling earth and looks at the powerful, sensuous figures which the artist has invested with the strength of the soil?

Captain John Robinson and his seafaring fathers before him became the models for Captain Ahab and the sturdy crew who sailed with him in quest of Moby Dick. And King Lear, known through numerous readings of the drama both as a plain reader and as an amateur actor, is the prototype of men whom Robinson has known and observed in many a day of confusion. The foibles of human nature which Edgar Lee Masters' lines depict in the *Spoon River Anthology*, the essential truths within character which eventually rise to the surface are familiar facets of the many-sided aspects of personality with which a painter who has never departed from his conviction that art cannot be far removed from life has long been acquainted.

When Robinson had completed the paintings which accompany the poems of the *Spoon River Anthology*, he said:

"Unlike a painting from nature, an illustration does not consist of plastic qualities alone; it must consist of both plastic and moral, or psychological, values. During the reading of these poems I *saw* a picture which seemed interesting and I went to work at once. In order to produce a spontaneous effect I allowed a drawing to come of its own accord, so to speak. Spontaneity in art, of course, is a cold-blooded business, for *spontaneous art* and *spontaneity* are a contradiction in terms. . . . .

"The practice of illustration, as I see it, is in one respect quite different from easel or mural painting, for it necessarily refers to something outside itself. The subject matter, the literary content, assumes a new significance and the illustration must reflect this. From my point of view the illustrator should not enter upon his task with too fixed a preconception; he should not have in mind too pronounced a pattern. The illustration is not pre-composed, but it must be allowed to grow, so to speak, from the seed of the impulse. Upon reading a poem or a work of fiction or history I *see* a picture and I go to work, usually without sketches, and I try to bring the picture to life, to develop and make actual that subjective impression. This subjective impression is by definition my own, not the author's—although he provides the stimulus. My impression is not his, nor is it that of any other reader."

There is a limit to what words can say about pictures. If Robinson had been satisfied with what he could say in writing, as he once wrote to his friend Cyril Kay-Scott, of the Denver Art Museum, he would not have turned to painting. "Isn't

form in every way superior to words as a means of expression?" he asked. To understand what he means by imagination based upon ideas and emotional expressions which are the result of experience; to comprehend what he implies in an understanding of the whole with its accompanying knowledge of human experience and behavior; to realize his conception of the moral and psychological values which complement and enlarge the meaning of a novel or a play, one must turn to the illustrations he has made for each text which inspired his paintings. The pictures speak for themselves and the artist.

Robinson's venture into the field of illustration came about when he was asked by the *Metropolitan Magazine* to accompany Reed to Russia. Strictly speaking, however, the artist was not the illustrator of Reed's text; rather, Reed and Robinson were two reporters who were sent out to give an account, each in his own manner, of the war on the Eastern Front. But this book marked the artist's first collaboration with a writer.

During that same year, 1916, in which *The War in Eastern Europe* was published, Robinson illustrated a book, *Colomba*, by Prosper Mérimée, which was published by Allyn and Bacon. More than ten years later, in 1927, Elizabeth Sage's *Rhymes of If and Why*, published by Duffield and Company, was illustrated by Robinson. These works, however, cannot be considered among that group of books in which, with his drawings and paintings, he revealed the keen human insight, the strength of draftsmanship, and the felicity of representation with which he is able to transfer a mental image to paper or canvas.

The six chief volumes upon which the artist's reputation as an illustrator has thus far been based are: *The Brothers Karamazov*, *The Idiot*, and *Leaves of Grass*, published by Random House and its recently inaugurated "Illustrated Modern Library"; and *King Lear*, *Spoon River Anthology*, and *Moby Dick*, all produced under the imprint of the Limited Editions Club.

For Bennett Cerf, of Random House, and for George Macy, of the Limited Editions Club, no praise may be written that is too eloquent for their efforts to produce well-designed and excellently illustrated volumes. But the fact that in America

1925—

the quality of the reproductions of paintings which are inserted in books has not equaled the best that may be found in books published in Europe before this war must be deplored. A fairly truthful impression of Robinson's work may not be obtained from the reproductions which have, thus far, been made of his paintings, although the black and white plates for *King Lear* are excellent.

As Emily Genauer has pointedly remarked, ".... often publishers and bibliophiles want not interpretation of text, but embellishment; not original and inventive work done with spontaneity and force, but elegant pastiche."[5] The problem, however, seems to be even more extensive than her statement suggests. Although many editors have not been averse to giving an artist a large amount of freedom in conceiving illustrations for their publications, the constant experimentation which occupies the time and the interest of so many publishers and printers in America prevents the achievement of the highest degree of excellence in the reproduction of the original work.

Wherever the original paintings which Robinson completed for the volumes of the works of Shakespeare, Dostoevski, Walt Whitman, Herman Melville, and Edgar Lee Masters have been shown, they have won high acclaim. "Robinson's King Lear is a strong, moving characterization,"[6] wrote Emily Genauer, when these drawings in black and white were exhibited in New York. "Of life and death, erring sons, lovelorn maidens and scheming justices, does Boardman Robinson eloquently speak," said Helen Boswell in the *Art Digest*, in 1942, when the C. W. Kraushaar Art Galleries exhibited some of his illustration-paintings.[7]

From Lewis Mumford, qualified to speak as art critic and as a lover of Melville, came the fullest applause when he saw the work which Robinson had done to show his meaning of the stirring life and death in *Moby Dick*, "No one else has come so close to the spirit of Melville and Melville's character as Robinson has. His pictures would remain as precious evidence of Melville's genius

[5] Emily Genauer, "Thirty-seven Famous Living Artists To Illustrate Shakespeare," *New York World-Telegram*, August, 1938.

[6] *Ibid.*

[7] Helen Boswell, "Spoon River Anthology," *Art Digest*, XVI (April 1, 1942), 23.

even if the words that prompted them should be destroyed."

As a merited honor Robinson was asked by Daniel Catton Rich and Frederick Sweet, of the Art Institute of Chicago, to become the featured artist in the Twenty-second International Exhibition of Water Colors; Robinson's paintings for *Moby Dick* and *Spoon River Anthology* were presented in an impressive one-man exhibition. In his evaluation, in the Foreword of the catalogue of this exhibition, Sweet wrote of Robinson's tempera-oil paintings: "He has interpreted the text with a dramatic touch and deep feeling."[8]

5

After their first year in Colorado, the Robinsons moved into a small ranchhouse not far from the Fountain Valley School, a place that was full of romance but meager in comfort. When Sally

proved, by the empirical method, that the electricity-producing unit in the utility room would not supply enough voltage to operate the bread-toaster, she decided that it was time the family moved into Colorado Springs. With the exception of the years 1932 and 1933, during the time of the revival plays under the direction of Robert Edmond Jones and the Central City Association, when Sally and the younger son, Bartlett, an actor, lived in a house the Robinsons maintained in Central City, "the Springs" has been their residence.

Robinson and his wife did not hope to recapture

[8] The Art Institute of Chicago, *The Twenty-second Exhibition of Water Colors*, Catalog, p. 2. Foreword by Frederick A. Sweet.

fully their early sentiments when they made a trip to Europe in 1939, but they were unprepared for the confusion of values which they saw in England and in France, where once they had seen balanced, happy people through the uncritical eyes of their youth. "It was deeply disturbing to us; we felt the effects of the depression upon the people; the results of the last war, and—what was worse—the threat of the recurrence of war seemed to envelop the security of everyone," the artist remembers.

In England, in the county of Surrey, the Robinsons felt the mood of appeasement which then paralyzed the minds of the residents, who, most reasonably, were utterly reluctant to believe what they were eventually forced to believe. "The English were so much more interested in their gardens than in their fates," said Robinson. "They were trying to be optimistic, though they knew they had no reason to be." It was a contrast to the state of mind which they found in France; there the people were gloomy and depressed with the knowledge of the fact.

In the home of Professor Albert Robert, a neighbor of Élie Faure, the Americans forgot their feeling of uncertainty and enjoyed themselves. It was a delightful interlude in a trip which was not a very happy adventure.

For the artist, who had seen the signs before and who had entertained no illusions at any time about a lasting peace in Europe, the trip was a revelation of a time, not too far ahead in the future, when the hot flames of war would again burn down the structure of European civilization. He and Sally went home to Colorado, troubled by the recollections of things they had seen and felt.

A simple cottage, affording them an uninterrupted view of Pikes Peak and the supporting range, was purchased by the Robinsons in 1943. This home, attractively bordered by a white picket-fence behind which Sally has planted varieties of flowers, is the rendezvous of the dozens of friends who come, unannounced, at all times of the day and evening to visit the artist and his wife. Here their granddaughter, Johanne, often discovers Sally working, in the back garden among the plants, which she continually sprays with water. She carries her small, gray head proudly; and, though she may claim the title of "grandmother," she is called "Sally" by those who know her, old and young.

The artist is comfortable and happy here. Six feet tall and one hundred and seventy pounds in weight, he seems still taller and larger than he is. Through the years he has, by vigorous living and by his reasonable habits, maintained a healthy physical form. He walks about his work with an easy, *fringant* gait, motivated by a quick and nervous energy which is controlled by the calm assurance which he has won from his life. His light-blue eyes, heavy-lidded, seem to give a softening touch to the Irish, flashing wit which is his steady defense against his daily problems. Paul Parker, who has worked with Robinson for years at the Colorado Springs Fine Arts Center, says, "This wit, and it is famous from Fifty-Seventh Street to San Francisco, is devastating and, like all good wit, tinged with malice. But when you are the victim you have no resentment; it is as though you were playing a scene in a Shaw play; your part is that of the straight man feeding lines to the brilliant lead. In true Shavian fashion, Mike Robinson's wit plays upon words, world politics, and social theory, but it is never precious. It runs from low to high comedy, from ribaldry to trenchant and well-informed commentary, from sentiment to irony."

One of the remarkable qualities of Robinson's mind is this: he pauses respectfully before each idea which is new to him, every expression that he has not been accustomed to use; he walks around and around this new word or idea, he examines it from all sides; he admits it tentatively into the reception chamber of his mind; he visits with it and gets acquainted with it; then he accepts it or rejects it, according to his evaluation of its merit. He has the mind and the techniques of thinking of a scholar.

To be critical of a new concept is not to be suspicious of it. An idea may be stubbornly resisted, without being obstinately repulsed, until its worth is ascertained by that individual who can make it a part of himself. "Criticism, of this sort, is the quest for the destination," says Robinson.

"Look at an idea as though it were an object," he advises his students, "and be sure to look at it from all sides." Then, "unless you *understand* the ideas you wish to disseminate, be still; otherwise your words may be misleading."

The artist has many tastes which are similar to

1925—

those of literary men. He remarks frequently: "I have more friends and acquaintances in the field of writing than I have in art." His library shows the diversity of his interests in the titles of the books, from *The History of the Ancient World*, by M. Rostovtzeff; *Hand-Atlas of Human Anatomy*, by Werner Spalteholz; *Troilus and Cressida*, by Chaucer to *The Writings of Thomas Paine*, and the authors whose works are well represented: Marcel Proust, Havelock Ellis, Thomas Mann, George Santayana, Ernest Hemingway, and Gertrude Stein.

"A book I don't care to re-read I should not consider a first-rate book," he says. Among the books which are the oldest friends of the artist, these are the best, the tried and true: *Plain Tales from the Hills; Brothers Karamazov; War and Peace,* which he has re-read four times; the works of Meredith; and, finally, the Bible and the plays of Shakespeare.

But when the day has given him weariness and the night refuses him sleep, Robinson will again take down the book which makes the way distinct: William Macneile Dixon's *The Human Situation*, "an highway which shall be for those: the wayfaring who need the light."

"How simple then is our duty—loyalty to life, to the ship's company, and to ourselves, that it may not be through our surrender that the great experiment of existence, whose issue remains in doubt, come to an end in nothingness."[9]

In August the evenings are cool in the Robinson's back yard, but the warmth which the sun has baked into the ground comes up reluctantly. We sat, silent, looking across the first low range, out upon the graded blue of the foothills. Up and beyond them rose the magnificence of the Rockies, the tips of the highest summits wreathed in gray-white shawls of clouds; above these, again, the orange streaks of light shot out a long way, blending finally over the flats of Kansas and Oklahoma. Here and there along the mountainside small points of light increased until, finally, the hour had come when the illuminated cog-track at Manitou, near the base of the range, which carries the tour-

[9] (New York, 1937), p. 438.

ists up to the Peak glowed like a phosphorescent chalk line upon a blackboard.

"This damned tree sprays stuff on me," growled Robinson. "Why don't we cut it down?"

"You know you wouldn't do it," returned Sally calmly, "else why didn't you cut it last summer?"

My cigarette made sweeping red arcs in the dusk as I raised it to inhale, then lowered it.

"What did you and Percy Hagerman talk about this afternoon?" asked Sally. "You were uncommonly serious, it seems to me."

"Percy and I have our heavy moments, now and again," Robinson shot a wicked grin at his wife. "We are, both of us, awfully serious men."

"Oh, be still. I've seen you sober with Percy, occasionally, but that was because you had nothing better to do. Anyway, what did you talk about?"

"We were talking men's talk. I forget just what it was."

"Now come, Mike, you were mighty preoccupied this afternoon; I noticed it, too," I urged. "It wasn't all about the art school, was it?"

"No, I guess we were in over our heads; we got to talking about philosophy and such immaterial things. Percy reads books, you know, and then tries out his secondhand ideas on me. He knows I am filled with ignorance, and it gives him confidence to talk to me."

"I can appreciate that," said Sally. "What did you say?"

"I said I didn't know much about religion or ethics, and Percy kept after me to give him my ideas about good and evil and such weighty matters."

"When did you grow this reticence?" smiled Sally. "I haven't noticed it for your beard, I guess; you must keep me informed about these changes in you."

"I have my private life," Robinson glared at us. "Don't you know I read books, too?"

"What did you say about this good and evil business?"

"Oh, I said lots of things," Robinson answered airily, "but mostly, I told Percy I'm agin evil and for good—when I know what it is."

"Give us a sample," Sally demanded. "What do you think is evil and what is good?"

"I don't know, for sure, just what either is unless it comes in a raw state. Anyway, I'd say that the paradox of good and evil is one of the terrors of living."

"That's pretty good," conceded his wife. "I'd like to hear more, but wait until I fill these glasses. Don't go on without me."

From the kitchen, through a door just next to our chairs, Sally brought iced drinks; we cooled the palms of our hands on them while she lit a cigarette. A fat bug crawled on Robinson's hand, making him jump. "Too many bugs out here under this tree," he complained. "It's worse in the dark; they catch you by surprise. How can I be a philosopher and a sage under these conditions?"

"Let's not get off on these bugs, Michael. You said something about a paradox. . . . ."

"Humph. I've forgotten that long ago. I'm on a new tack now."

"Well, I've heard you talk about a paradox before, anyway, so we can pick up in the general area of mysterious things. Does this bore you?" she turned to me.

"Not at all," I assured her. "I've read a book too."

"Then, Michael, you may go on. I must be getting beyond my most youthful days because I seem to be interested in these subjects. They say youth and metaphysics are wasted upon children."

"Shaw said part of that; I heard him," said Robinson. "I'm thinking, too, that it's high time a man had an idea about where men go when they leave here. An interesting speculation; one which occupies more of your time when you get over fifty, I hear."

"And what do you think about immortality, Mike?" I asked.

There was a lengthy silence while Robinson emptied his glass. He breathed deeply and looked at the faint glow which barely outlined the farthest mounds in the distance, which, for our dark-accustomed eyes, seemed now more like believable hills than the fantastic western heights.

"I do more than faintly trust the larger hope, as the country prelate said, when I turn my thoughts to after-life," the deep voice returned to me. "I feel a rhythm of a great plan; after death I hope to continue to be a part of it."

There was silence. Then the voice went on:

"However, though I have faith in that, one of the greatest confusions that comes to me now is the close proximity, seemingly, of what we like to think of as ultimate value to that which is just

plain expediency. As Lincoln Steffens discovered, the right course isn't very clearly marked on the road to heaven."

"Sally," Robinson continued in a tone which dismissed seriousness, "these bugs are awful; don't you want me to cut down this maple tree?"

"Oh, Michael, pull down your eyebrows and take a nap," said a soft voice, and Sally laid a hand on his arm.

"Mountain Anatomy," Robinson called the new work which he studied there in his studio. For weeks it had been hanging there, the object of his concern.

"It's difficult to get at the very essence of mountains," he said as he examined the painting, a strong work, low in color intensities, powerful in drawing, direct and structural in design. The searching brush lines, penetrating to an indescribable depth, explained the mountain from top to base.

Struggle through action and counteraction, that is the breath of life and the spirit which lives in Robinson's painting. His art is an intensification; there is no ease through thoughtlessness, no simplicity by clever manipulations.

The artist removed the painting from the wall and set it upon his easel. He mixed paints; he began to work. An hour passed, and the second was well spent when he sat back to study. Through his contemplation of nature he knew that, though she is the source of the artist's knowledge, she may be the cause of his confusion. But he who sees her altogether and understands her, whole and clear, can know what Emerson realized when he gave praise to the lines:

The innocent brightness of a new-born Day
                                        is lovely yet;
The clouds that gather round the setting sun
Do take a sober coloring from an eye
That hath kept watch o'er man's mortality;
Another race hath been, and other palms are won.
Thanks to the human heart by which we live,
Thanks to its tenderness, its joys, and fears,
To me the meanest flower that blows can give
Thoughts that do often lie too deep for tears.

THE CHRONOLOGY

1876	September 6	Born in Somerset, Nova Scotia
1880		His mother, brother, and sister started with father on a five-year trip around the world
1885	September	Left Nova Scotia with Grandfather Parker to join his family in Cardiff, Wales
1885–90		Attended private school in Cardiff
1890	January 22	Father died in Cardiff
1890–94		Attended school in Berwick, Nova Scotia
1894		Went to Boston
1894	September	Entered Massachusetts Normal Art School
1894–97		Studied in Massachusetts Normal Art School under E. Wilbur Dean Hamilton
1896		Saw murals by Puvis de Chavannes and Sargent in Boston Public Library
1896	April	Met patrons, Hannah Parker Kimball and Mrs. Henry Kimball
1898	June	Sailed for Paris, France
1898		Visited Colorossi's, the Académie Julian, and Leon Gérôme's class at the Ecole des Beaux Arts
1898		Friends, William King and Arthur Atkins, introduced him to Sally Whitney, a San Franciscan studying with Rodin
1899		Lived with Arthur in the apartment of Frederick Keppel, Sr., Atkins' uncle
1899		Sailed for Naples, Italy, as Frederick Webb's companion
1899		Visited Naples, Pompeii, Rome, and Florence
1899		Returned to Paris
1899		Sailed for Boston
1900		Remained in Boston eight months; worked at plaster cast of city, which was sent to Paris Exposition in 1900
1900	March	Went to San Francisco to visit Sally Whitney
1901		Associated in San Francisco with Bruce Porter and Arthur Putnam
1901		With Arthur Putnam attempted to establish San Francisco Art Students League
1901		Returned to Paris to work for Mrs. Annie Bertram Webb
1903	November 27	Married Sally Senter Whitney in Paris
1903		Worked in studio on Boulevard Rochechouart
1904		Sailed with his wife for New York

1904	Summer	Moved into barn-loft near Fort Washington Park
1905		Abandoned his studio and obtained a job as field worker for the Association for the Improvement of the Condition of the Poor
1905–6		Worked for Association for the Improvement of the Condition of the Poor
1905		Daughter, Barbara, born
1906–7		Art editor of *Vogue*
1907–10		Illustrator on the *Morning Telegraph*
1908		First son, John Whitney, born
1909		Infant daughter, Barbara, died
1910		Became member of the Players Club
1910–14		Cartoonist on the *New York Tribune*
1912		Second son, Bartlett Whitney, born
1912		Began construction of home in Forest Hills, H. T. Lindeberg, architect
1914		Became free-lance illustrator for such magazines as *Collier's, Harper's Weekly, Puck, Leslie's Weekly,* and *Scribner's*
1915		Sold home at Forest Hills and moved to Croton-on-the-Hudson
1915		Publication of Robinson's *Cartoons of the War*
1915	March	Selected by *Metropolitan Magazine* to become war correspondent, with John Reed, on the Eastern Front
1915	April 1	Sailed with John Reed for Europe, where they traveled through Serbia, Rumania, Bulgaria, and Russia
1915	October	Returned from European trip
1916	January–February	First exhibition, war drawings, at Thumb Box Gallery, New York
1916	May	Publication of John Reed's *The War in Eastern Europe*, illustrated by Robinson
1916		Lectured on his experiences on the Eastern Front under the auspices of the Pond Lecture Bureau
1916	September	Publication of Mérimée's *Colomba*, illustrated by Robinson
1916		Began to contribute to the *Masses*
1916–19		Worked as free-lance artist
1917	Summer	Started spending summers at Martha's Vineyard
1917	November	The *Masses* trial
1918		Birth of the *Liberator*, to which Robinson contributed until 1922
1919–22		Taught drawing and pictorial design at the Art Students League
1919	November	Drawings shown at Knoedler Galleries
1920		Worked as anonymous cartoonist on *Harvey's Weekly*
1920		Attended Republican Convention in Chicago
1921		Cartoonist for the *New York Call*
1921	November 12	Disarmament Conference assembled in Washington; Robinson went as cartoonist for the *Baltimore Sun*
1922	Spring	Joined Sir Charles Ross in London
1922–23		Worked as cartoonist on the *Outlook*
1923	Spring	Wife returned to America

1923	Summer	Motored through southern England with Mr. and Mrs. Frazier Hunt and Sinclair Lewis
1923	September 1	Visited father's grave at Cardiff
1923	November	Sailed for Boston with Bartlett, the younger son
1923		Joined wife and sons in Stanley King home, Boston
1923	Winter	Established studio in residence of Wolcott H. Pitkin in New York
1924	February	Exhibition of drawings at Dunster House, Cambridge
1924		Exhibition at E. Weyhe's Gallery, New York
1924		Met A. R. Orage
1924–30		Taught at Art Students' League; turned out thirteen or fourteen lithographs
1925		Bought house at Tenth Avenue and West Twenty-fourth Street, New York
1927		Publication of Elizabeth Sage's *Rhymes of If and Why*, illustrated by Robinson
1927		Commissioned by Edgar Kaufmann, of Pittsburgh, to paint murals for his department store
1929	December	Murals first exhibited at Art Students League
1930	January	Exhibition at Delphic Studios, New York
1930–44		Director of art department at Fountain Valley School, Colorado Springs, Colorado
1931		Became director of the art school at Broadmoor Art Academy, Colorado Springs
1931	January	Exhibition at Denver Art Museum
1932	April	Exhibition of water colors at Brownell-Lambertson Gallery, New York
1932	October 14	Completed mural for R.K.O., Radio City, New York
1933		Publication of Dostoevski's *Brothers Karamazov*, illustrated by Robinson
1935		Publication of Dostoevski's *The Idiot*, illustrated by Robinson
1935		Painted frescoes at Colorado Springs Fine Arts Center
1936		Became director of the art school of new Colorado Springs Fine Arts Center
1937	November 19	Murals completed in Department of Justice Building, Washington, D.C.
1938		Publication of Shakespeare's *King Lear*, illustrated by Robinson
1939	Spring–summer	Trip to England and France with wife
1940		Painted mural for Englewood, Colorado, post office
1940		Exhibition at Walker Galleries, New York
1942		Publication of Masters' *Spoon River Anthology*, illustrated by Robinson; exhibition at the C. W. Kraushaar Art Galleries, New York
1942	May	Featured exhibition in connection with the Twenty-second International Exhibition of Water Colors at the Art Institute of Chicago
1943		Publication of Melville's *Moby Dick*, illustrated by Robinson
1943	May 5–July 1	Comprehensive exhibition, Colorado Springs Fine Arts Center, Colorado Springs
1944		Publication of Whitman's *Leaves of Grass*, illustrated by Robinson
1945	Winter quarter	Guest artist at Michigan State College, East Lansing, Michigan
1946	January	Exhibition, Dallas Museum of Fine Arts, Dallas, Texas
1946	October	Retrospective exhibition, C. W. Kraushaar Art Galleries, New York

BOARDMAN ROBINSON
THE TEACHER

By ARNOLD BLANCH

MY FIRST acquaintance with Boardman Robinson came through seeing his drawings. It must have been around 1916 that Adolf Dehn, a fellow-student at the Minneapolis Art Institute, brought several copies of the *Masses* to school. To a few of us they became almost textbooks, giving us an intellectual escape from the commercial attitudes that prevailed at the school. Their content, artistic as well as political, caused many arguments.

And so Boardman Robinson became one of our heroes and New York a place where great men lived. Someday, somehow, I would go there and perhaps see Robinson. It was a remote wish; but then in a year I was there. One early Sunday morning, coming down lower Fifth Avenue, I saw him. He was evidently coming home from a party, still reflecting Saturday-night gaiety. This first impression of Mike has always remained. He was walking as if his feet enjoyed the earth, and he still walks that way, even if it is just across the room.

In 1917, along with a number of other art students, I attended the famous *Masses* trial, which became a political education for us all. However, it was not until after the first World War that I was able to study with Boardman Robinson at the Art Students League.

To write of him only as a teacher becomes difficult. His relationship to his students was never the conventional teacher-student relationship but rather the attitude of a friendly fellow-artist. Mike Robinson more than anything else is an inimitable human being, and he never escapes being one. Pedagogy is not a part of him. Even with an unintelligent or unsympathetic student, he may become indignant or outraged but never pedantic.

Among the many who have studied with him, I would say there is not one who could have failed to know that here is an intensely civilized man and one who has not lost virility or wit in the process of becoming civilized. Perhaps in my personal relationship with him this realization and enjoyment of his human and intellectual richness has become an influence more basic than that exerted by his ideologies of art, although the ideological influence, too, has been important.

I shall always remember the first time Mike criticized my drawings. I have related the incident to many of my students, especially to those who seem to be more interested in displaying their talent than in adding to it. In that time of early development, before my ego had received critical ballast, Mike viewed my drawings, one by one. With great consideration, he would say after observing each one, "a beautiful drawing." By the time he had seen them all, I was completely convinced of my genius. Then, in the same manner in which he had examined the drawings, he looked at me and said: "Why do you come to art school? Why make these in class when you could do them at home as well? There is a model on the stand which you are pretending to draw, but your drawings have no relationship to the model. That is why I ask you why you are here." A listening silence filled the classroom. Although I knew it was not Mike's intention to embarrass me, my ego was taking a beating, so I replied with some heat: "Mr. Robinson, are you asking me to sit here and make a copy of the model?" "No," he said, "I do not ask anything of you, but I would like you to ask yourself why you are here—to accumulate knowledge or to display your virtuosity. This

1919—

model possesses a structure, which is like and yet unlike any other model, and each pose or gesture this model takes has a structure of its own. Do your drawings possess these differences, or are they repetitions of fluency?"

I was probably an irritating student because I often questioned Mike's statements, even at times when he was criticizing other students. He was never impatient but sometimes rather sharp. He never talked down to his students; often the meaning of his statement escaped us, because the ears of most of us were not accustomed to language conceived from abstract thought. He hated a platitude, although he swore occasionally. His use of words in criticisms was spontaneous and imaginative, and he was capable of being a great showman. Just a year or so ago, hearing him give a talk on composition, I was amazed to see that, after all these years of teaching, he was so able to give his subject fresh words and meaning.

In the content of his teaching there was very little that was unusable; perhaps not always at the time of its origin was the thought applicable, but later a need would bring to memory the few words that illuminate. To present his theories of art or his particular methods of teaching is something I cannot do, because if they exist I do not know them. He has given many ideas on art to students, some of them contradictory, but they have fitted well in time and purpose. One of his most definite statements on teaching is one he made some years ago when he said: "I believe in the classical method of teaching"; and even now I do not know precisely what he meant. Surely it was not the Academy Julian method, nor is it like that of the academic schools of today which claim to use and believe in classical form. When Mike demonstrated a point in criticism by sketching on the margin of a student's drawing, his emphasis was on the movement and structure of the forms—not on classical proportions. He had a violent antagonism to formulas; and when he saw them in a student's work, he never refrained from demolishing them. He also disliked cleverness, and when a student possessed it to any degree Mike was likely to have a prejudice against him. Many times in art schools one will find a very talented art student who is also clever. It was such a type of preco-

ciousness that seemed to disturb Robinson the most.

When he talked with his students about contemporary artists, it was noticeable that he seldom mentioned their work, but often, without being critical, he described their personalities.

He used to say of French artists in the school of Paris: "They are such clever bastards!" But there were exceptions, Rouault being one. I always suspected him of having a secret admiration for Picasso, in spite of his being "a clever bastard." At the Art Students League he continually brought to our attention the work of old masters and advised us to make some free copies of Giotto in line, then in masses. In the composition classes in Colorado Springs Fine Art Center, when he gave the students reproductions to analyze, he would frequently demonstrate his method of design analysis, emphasizing the rhythm of form and the balance of dark and light and the emotional content of shapes.

Of the actual method or technique of painting and drawing he said very little. In a recent letter to a young artist he wrote: "Of course, one's valid growth doesn't depend on method, but method can influence it—look at Cézanne's early method. Isn't Cézanne's attitude the best of all? He eschewed all preconception, leaving himself completely open to the subject. Your work is fine; I can only wish for it what I wish for my own, that it be better."

In 1930 Mike went to live, work, and teach in Colorado Springs. In March, 1939, he came to my studio and invited me to come to the Art Center to teach for a summer. I went that summer and also for the three succeeding. Mike had fathered the Art Center until it became one of the best art schools in the country; the summer months I spent there were very stimulating and enjoyable. In this school the students seemed to reflect the abundance and vigor of Mike's personality. In the classrooms there were violent discussions about art, science, music, marriage, or anything that might come to mind.

Often there were school picnics, where we would play baseball. Mike was umpire, and always the game would end in a loud but genial scrap. There were costume parties, too, and "Uncle Mike," as the students called him, once came clothed in vegetables. We would drink beer and dance noisily, often to the consternation of the gentle neighbors of the Center. The next morning at eight found us all at work again.

Boys and girls were always going in or coming out of Robinson's studio. With kindliness he would listen to their troubles, give them advice, and then perhaps ask them to criticize what he was working on at the time. These opinions from students he never took lightly. Some of his friends from time to time have said, "Why doesn't Mike retire from teaching?" I don't think he ever will, voluntarily, not only because he loves teaching, but because, as a creative man, he cares for the as-

sociation of those whose minds are plastic and adventurous. He finds these qualities in his students.

I hope I have made clear why it is difficult to write of Boardman Robinson, the teacher. Teachers so often seem to come out of molds. But there was never one made that would fit Mike.

Arnold B. Ronnebeck

BOARDMAN ROBINSON
THE ARTIST

By ADOLF DEHN

BACK in the year 1915 at the Minneapolis Art School, in the center of that great wasteland—our Middle West—the Gibson Girl was the peak of inspiration to students of illustration like me. But a great light broke through that halo of inspiration one day when I discovered the *Masses*, with the reproductions of Sloan, Bellows, Henri, Robert Minor, Stuart Davis, Maurice Becker, Art Young, and Boardman Robinson. These pictures seemed crude and vulgar, but they were a powerful contrast to the perfumed drama of Howard Pyle and the drab literalism of the Munich School. It was a bright light, but a demoralizing one; for now the student of illustration dared think of being an artist.

I admired all these works immediately, but the drawings by this man Robinson stood out. For me they were great. His line sang; it had delicacy and power. It was startling and wild, but it never really went astray. It always told the story it had to tell; it created the form it had to create. As students will, I went overboard for this work. This cartoonist was the "one and only" draftsman. To-day, after these many years, Boardman Robinson is not a "one and only." Nevertheless, despite the fact that I have been looking at pictures for thirty years, I am still able to say that no artist is his superior as a draftsman and that he is one of the great artists of our time. My first hero is still a hero.

In New York, at the Art Students League in 1918, it never occurred to me that one could dare visit the great man until, by chance, Floyd Dell, at that time one of the editors of the *Masses*, assured me that Mr. Robinson was like other people and would not mind the admiration of an art stu-

dent. Weeks later with a trembling hand the art student rapped at a little door on East Twenty-third Street, at the ungodly hour of eleven in the morning; and there appeared a Viking in a leather apron, with an underbrush of unruly red hair, devil's eyebrows, piercing light-blue eyes—and, with all that, a smile. That was the master, Boardman Robinson.

The one episode I remember from this visit was that I, the novice, was asked to criticize the picture he was working on. With some desperation I did. I was amazed that he decided to make the changes I suggested. After doing so, he agreed that the picture was improved. The ice was broken; I was treated like a fellow-artist, even though I was only a student. I was asked to come again and again, and I had some fine, square meals prepared by Sally, his wife.

How rarely a hero measures up to his work! Robinson the man had all the power and poetry of his drawings. He had a sharp wit, which could destroy or stimulate his opponent. He had strong convictions and stood by them during the days of the first World War, losing prestige and security thereby. It would have been so much easier to have remained silent. Along with a fierce contempt for pompous and greedy politicians, bankers, and industrialists and for stupidity and hypocrisy, wherever it is found, he had a feeling for the lost cause, for the underdog.

I remember an episode he told me about, which shows how his sympathy and humor went out to a poor devil whom he probably did not respect at all. At the Republican Convention held at Chicago in 1920, he was drawing caricatures for *Harvey's Weekly* and found himself in a room full of cigar smoke and big-shot politicians. The poor devil in question, a well-meaning fellow from Ohio, pulled out a plug of tobacco and made the unholy *faux pas* of offering it to such a rare gentleman as Senator Lodge! During the frozen silence that followed, Robinson said: "Sure, I'd like a chew." And so Boardman Robinson and a certain dark horse—the future President of the United States, Warren Gamaliel Harding—had a chew together.

Robinson's days of teaching began after my own art-school days, so I never had the good fortune to study with him. Nevertheless, he influenced me more than any of my instructors. His influence on me came through watching him at work, through many conversations, but chiefly through his paintings themselves. This influence went, beyond the principles of art, to the business of life—how to live, how to behave, how to work, and how to think. He became a second father to me; and, as the years have gone by, I have found him to be a second father to many a young artist.

During the 1920's, when Robinson made the great change—giving up cartooning to devote himself to painting—I was off in Europe. Occasional letters from him gave me a picture of his struggles, the struggle with paint and the struggle to earn a decent living. This need to earn a living made a teacher of him, which was a fine thing for hundreds of our most talented young artists. But though a limited amount of teaching can be stimulating to an artist, Robinson devoted perhaps too much time to that end. During these many years he has not had enough time to paint.

It took courage in his early middle age to give up the greater security, which came from drawing for the press, to face the uncertainties of an existence by devoting his time to painting. Along with this desire to paint there was the desire for the heroic. Big murals attracted his attention. Boardman Robinson is a heroic fellow. He loves Michaelangelo and Rabelais, the ocean and the Rocky Mountains. But his big murals, however good they may be, never touch his greatest drawings. His murals are good. I am sure his drawing "The Hands of Moses" is great. He showed me the sketches for the murals in the Kaufmann Store, in Pittsburgh. They were tremendous and alive. The murals, by comparison, are good designs, but they have not the breath of life. I can only guess why this should be so. His great gift is his calligraphic touch, the daring line that holds and makes the form and creates the design. It is done with passion, spontaneity, and speed. Working for months on large walls and adapting his style and design to an architectural setup watered his passion and impaired his spontaneous touch. In art, at least, the size of a picture has nothing to do with the heroic. I think of one of Rembrandt's etchings and also of a mural one-half mile long which was done, I believe, by Rockwell Kent and which died as soon as the newspaper headlines featuring it had dried. Boardman Robinson is the greater artist and the more heroic when he tries less hard to be great and heroic.

It is particularly gratifying to find his best work has lost none of the fire of his earlier work. It has grown, rather, in maturity and power. His paintings for *Moby Dick* stand above his earlier works and are the finest illustrations done in America, past or present. I was around while many of them were being made, and occasionally Mike would saunter down to my studio and ask me to come up and take a look. When he asked me to "take a look" he did not mean that I should admire his work; he meant that I should tear it apart. So, with some of the same feeling that the young art student had had when he first criticized the master's work, I tackled the job of criticism. When he agreed with me, he made changes, and quite often the picture was improved.

As an instructor of lithography, I tried to make a lithographer out of him. He had a stubborn and foolish resistance to the stone. His talent is a natural one for lithography. No reproduction medium gives the spontaneity of the drawing line as does the lithograph stone. If Robinson, like Rembrandt, would give us a hundred great prints, they would have a far better chance of rattling along through posterity than all his murals. The same is true for water color. In friendly arguments he would pick on water color as a bastard affair, more related to batiks than to painting; for he had seen far too many anemic water colors by weak sisters who wallow daintily in the beautiful washes and textures which are inherent possibilities of the medium. If he had ever allowed himself free play with water color, his power to create form with bold, sure strokes would have opened up a door for his very special gifts.

(77)

BOARDMAN ROBINSON: *Artist*

1918— His love of the mountains is in line with his love of the heroic. He loves them—and fears them as a painter. Shortly after my arrival in Colorado Springs, where I taught at the Fine Arts Center, I started to sketch the mountains. Mike, with a sharp glint in his eye, would pull his high-sounding line which went something like this: "Ah, so you're going to paint the mountains. Nobody can paint the mountains until he knows them; you can't know them till you have lived with them for ten years, and after you know them you know better than to try to paint them. Only the Chinese could paint mountains. Go look at the Chinese, you young upstart!" To me this was perverse casuistry, and my retort was: "Of course, the Chinese could paint a mountain and also a bird and a leaf, as we can never do; but I have painted manure piles in Minnesota. They, too, stand in time and place. If one can dare paint a manure pile ten feet high, he can also dare paint a mountain ten thousand feet high." I am bold enough to believe that if Robinson could have more of the approach which I expressed and less of that dreadful awe of the monumental, his painting would be greater.

Some day, after another ten years, when I know my mountains well enough, I shall make a sublime portrait of my great friend, Boardman Robinson, sitting on top of Pikes Peak with one foot in Colorado Springs, the other in Cripple Creek, painting a miniature of God who sits for him on one of the lesser peaks near by.

Adolf Dehn

(78)

BIBLIOGRAPHY

THE ART INSTITUTE OF CHICAGO. *The Twenty-second Exhibition of Water Colors*. Foreword by FREDERICK A. SWEET. Catalog, p. 2.

BIDDLE, GEORGE. *An American Artist's Story*. Boston: Little, Brown & Co., 1939.

"Boardman Robinson," *Outlook*, CXXX (January 18, 1922), 86.

"Boardman Robinson: Artist and Student of Humanity," *Touchstone*, VI (January, 1920), 207–11.

"Boardman Robinson Depicts 'Trade' for a Department Store," *Art Digest*, IV (December 1, 1929), 32.

"Boardman Robinson—His Paintings for Some Pittsburgh Walls," *New York Herald Tribune*, December 8, 1929.

"Boardman Robinson Honored In Colorado," *Art Digest*, XVII (June, 1943), 5.

"Boardman Robinson's Work as a Cartoonist," *Current Literature*, LIII (October, 1912), 461–64.

BOSWELL, HELEN. "Spoon River Anthology," *Art Digest*, XVI (April 1, 1942), 23.

BYWATERS, JERRY. "Toward an American Art," *Southwest Review*, XXV, No. 2 (January, 1940), 128–42.

CAHILL, HOLGER, and BARR, ALFRED H., JR. (eds.). *Art in America in Modern Times*. New York: Reynal & Hitchcock, 1934.

CHENEY, MARTHA CHANDLER. *Modern Art in America*. New York: Whittlesey House, 1939.

CHENEY, SHELDON. *A Primer of Modern Art*. New York: Liveright Publishing Corporation, 1932.

"Colorado—Boardman Robinson," *Contemporary Art of the Western Hemisphere* (Canada: International Business Machines Corp., 1941), p. 56.

CRAVEN, THOMAS. *Men of Art*. New York: Simon & Schuster, 1931.

"Design in Cartoons," *Touchstone*, VI (October, 1919), 78.

DIXON, WILLIAM MACNEILLE. *The Human Situation*. New York: Longmans, Green & Co., 1937.

"A Dozen of the Most Distinguished Illustrators," *Vanity Fair*, August, 1915.

DU BOIS, GUY PÈNE. *Artists Say the Silliest Things*. New York: American Artists Group, Inc., 1930.

EASTMAN, MAX. "Lot's Wife," *Liberator*, I, No. 3 (May, 1918), 26.

GÁG, WANDA. *Growing Pains*. New York: Coward-McCann, Inc., 1940.

W. J. Gaynor. New York: William L. West, 1913.

GENAUER, EMILY. "Thirty-seven Famous Living Artists To Illustrate Shakespeare," *New York World Telegram*, August, 1938.

GOLD, MICHAEL. "On to Harding, Then Home Again," *Liberator*, V, No. 1 (Serial No. 46) (January, 1922), 14–17, 20.

HARRIS, RUTH GREEN. "Drawings," *New York Times*, January 12, 1930.

JEWELL, EDWARD ALDEN. "Murals Done in Auto Paint," *New York Times*, December 8, 1929.

KENYON, DOROTHY. "Mr. Robinson as Satirist," *Freeman*, VII (March 21, 1923), 39.

LA FOLLETTE, SUZANNE. *Art in America*. New York: Harper & Bros., 1929.

"A Letter from Boardman Robinson," *Liberator*, V, No. 7 (Serial No. 52) (July, 1922), 29.

McBRIDE, HENRY. "Boardman Robinson's Bible Drawings," *New York Sun*, February 17, 1919.

MELLQUIST, JEROME. *The Emergence of an American Art*. New York: Charles Scribner's Sons, 1942.

MELTZER, CHARLES HENRY. "An Appreciation of Vigor and Imagination in Art: Boardman Robinson —'An American Daumier,'" *Arts and Decoration*, XV (August, 1921), 228–29.

Metropolitan Magazine. Photograph with small biography and criticism, October, 1915, p. 28.

"Mountain-Chaser," *Time*, XXXV (March 18, 1940), 40.

"Murals in Department Store Tell History of Commerce," *New York World*, December, 1929.

BOARDMAN ROBINSON: *Bibliography*

1913–44

MURRELL, WILLIAM. *A History of American Graphic Humor*. New York: Macmillan Co., 1938.

NOCK, A. J. Editorial, *Freeman*, August 28, 1920.

ORAGE, A. R. *Selected Essays and Critical Writings*. London: Stanley Nott, 1935.

PARKER, PAUL. "Boardman Robinson: Master of Conflict," *Pacific Art Review*, III (1944), 40.

———. "Post Office Mural for Englewood, Colorado," *Parnassus*, XII (October, 1940), 29.

"Powerful Illustrations; Exhibition, Walker Galleries," *Art News*, XXXVIII (March 9, 1940), 19.

"Retrospective Exhibition at the Colorado Springs Fine Arts Center," *Art News*, XLII (May 15, 1943), 25.

ROBINSON, BOARDMAN. "American Art of the Future," *Art Register* (published by the Denver Art Museum) I, No. 2 (January, 1931), 1.

———. "In Chicago," *Liberator*, III, No. 8 (Serial No. 29) (August, 1920), 22.

———. *Ninety-three Drawings*. With an Introduction by GEORGE BIDDLE. Colorado Springs: Colorado Springs Fine Arts Center, 1937.

———. "Regionalism in Art," *Colorado College Bulletin: Four Lectures on the Fine Arts*. Colorado Springs, March, 1936.

SAINT-GAUDENS, HOMER. *The American Artist and His Times*. New York: Dodd, Mead & Co., 1941.

SCHMECKEBIER, LAWRENCE E. *John Steuart Curry's Pageant of America*. New York: American Artists Group, Inc., 1943.

SCHOOLMAN, REGINA, and SLATKIN, CHARLES E. *The Enjoyment of Art in America*. New York: J. B. Lippincott Co., 1942.

SLOAN, JOHN. *Gist of Art*. New York: American Artists Group, Inc., 1939.

TAGGARD, GENEVIEVE. "May Days," *Nation*, CXXI (September 30, 1925), 353–56.

"Topic of the Times," *New York Times*, November 21, 1927.

VINCI, LEONARDO DA. *The Notebooks*. Arranged, rendered into English, and introduced by EDWARD MACCURDY. New York: Garden City Publishing Co., 1941–42.

WELLER, ALLEN. "Drawings by Boardman Robinson," *Magazine of Art*, XXXIV (June–July, 1941), 318–21.

WICKEY, HARRY. *Thus Far—the Growth of an American Artist*. New York: American Artists Group, Inc., 1941.

WRIGHT, WILLARD HUNTINGTON. *Modern Painting*. New York: Dodd, Mead & Co., 1930.

CATALOGUE

This catalogue is not complete, nor can its absolute accuracy be guaranteed. It is hardly possible that all the drawings made by the artist from 1907 to 1915, for example, could be listed completely. This catalogue does include a list, compiled from all known sources of information, of the outstanding work of the artist.

Abbreviations used in describing places of signature:

l.l. —lower left   l.c.l. —lower center left
l.r. —lower right   l.c.r. —lower center right
l.c. —lower center   u.c.l.—upper center left
u.l.—upper left   u.c.r.—upper center right
u.r.—upper right

DRAWINGS

AUGUSTE RODIN   About 1899
Pencil drawing.
Head of Rodin with beard.
Signed: (on Rodin's left shoulder) "B.R."
Reproduced in *Ninety-three Drawings*, Pl. 11.

80. NUDE   1900
Wash drawing. $7\frac{1}{4} \times 5\frac{1}{4}$ inches.
Three-quarter-length female figure, back view. Tones blotted out to obtain light value of flesh. Outline of figure described by pencil lines. Great value contrast between light tone of figure and dark background.
Signed u.r.: "B.R."
Collection of the artist.

85A. SALLY'S HANDS   1904
Pencil drawing.
Four sketches of Sally's hands in varying positions.
Signed l.l.: "S's hands
Chateau du Plum-Trèvin
February 20 '04."
Collection of the artist.

85. SALLY   1905
Drawing. $6\frac{1}{2} \times 5\frac{1}{2}$ inches.
Three-quarter view of Sally Robinson, sewing.
Signed l.r.: "Boardman Robinson."
Collection of the artist.
Listed in the *Comprehensive Exhibition Catalogue*, No. 59.

ILLUSTRATION   1907–10
Drawing.
"And that baby and her nurse are sleeping right in thar behind them blankets."
Two male figures sit in center, facing each other. Large hound dog lies asleep on the floor at their feet.
Unsigned.
Published in the *Morning Telegraph*, 1907–10.

ILLUSTRATION FOR "HATS IS HATS"   1907–10
Pen and ink. $8\frac{1}{2} \times 9\frac{1}{2}$ inches.
Calf smashing large hatbox. Bold, strong lines.
Signed l.r.: "B.R."
The Henry Schnakenberg collection of the Robert Hull Fleming Museum of the University of Vermont, Burlington.
Illustration for a magazine story, "Hats Is Hats."

BROADWAY CONTRASTS   1907–10
Drawing.
Mr. W. J. Ferguson and Mr. Étienne Girardet. Caricatures of two male figures. Full-front view of one at left shows tall, thin man, wearing Chesterfield coat and derby. Profile view of one at right shows short, bald, high-collared man in profile.
Signed at left of right figure: "B.R."
Published in the *Morning Telegraph*, 1907–10.

BROADWAY CONTRASTS   1907–10
Drawing.
Two women in fashions of the period, wearing extremely large hats. Figure on left faces full front. Figure on right stands so that she shows three-quarters back view, with face in profile.
Unsigned.
Published in the *Morning Telegraph*, 1907–10.

ILLUSTRATION   1907–10
Drawing.
"Who—where'd you get them?" queried Dean.
Two male figures sit on bunk bed at left. The one at far right faces a male figure standing at center right, who wears a large hat and gun in holster. At right a fourth male figure, wearing a hat, sits looking on.
Signed l.c.r.: "B.R."
Published in the *Morning Telegraph*, 1907–10.

ILLUSTRATION   1907–10
Drawing.
Family stands at right, facing right. The bearded father in derby hat and dark suit holds an infant. The

1907–12 mother, with four children, stands behind him.
Signed l.l.: "B.R."
Published in the *Morning Telegraph*, 1907–10.

MADAME FREMSTAD FEEDING PARK SQUIRRELS 1907–10
Drawing.
Fashionably dressed woman, in dark, heavy cloak
and large hat with light feathers, stands at center left,
facing a squirrel on a bench at left. Another squirrel
stands at her feet. Large tree at right.
Signed l.l.: "B.R."
Published in the *Morning Telegraph*, 1907–10.

GETTING READY FOR EASTER   1907–10
Drawing.
Scene in milliner's shop shows woman customer at
left, sitting in front of mirror admiring herself in a
large hat. Man in black stands beside her, looking on,
his top hat, gloves, and cane lying on table beside him.
Devil-figure at far right looks on from shadows. Large
hat on display in center right foreground.
Signed: l.c.l.: "B.R."
Published in the *Morning Telegraph*, 1907–10.

JAMES HUNEKER   1908
Pen and ink. 8×12 inches (approximately).
Portrait. Three-quarter view of seated figure.
Collection of Mrs. Malcolm L. McBride, Cleveland,
Ohio.

51. ADOPTED CHILDREN   About 1910
Ink drawing. 9½×7½ inches.
Two children lie in bed in barnlike room. Large
structural rafters form corner above them.
Signed l.r.: "Boardman Robinson."
Collection of the artist.

MAYOR GAYNOR   1910–14
Drawing. 14×18 inches (approximately).
Bust of Gaynor. A wreath lies on railing in front of
him at lower right.
Signed l.r.: "Boardman Robinson."
Published in the *New York Tribune*, 1910–14; repro-
duced in *Ninety-three Drawings*, Pl. 13.

FOG   1910–14
Drawing. 14×10 inches (approximately).
A shrouded, indistinct figure sweeps along; its head
is a skull.
Signed l.r.: "Boardman Robinson."
Collection of the artist.
Published in the *New York Tribune*, 1910–14; repro-
duced in *Ninety-three Drawings*, Pl. 39.

DEATH AND THE BABIES   1910–14
Drawing.
Black-shrouded Death holds many babies in his arms.
A mother at lower right shields hers from him.

Signed l.l.: "Boardman Robinson."
Published in the *New York Tribune*, 1910–14; reproduced in *Ninety-three Drawings*, Pl. 21.

HUERTA   1910–14
Drawing. 24×14 inches (approximately).
Male figure, wearing eyeglasses, sits on grave bear-
ing headstone labeled "Francisco Madero." In his left
hand he holds a bloody sword.
Signed l.r.: "Boardman Robinson."
Published in the *New York Tribune*, 1910–14; repro-
duced in *Ninety-three Drawings*, Pl. 41.

PORTRAIT OF ANDREW CARNEGIE   1911
Drawing. 18×14 inches.
Wears a "canny Scot" smile.
Signed: "B.R."
Collection of Harry Schoen, New York City.

MEXICO   1911
Drawing. 20½×14 inches.
Female figure at right, standing knee-deep in human
corpses. Smoke in background.
Signed l.r.: "Boardman Robinson."
Collection of the artist.
Listed in the *Comprehensive Exhibition Catalogue*, No. 85.

VIVA MEXICO   1912
Drawing. 18×13 inches.
Draped female figure, with flowing hair, stands tri-
umphant over fallen figure, bloody sword in her right
hand, her left hand upraised. In center background,
smaller figures with cannon.
Signed l.l.: "Boardman Robinson."
Collection of the artist.
Published in the *New York Tribune;* reproduced in *Nine-
ty-three Drawings*, Pl. 18; listed in the *Comprehensive
Exhibition Catalogue*, No. 89.

50. THE BREAD LINE   1912
Drawing. 11¼×21 inches.
Fourteen figures line up to receive food at window
at extreme left. At top left a sign reads, "Line forms
on this side."
Signed l.r.: "Boardman Robinson '12."
Collection of the artist.

54. STATEN ISLAND FERRY   1912
Wash drawing. 14½×20¼ inches.
Eight figures aboard Staten Island ferry. Central
group, two women and two men, look out over railing.
Woman in dark cloak and large hat in lower left corner
of composition. Drawing in black, supported by brown
washes.
Signed l.r.: "Boardman Robinson 1912."
Collection of the artist.

WAKE UP JERRY—TEDDY'S HOME   1912
Ink drawing. 17×14 inches.
Two tramps on a park bench.
Collection of the artist.
Listed in the *Comprehensive Exhibition Catalogue*, No. 83.

VILLA IS CLOSING IN   1912

Crayon and brush drawing. 12×16 inches (approximately).

Male figure, labeled "Huerta," sits at left in chair, looking backward over his left shoulder at shadowy figure of Villa, rising above a mountain peak at upper right. Villa clenches small dagger in his right hand. Grave with stone, labeled "Madero," lies at lower right.
Signed l.r.: "Boardman Robinson."
Collection of the artist.
Published in the *New York Tribune*.

WELCOME HOME, COLONEL   1912

Crayon. 16½×10½ inches.

Uncle Sam, at left, welcomes Teddy Roosevelt, who walks off ship's gangplank from right. They are about to shake hands. Small figure dances in front of ship in background.
Signed l.c.l.: "Welcome Home!"; l.r.: "Boardman Robinson."
Collection of the artist.
Listed in the *Comprehensive Exhibition Catalogue*, No. 82.

LADIES OF THE EVENING   1912

Crayon drawing. 13¾×11 inches.

Two-column cartoon of two prostitutes, sitting in cafe. Figure of devil. Men seated at rear.
Signed l.r.: "Boardman Robinson."
Collection of the artist.
Published in the *New York Tribune*.

TRIO   About 1912

Black and white wash drawing. 25×15 inches.

View from gallery of Carnegie Hall. A group of musicians playing on stage.
Collection of Carl Ruggles, Arlington, Vermont.

INVESTIGATION   1912–14

Drawing.

Nine male figures sit at table, looking upward at the "handwriting on the wall." Door at left in background. Placard on wall at right bears one word, "Investigation."
Published in the *New York Tribune*, 1912–14.

THE GOD OF WAR   1913

Charcoal. 13×20 inches.

Words appear in drawing: "1913 Peace on Earth Goodwill to Men." Original done by Robinson for the Christmas issue of the *New York Tribune*, 1913.
Signed: "Boardman Robinson to Gertrude Besse King 1917."
Collection of Stanley King, Amherst, Massachusetts.

THE CRUCIFIXION   About 1913

Brush and ink. 21⅛×16⅕ inches.
Christ on the cross.
Signed: "Boardman Robinson"; inscribed (in pencil): "It Was the Wrong Time To Say the Right Thing."
Collection of the Metropolitan Museum, New York.

LOUVAIN, 1914   1914

Wash drawing. 20×24 inches.

Female figure in dishabille, with bowed head and hair falling forward, sits at right beside tree stump. At left a helmeted warrior wanders off.
Signed l.c.r.: "Boardman Robinson."
Collection of the artist.
Published in *Harper's Weekly*, 1915; reproduced in *Ninety-three Drawings*, Pl. 25; listed in the *Comprehensive Exhibition Catalogue*, No. 110.

VON QUIXOTE   1914

Drawing.

Figure on horse, "Militarism," jousts with windmills, whose four arms are labeled "England," "France," "Belgium," and "Russia." His sword flies upward as he falls backward.
Signed l.r.: "Boardman Robinson."
Published in the *New York Times*, 1914; reproduced in *Ninety-three Drawings*, Pl. 36.

THE MOTHER AND THE FATHER   1914

Wash drawing. 22¾×18½ inches.

"Greed" and "Pride" stand with their son, "War," who is armed with shield, sword, and horns on his head.
Signed l.r.: "Boardman Robinson."
Collection of the artist.
Published in the *New York Tribune*; listed in the *Comprehensive Exhibition Catalogue*, No. 90.

WESTWARD   1914

Crayon drawing. 18½×16 inches.
Russian bear holding rifle and club.
Signed l.r.: "Boardman Robinson '14."
Collection of the artist.
Published in the *Masses*; listed in *Comprehensive Exhibition Catalogue*, No. 102.

CIVILIZED BOMBARDMENT   1914

Ink drawing. 21×16½ inches.

Street scene shows figures seeking shelter from planes dropping bombs.
Signed l.r.: "Boardman Robinson"; l.l.: "Civilized Bombardment."
Collection of the artist.
Published in the *New York Tribune*; listed in the *Comprehensive Exhibition Catalogue*, No. 93.

THE FIELD   1914

Ink drawing. 16×13¼ inches.
Published in the *New York Tribune*; listed in the *Comprehensive Exhibition Catalogue*, No. 94.

UNTITLED   1914

Drawing. 14×8 inches (approximately).
"What's the celebration about, M's Milligan?"
"Sure, me boy's comin' home today. He was sentenced to ten years in the penitentiary, but he got three years off for good conduct."

1914–15

"Ah, I wish I had a son like that."
Two Irish scrubwomen meet, one on the left, laden with market basket and groceries.
Signed l.r.: "Boardman Robinson '14."
Published in the *Masses*, May, 1915, p. 17 (full page).

MOTHER EARTH   1914
Drawing. 10×20 inches (approximately).
Earthquake in Italy. Nude female figure lies across the width of the composition. Her right arm reaches forward to grasp at burning cities and other scenes of destruction. At lower right, small figures flee.
Signed l.l.: "Boardman Robinson."
Collection of the artist.
Reproduced in *Ninety-three Drawings*, Pl. 46.

ON THE MAIN STREET OF BELGRADE   1915
Charcoal drawing. 11½×7¾ inches.
Signed: "Boardman Robinson" (in Prints Division of the New York Public Library, February 14, 1927).
Collection of the New York Public Library.

VICTORY *or* EUROPE LURED TO DESTRUCTION   1915
Drawing. 15×10 inches.
A poor, bowed, and shrouded figure, mounted on an ass, induces his beast to go forward by dangling a carrot, "Victory," in front of his nose. The carrot hangs from a string at the end of a long pole over the brink of a precipice.
Signed l.r.: "Boardman Robinson."
Published in the *Masses*, 1915; reproduced in *Ninety-three Drawings*, Pl. 37, and in *A History of American Graphic Humor*, by William Murrell, Pl. 179.

TYPHUS HOSPITAL, SERBIA   1915
Wash drawing. 11¾×10 inches.
A long row of typhus sufferers lie stretched out beside a wall with two windows. Two patients at center sit up, with heads bowed. Three men in the background lift a patient onto a blanket.
Signed l.r.: "Boardman Robinson, Lasnitla, Serbia."
Collection of the Colorado Springs Fine Arts Center, Colorado.
Reproduced in *Ninety-three Drawings*, Pl. 49; listed in the *Comprehensive Exhibition Catalogue*. No. 138.

AT THE MOUND OF SKULLS, NISH   1915
Pen-and-ink drawing. 7×4⅜ inches.
Small sketch.
Signed: "Boardman Robinson" (in Prints Division of the New York Public Library, February 14, 1927).
Collection of the New York Public Library.

RUSSIAN SOLDIER DANCING   1915
Pen, lithograph crayon, and wash drawing. 14×10 inches.
Dancing soldier, one leg raised.
Signed l.l.: "BR"; l.r.: "Boardman Robinson."
Collection of the Philadelphia Museum of Art.

SCENE IN LOBBY OF HOTEL ASTORIA, PETROGRAD 1915
Colored crayon. 15×13 inches.
Signed l.l.: "BR"; l.r.: "To Stanley King—a memory of Petrograd 1915. BR 1919."
Collection of Stanley King, Amherst, Massachusetts.

GYPSY WOMAN WITH BASKET   1915
Pen drawing with ink washes. 15×19½ inches.
Signed l.l.: "Boardman Robinson."
Collection of the Philadelphia Museum of Art.

RUSSIAN PRISONERS   1915
Drawing. 10×8 inches.
Collection of Mrs. Meredith Hare, New York City.

WOUNDED, RUSSIA   1915
Lithograph (edition of 25). 14×10 inches.
Two wounded Russian soldiers stand together. The one at right has bandaged right hand. He leads another, whose eyes and right arm are bandaged.
Signed l.r.: "Boardman Robinson."
Reproduced in *Ninety-three Drawings*, Pl. 50; listed in the *Comprehensive Exhibition Catalogue*, No. 161.

93. TWO CIVIL PRISONERS   1915
Drawing. 14×8 inches.
A woman, bareheaded, stands at right. At left beside her stands a man, with short beard and a hat. Behind them is an indistinct head of a man.
Signed l.l.: "Boardman Robinson 1915."
Collection of Mrs. Meredith Hare, New York City.
Reproduced in *Ninety-three Drawings*, Pl. 51.

SOLDIER PRAYING BY THE ROADSIDE, GALICIA   1915
Drawing. 6×4 inches.
A soldier kneels, facing left, his cap in hand, a pack slung over his back.
Signed l.r.: "Boardman Robinson."
Collection of the artist.
Published in the *Masses*, April, 1916, p. 4 (full page).

THE GENERAL HASTENS TO BATTLE *or* THE GENERAL
                                                   1915
Pen and ink with black crayon and ink wash. 4×8 inches.
A very broken-down horse, a remarkably fat driver, and a Russian general of great importance proceed at a snail's pace. Drawing originally done as illustration for *The War in Eastern Europe*. Not published in the book.
Signed l.r.: "Boardman Robinson."
Collection of Connie Zachritz, Colorado Springs, Colorado.
Reproduced in *Ninety-three Drawings*, Pl. 53.

ISTVOSTCHIKI (ISTVOSTCHIK)   1915
Drawing. 13½×10½ inches.
Head of a white-bearded Russian, who wears dark hat with small rounded brim. Light buckle on the hat band, in front.
Signed l.r.: "Boardman Robinson."
Collection of the artist.
Listed in the *Comprehensive Exhibition Catalogue*, No. 45.

SLAVIC SOLDIER   1915
    Pen-and-ink drawing. 16½×12½ inches.
    Soldier, standing, cap in left hand. Index finger of
right hand placed on forehead. (On back, a map of Hun-
gary, Rumania, and Black Sea region in pen and ink.)
Signed: "Boardman Robinson" (in Prints Division of
    New York Public Library, February, 14, 1927).
Collection of New York Public Library.

TURKOMAN   1915
    Wash drawing. 8×12 inches (approximately).
    Head.
Signed: "Boardman Robinson."
Collection of Mrs. Malcolm L. McBride, Cleveland,
    Ohio.

GROUP OF SKETCHES, Moscow   1915
    Drawings.
    Moscow in wartime.
Collection of the artist.
Listed in the *Comprehensive Exhibition Catalogue*, No. 176.

GROUP OF SKETCHES, PETROGRAD   1915
    Drawings.
Collection of the artist.
Listed in the *Comprehensive Exhibition Catalogue*, No. 177.

BATHER DRESSING   1915
    Pen drawing with water-color washes. 10½×8
inches.
Signed l.r.: "Boardman Robinson."
Collection of Philadelphia Museum of Art.

THE KAISER AND HINDENBERG   1916
    Drawing. 17×12 inches.
    Half-figure of the Kaiser, with the head and shoul-
ders of Hindenberg behind him.
Signed l.r.: "Boardman Robinson."
Collection of the artist.
Listed in the *Comprehensive Exhibition Catalogue*, No. 84.

THIRD AVENUE BUM   1916
    Lithograph (edition of 25). 7½×5 inches.
    Man walking along street.
Listed in the *Comprehensive Exhibition Catalogue*, No. 163.

SERBIAN BEGGAR   1916
    Lithograph (edition of 25). 7½×5 inches.
    Male figure, who wears high fur cap and a long shirt
strapped at waist, extends his hand.
Listed in the *Comprehensive Exhibition Catalogue*, No. 162.

100. WEIGHT HANDLERS   1916
    Crayon and wash drawing. 16½×12½ inches.
    Two male figures, the lower of which is lifting a can
to the upper. Lithograph crayon used for solid black
lines, supported by gray washes and sepia crayon.
Signed l.r.: "Boardman Robinson '16."
Collection of the artist.

OVER THE BARRICADE   1916
    Ink drawing. 21×16 inches.
    Male figure, "Revolutionary Story," leaps forward
over barricade. Indistinct mob and buildings in background.

Signed l.r.: "Boardman Robinson."
Collection of the artist.
Listed in the *Comprehensive Exhibition Catalogue*, No. 86.

THE MASQUE OF THE RED DEATH   1916
    Drawing. 19½×13 inches.
    Dark background contrasts starkly with light at
left, toward which walks the grim, shrouded figure of
Death. Horror expressed by numerous figures around
the central figure, all in semidarkness.
Unsigned.
Collection of the artist.
Published in the *Masses*, October, 1916, p. 6 (full
    page).

UNTITLED   1916
    Drawing. 18×8 inches.
    Soldier in trench, with spade in hand, being inter-
viewed by civilian in hat and overcoat.
    Civilian: "Well, what do you think of war?"
    Soldier: "Rotten—there's no time for atrocities."
Signed l.r.: "Boardman Robinson."
Published in the *Masses*, June, 1916, p. 10 (full page).

BILLY SUNDAY   1916
    Crayon drawing.
    "I got him. He's plumb dippy over going to war!"
At left, a rough, peasant-like figure, wearing vest and
cap, strides toward left, pulling the figure of Jesus behind him. Jesus' hands are bound, and he is being led by
a rope tied around his neck.
Signed l.c.r.: "Boardman Robinson."
Reproduced in *Ninety-three Drawings*, Pl. 32.

THE DESERTER   1916
    Drawing. 15½×22½ inches.
    A satire on wartime Christianity. A Christ-figure,
with his back against a wall, over the top of which are
suggested the towers and minarets of a Russian city,
faces a firing squad of five military figures—the Kaiser,
John Bull, Teddy Roosevelt, etc. Rifles form one con-
tinuous line pointing to the heart of the Christ-figure.
Signed l.l.: "Boardman Robinson."
Collection of Dorothy Kenyon, New York City.
Published in the *Masses*, July, 1916, pp. 18–19 (double-
    page spread).

APE-MAN   1916
    Drawing.
    Large head of ape-man—dark hair, prominent jaw,
aquiline nose. He faces left.
Signed l.r.: "B.R. '16."
Published in the *Masses*, October, 1916, cover (full
    page).

GOD   1916
    Drawing.
    Nine heads of bearded, stern-looking warriors, wear-
ing a variety of military headgear, merge into one enor-

1917

mous seated figure, holding a sword upright on knees and facing left. Around the sword play a circle of tiny cherubs, each brandishing a sword. At lower right foreground rise masses of almost indistinguishable Lilliputian figures bearing three small flags.
Signed l.r.: "Boardman Robinson."
Published in the *Masses*, August, 1916, p. 9; reproduced in *Ninety-three Drawings*, Pl. 19.

105. SAMUEL GOMPERS   1917
Crayon drawing. $15 \times 12\frac{1}{2}$ inches.
Head of Samuel Gompers wearing spectacles and hat.
Signed l.l.: "Samuel Gompers"; l.r.: "Boardman Robinson."
Collection of the Colorado Springs Fine Arts Center, Colorado.
Listed in the *Comprehensive Exhibition Catalogue*, No. 101; reproduced in *Ninety-three Drawings*, Pl. 2.

PEACE ONLY WITH HONOR   1917
Drawing.
POLITICIAN: "We must have peace only with honor!"
VOICE: "How do you mean—honor?"
Top-hatted politician speaks, with brandished, upraised right fist. In left hand he holds long document, which reaches his feet. At right foreground, a bending soldier attempts to lift a recumbent soldier. Small soldier figures distinguishable in the right distance.
Signed l.r.: "Boardman Robinson."
Published in the *Masses*, February, 1917, p. 9 (full page).

SIBERIA   1917
Drawing. 14×8 inches (approximately).
Man stands with hands upraised at center, dominating the composition. Chains hang from his wrists, his waist, his ankles. Following him in a curved row stands a line of prisoners, all chained.
Signed l.r.: "Boardman Robinson '17."
Published in the *Liberator*; reproduced in *Ninety-three Drawings*, Pl. 38.

PISCHA SCHNOOFITZ   1917
Ink drawing. 10×13 inches.
Baby in carriage, a violin case lying across its chest, is being wheeled by nurse to concert.
Collection of Mr. and Mrs. Roy Harris, Colorado Springs, Colorado.
Published in *Good Morning*; listed in the *Comprehensive Exhibition Catalogue*, No. 113.

ALL READY TO FIGHT FOR LIBERTY   1917
Drawing.
Uncle Sam, handcuffed by "Censorship," with the ball "Conscription" attached to his bound feet, looks dejected and helpless. The figure of "Liberty" stands in background, arms upraised, hands on head in gesture of despair. Hill in background at lower left.
Signed l.r.: "Boardman Robinson."
Published in the *Masses*, June, 1917, p. 7 (full page).

UNTITLED   1917
Cartoon drawing.
Woman suffragette, at right, holds hammer, on which is printed: "Kaiser Wilson, have you forgotten your sympathy with the poor Germans because they are not self-governed? 20,000,000 American women are not self-governed. Take the beam out of your own eye." She faces top-hatted Wilson, being driven in limousine with no top. Two figures sit in front seat; one, top-hatted, in back with him. Editor's note at bottom says: "This is one of the banners for which the suffragists were jailed."
Signed l.r.: "Boardman Robinson."
Published in the *Masses*, October, 1917, p. 17 (two-thirds of page).

43. THE PRODIGAL SON AND HIS FATHER *or* THE PRODIGAL SON   1917
Wash drawing. $16\frac{1}{2} \times 12\frac{1}{2}$ inches.
"The third in a Series of Biblical Designs and Character Studies by Boardman Robinson." In center of composition the father, facing left, greets son, who is bowed facing him. Both are in semimodern dress. Tree trunk grows at side of road on left, small boulder stands behind the son. A half-figure of a hatted onlooker is at center right.
Signed l.c.: "Boardman Robinson '17."
Collection of the artist.
Published in the *Liberator*, June, 1918, frontispiece (full page); reproduced in *Ninety-three Drawings*, Pl. 58; listed in *Comprehensive Exhibition Catalogue*, No. 173.

THE DOCTOR   1917
Ink drawing. 17×14 inches.
Female figure, "Columbia," lies in bed being interviewed by a doctor, "Wilson."
Signed l.l.: "Boardman Robinson '17."
Collection of the artist.
Published in the *New York Call*; listed in the *Comprehensive Exhibition Catalogue*, No. 108.

TWO DEPORTATIONS—TAKE YOUR CHOICE   1917
Two drawings.
One page, entitled "Belgium," shows soldier in German uniform at far right, directing milling crowd walking toward left on boat dock. Various military guards stationed at intervals. Other page, entitled "U.S.A.," shows fat, top-hatted businessman, labeled "Phelps-Dodge Corporation," directing with thumb the activities of a group of men carrying guns and clubs, who beat at a crowd of people being herded into a boat. Man at lower right stands over supine figure, beating him with revolver butt.
Both signed l.r.: "Boardman Robinson."
Published in the *Masses*, September, 1917, pp. 22–23 (double-page spread).

As It Might Work   1917

Pen and ink, black and white chalk. $19\frac{1}{2} \times 15\frac{1}{4}$ inches.

Inscribed: (on blindfold across Uncle Sam's eyes) "Espionage Bill"; (across bottom in pencil in script) "As It Might Work." Incompetent officers: "Now, in case we make mistakes, he can't bother us."

Signed: "Boardman Robinson '17."

Collection of the Metropolitan Museum, New York.

Published in the *New York Tribune*, 1917.

The Watchman's Daughter   About 1917

Pen and ink, washed. $23\frac{1}{4} \times 18\frac{3}{4}$ inches.

The daughter, who stands, speaks to watchman seated.

Signed: "Boardman Robinson."

Collection of the Metropolitan Museum, New York City.

Adam and Eve   About 1917

Ink and wash. $12\frac{3}{4} \times 9\frac{1}{2}$ inches.

Three figures. Few strong lines. A study in design.

Signed l.c.: "Boardman Robinson."

Collection of the Robert Hull Fleming Museum, University of Vermont, Burlington.

An Interruption   1918

Drawing.

Many figures in evening dress—Wilson in center, other figures surrounding him, labeled "Clemenceau," "Lloyd George," "Big Business Conservation." A large woman, labeled "Privilege," with arms outstretched, stands at far right. Through the floor a powerful arm, "Bolsheviki," thrusts upward. Toward it Wilson extends a hand.

Signed l.l.: "Boardman Robinson."

Published in the *Liberator*, March, 1918, pp. 22–23 (double-page spread).

99. Street Car   1918

Lithograph (edition of 25). $10 \times 12\frac{1}{2}$ inches.

Three heads. At left, a man wearing a hat. In center, a Negress wearing exceptionally large black hat. At right, a plump housewife in flat hat with flowers.

Signed l.r.: "Boardman Robinson."

Listed in the *Comprehensive Exhibition Catalogue*, No. 158; reproduced in *Ninety-three Drawings*, Pl. 75.

The International Labor Situation   1918

Drawing.

Four male figures—one, Arthur Henderson, stands at center back of the table. Seated are Albert Thomas, far left; Ramsay MacDonald, center left; and diminutive, vociferous Samuel Gompers at far right, with fist upraised and clenched.

Signed l.l.: "Boardman Robinson."

Published in the *Liberator*, August, 1918, pp. 18–19 (double-page spread).

44. Exodus 17 *or* The Hands of Moses   1918

Drawing supported with color washes.

The aged, bearded Moses sits on hilltop, his hands held high by two male figures, Aaron and Hur. "Exodus 17:11–12" is printed beneath as a caption.

Signed l.r.: "Boardman Robinson '18."

Published in *Living Art*, and in the *Liberator*, July, 1918, frontispiece (full page); reproduced in *Ninety-three Drawings*, Pl. 56.

Untitled   1918

Cartoon drawing.

"Kaiser" stands in regal robes, with scepter and crown, at far left. Behind him, reaching toward the crown, stands "German Democrat." Pulling him back by the coattails is top-hatted figure at lower right of "Allied Imperialist." Houses in center background. Caption: "This class of pampered and privileged traitors intends to have peace while the Kaiser is still on his throne. . . . . They maintain a dangerous vagueness about the Allied peace terms, with the sole object of preventing a revolutionary movement in Germany.—H. G. Wells."

Signed l.r.: "Boardman Robinson."

Published in the *Liberator*, April, 1918, p. 7 (two-thirds page).

The Temptation   1918

Drawing.

Figure of Christ is seated on hilltop. Behind him stands large, portly figure in businessman's clothes, black top coat, white vest. His arms, with hands spread wide, stand out from his sides.

Signed l.r.: "Boardman Robinson '18."

Collection of Eugene Boissevain, Austerlitz, New York.

Published in the *Liberator*, May, 1918, p. 27 (full page).

Backing the Wrong Horse   1918

Drawing.

"It is rumored that Mr. Gompers has lost favor with the Administration after his debacle abroad and that Mr. Walsh is now chief adviser to the White House." Uncle Sam, holding binoculars in front of him, stands with male, derby-hatted figure in front of race track, over which is placard which says: "Labor Leadership Stakes—Entries—War Labor Board—Walsh Up; A.F. of L.—Gompers Up." On fence in front of race track, "Big Biz" droops dejectedly.

Signed l.l.: "Boardman Robinson."

Published in the *Liberator*, November, 1918, p. 24 (half-page).

Portrait   1918

Lithograph crayon and ink. $12\frac{3}{8} \times 8\frac{5}{8}$ inches.

Signed l.r.: "Boardman Robinson."

Collection of the Whitney Museum of American Art, New York City.

The Third Degree in the Middle West   1918

Drawing.

"Are you a Republican?"

"No."

1918–19
"Are you a Democrat?"
"No."
"Then you're a traitor!"
Seated man at left faces portly inquisitor, who points at him across near table. Behind table at right stand two male figures, one fat and hatted, the other hatless and bespectacled. Behind seated figure at upper left stands menacing figure with gun, which points at back of seated man's head. Gunman wears large hat and large mustaches.
Signed l.c.r.: "Boardman Robinson."
Published in the *Liberator*, October, 1918, pp. 26–27 (double-page spread); reproduced in *Ninety-three Drawings*, Pl. 28.

PUTTING DEMOCRACY AT HOME UNDER LOCK AND KEY
1918
Drawing.
Uncle Sam in uniform closes outside cellar door on female figure of "Democracy." Padlock lies at his feet, Capitol building in distance.
Signed l.r.: "Boardman Robinson."
Published in the *Liberator*, 1918; reproduced in *Ninety-three Drawings*, Pl. 29.

CITIZEN HOHENZOLLERN 1919
Charcoal. $12\frac{1}{2} \times 16\frac{1}{2}$ inches.
Collection of Dr. S. W. Schaefer, New York City.

LABOR AND THE PEACE CONFERENCE 1919
Drawing. $14\frac{1}{2} \times 18\frac{1}{2}$ inches.
Large figure of "Labor" sits at right, holding in his hand diminutive figures of five men, who sit deliberating at table.
Signed l.r.: "Boardman Robinson."
Collection of the artist.
Published in the *Liberator*, 1919; listed in the *Comprehensive Exhibition Catalogue*, No. 98; reproduced in *Ninety-three Drawings*, Pl. 23.

SIGNED, JUNE 28TH, 1919 *or* THE DEAD HAND ON THE VERSAILLES TREATY 1919
Pen and crayon drawing. 16×13 inches.
A skeletal hand at left signs scroll, on which the words, "Versailles, June 28, 1919 Treaty of Peace, League of Nations," appear. Mouse in lower foreground. A bat hovers in indistinct darkness at upper right.
Signed l.l.: "Boardman Robinson."
Collection of the artist.
Published in the *Liberator*, 1919; reproduced in *Ninety-three Drawings*, Pl. 24, and in William Murrell, *A History of American Graphic Humor*, Pl. 182; listed in the *Comprehensive Exhibition Catalogue*, No. 157.

STOP! THE WARNING OF THE BROTHERHOODS 1919
Drawing.
A railway brakeman flags what the onlooker assumes to be a train in the distance coming from left. He stands on track with left hand upraised, palm facing left. In his right hand he holds high his flag.
Signed l.r.: "Boardman Robinson."
Published in the *Liberator*, December, 1919, p. 15 (full page).

IS THIS THE REAL WILSON? 1919
Drawing.
Subtitle: "Germany shall be compelled to deliver 140,000 milch cows to the victors.—The Peace Treaty." On left, a German mother holds up for inspection her baby, almost a skeleton. Behind a fence, facing her, are Wilson, most prominent, with hand raised over fence, palm of hand facing her, and Clemenceau. Behind them are two indistinguishable figures wearing top hats. In the middle distance, on the Allied side of the fence, a cow grazes.
Signed l.c.: "Boardman Robinson."
Published in the *Liberator*, October, 1919, p. 4 (half-page).

SOVIET RUSSIA *or* RUSSIA SURROUNDED 1919
Drawing.
Soviet Russia, young and virile, stripped to the waist, attempts to defend himself with lighted torch upheld in left hand, sword upheld in right, against ravenous animals—lions, snakes, boars.
Signed l.r.: "Boardman Robinson."
Published in the *Liberator*, August, 1919, pp. 26–27 (double-page spread); reproduced in *Ninety-three Drawings*, Pl. 33.

16. LINCOLN, NUMBER 2 1919
Lithograph (edition of 50). 15×11 inches.
Head of Lincoln, unbearded.
Signed l.r.: "Boardman Robinson"; "B.R. '19."
Published as cover for the *Liberator*, February, 1919; listed in the *Comprehensive Exhibition Catalogue*, No. 165; reproduced in *Ninety-three Drawings*, Pl. 1.

LINCOLN, NUMBER 3 1919
Lithograph (edition of 50). $16\frac{1}{4} \times 12\frac{1}{2}$ inches.
Mask of Lincoln, bearded.
Signed l.l.: "B.R. '19."
Listed in the *Comprehensive Exhibition Catalogue*, No. 159.

THEY'VE SIGNED IT! 1919
Drawing.
Spirit of Lenin in upper left holds transparent roll of paper, "Death Warrant of Capitalism," which covers "Treaty of Versailles," lying on a table at which Wilson sits, pen in hand, writing signature. Behind and back of him stand Clemenceau, Orlando, and Lloyd George.
Signed l.r.: "Boardman Robinson."
Published in the *Liberator*, August, 1919, p. 4 (full page).

JUSTICE FOR WORKING MEN 1919
Drawing.
Subtitle: "Tom Mooney has been sent to prison for life after an impartial commission appointed by the President declared that he was unjustly condemned."

"Justice," a completely blindfolded hag, points right as she sits in judge's stand. Below sits a man with spectacles, apparently a recorder. At right stands Tom Mooney, facing right, hands cuffed behind him, being shoved out of the courtroom by a burly, baldheaded figure.
Signed l.l.: "Boardman Robinson."
Published in the *Liberator*, p. 13 (full page) (with "Justice for Capitalists" it forms double-page spread).

JUSTICE FOR CAPITALISTS   1919
   Drawing.
   Subtitle: "The indicted officers and gunmen of the Arizona Copper Trust have been set free without trial after an impartial commission appointed by the President demanded their prosecution." "Justice," an old crone, sits smilingly behind judge's stand, reaching down to clasp the hand of one of a group of four portly businessmen.
Signed l.r.: "Boardman Robinson."
Published in the *Liberator*, p. 12 (full page) (with "Justice for Workingmen" it forms double-page spread).

THE STEPMOTHER DRIVES OUT THE FIRST BORN 1919
   Drawing.
   Uncle Sam with wife, "Capitalism," a portly woman in coat and hat, who holds a tiny pet dog, "Press," make pointing gestures to the first born, "Spirit of 76," who stands at far right. Behind them all stands a figure of a military guard with gun. At back left stands monument, on which is inscribed the words: "Sacred to the memory of Columbia, beloved spouse of the American Republic. Died after long illness, on 15th June Anno MCMXVII R.I.P."
Signed l.r.: "Boardman Robinson."
Published in the *Liberator*, April, 1919, p. 15 (two-thirds page).

124. ANOTHER KNOCKOUT *or* LAW AND ORDER   1919
   Drawing. 17×13½ inches.
   At upper left stands a fat, baldheaded, pot-bellied male figure in vest, with shirt sleeves rolled up, wearing brass knuckles. In center foreground, on the floor, is the figure of man, apparently beaten, who is attempting to rise. He braces his shoulders with hands flattened on floor. His head is bowed.

Signed l.r.: "Boardman Robinson."
Collection of the artist.
Published in the *Liberator*, December, 1919, p. 9 (full page); listed in the *Comprehensive Exhibition Catalogue*, No. 96; reproduced in *Ninety-three Drawings*, Pl. 22.

WALT WHITMAN—IN HONOR OF HIS BIRTHDAY *or*
   WALT WHITMAN, NUMBER 1   1920
   Lithograph (edition of 25).
   Head of Whitman, flowing beard, flowing white hair.
Signed l.l.: "B.R. '20"; l.r.: "Boardman Robinson."
Published in the *Liberator*, May, 1920, p. 4 (full page); listed in the *Comprehensive Exhibition Catalogue*, No. 167; reproduced in *Ninety-three Drawings*, Pl. 5.

OUR CANDIDATE   1920
   Drawing.
   Prisoner, facing left, sits at right in his small cell, his hands clasped. A book lies on the seat beside him, a jug is on the floor; prison bars of door are visible in the background.
Signed l.r.: "Boardman Robinson."
Published in the *Liberator*, April, 1920, frontispiece (full page).

WARREN G. HARDING   1920
   Drawing, pen and wash. 14×11 inches.
   Caricatured head of Harding. Bold value contrasts.
Signed l.r.: "Boardman Robinson."
Collection of the artist.
Reproduced in *Ninety-three Drawings*, Pl. 12.

77. DANCING NUDE   1920
   Wash drawing. 9½×6½ inches.
   Female nude, poised on right foot. She faces left. Full-length back view.
Signed l.r.: "Boardman Robinson."
Collection of the artist.

FEODOR CHALIAPIN   1920
   Pencil drawing. 6¼×4¼ inches.
   Profile view of head.
Signed l.l.: "F. Chaliapin"; l.r.: "Boardman Robinson '20."
Collection of the artist.

SIMON LEGREE PALMER   1920
   Drawing.
   At left stands a figure, reminiscent of the southern character. He wears goatee, hat, vest, revolver in holster, and riding boots. In his right hand he swings a whip. Tied to a whipping post at right are two beaten figures, labeled "Communist Party" and "Communist Labor Party." Other almost indistinguishable figures cower beside them at center.
Signed l.c.l.: "Boardman Robinson."
Published in the *Liberator*, March, 1920, p. 9 (full page).

SERMON ON THE MOUNT   1920
   Red-chalk and black-pencil drawing. 14×17 inches.
   A study for a larger fresco. Christ is seated on a rock, surrounded by his disciples. His right hand is raised. Figures form an oval contour, some seated, some standing, some lying down. Line figure of Judas stands in background to the left of center.
Signed: "Boardman Robinson."
Collection of Eugene Schoen, New York City.

CHECKMATE, GENTLEMEN   1920
   Lithograph (edition of 25). 13×19 inches.
   Lenin plays chess with Clemenceau, Lloyd George, and Wilson. Lenin sits at left, smoking cigarette. Clemenceau sits at table opposite him, with Wilson around

1920

corner at center left. Lloyd George stands behind them.
Signed l.l.: "Boardman Robinson."
Published in the *Liberator*, February, 1920, pp. 26–27
(double-page spread); listed in the *Comprehensive
Exhibition Catalogue*, No. 155; reproduced in *Ninety-
three Drawings*, Pl. 34.

MAY DAY, 1920   1920
Drawing.
Labor, represented by a man in shirt sleeves and
overalls, lies sleeping at the foot of a tree, which rises
at left. His eyes are closed, his left arm upraised. Behind him at left stands soldier in alert position, a bay-
onet in hand. In semicircular background are large guns
trained on him and other soldiers aiming in his direction.
Signed l.r.: "Boardman Robinson."
Published in the *Liberator*, June, 1920, p. 4 (full page).

HE PUT ON THE LID AND THE BOTTOM FELL OUT 1920
Ink and line. 8×12 inches.
A portly, seated, bulging figure in top hat holds ket-
tle with cover. Out of the bottom of the kettle swarm
small figures, "Hatred," "Mob Rule," "Terrorism,"
and "Crime."
Signed l.r.: "Boardman Robinson."
Collection of Mrs. Malcolm L. McBride, Cleveland,
Ohio.
Published in the *Liberator*, January, 1920, p. 20 (full
page).

THE SAILING OF THE "BUFORD"   1920
Drawing.
Small ship sails, left, out of New York Harbor. Be-
hind it trails long smoke column, which obscures the
face of the Statue of Liberty at right.
Signed l.c.l.: "Boardman Robinson."
Collection of the artist.
Published in the *Liberator*, February, 1920, p. 4 (full
page).

RASPUTIN AND THE EMPRESS   1920
Crayon drawing. 14×8½ inches.
Figure of Rasputin stands at left, the Empress at
right, seated. They are posed as for a photograph.
Signed l.r.: "Boardman Robinson."
Collection of the artist.
Listed in the *Comprehensive Exhibition Catalogue*, No. 115.

123. THE RETREAT FROM RUSSIA *or* RETREAT FROM
MOSCOW *or* DIPLOMATIC RETREAT   1920
Drawing.
Five figures on horseback (two of whom are labeled
"Churchill" and "Imperialism," respectively) file de-
jectedly toward left, among crosses marking graves and
skulls and bones.
Signed l.r.: "Boardman Robinson." [Signed later,
"1918"]

Collection of the artist.
Published in the *Liberator*, September, 1920, pp. 18–19;
listed in the *Comprehensive Exhibition Catalogue*, No.
100; reproduced in *Ninety-three Drawings*, Pl. 48.

GEORGE HARVEY   1920
Caricature-drawing.
Head of George Harvey, who wears tall hat and
black-rimmed spectacles.
Signed l.r.: "Boardman Robinson."
Reproduced in *Ninety-three Drawings*, Pl. 9.

42. JESUS TO A CERTAIN RICH MAN   1920
Drawing.
"Go and sell that thou hast and give to the poor."
Jesus, on right, with left arm gesturing, faces left, with
his right hand on the arm of a richly clothed man in
turban, who confronts him. At far right stands male
figure, behind Jesus. At far left stand two indistinguishable men with turbaned heads.
Signed l.r.: "Boardman Robinson."
Published in the *Liberator*, July, 1920, p. 12 (full page)
(with "Roger Babson to the American Financier" it
forms double-page spread).

ROGER BABSON TO THE AMERICAN FINANCIER   1920
Drawing.
"The value of our investments depends upon the
strength of our churches. The religion of the community is really the bulwark of our investments. Let
us businessmen get behind the churches!" Roger Babson, center left, in formal clothes with top hat, admon-
ishes a portly financier, center right, also in formal
clothes. At far left stands meek figure, wearing flat hat,
stiff collar, and eyeglasses, who represents the clergy.
Signed l.r.: "Boardman Robinson."
Published in the *Liberator*, July, 1920, p. 13 (full page)
(with "Jesus to a Certain Rich Man" it forms
double-page spread).

IN CHICAGO   1920
Drawings.
Sketches of the National Republican Convention.
Figures include Harding, the candidate; Johnson, a gen-
eral; Judge Gary and Nicholas Murray Butler together;
Coolidge; Senator Lodge; ex-Senator Crane; and two
unknown men, drinking bootleg liquor.
Most of the sketches are signed: "B.R."
Published in the *Liberator*, August, 1920, pp. 22–23
(double-page spread).

37A. SUZANNAH AND THE ELDERS   1920
Crayon and pencil drawing. 14×10 inches (approxi-
mately).
Female nude bends forward on left knee to dry right
leg with towel. Behind and above her, eyes in indistinct
faces peer at her.
Signed l.r.: "Boardman Robinson."
Collection of Willard Helburn, Cambridge, Massachu-
setts.
Reproduced in *Ninety-three Drawings*, Pl. 83.

HISTORY WRITES   1920

At lower right, Wilson feels with his hands the crown upon his head, while above and behind him, at center right, "History" writes in her large book the one word: "Hypocrite."
Signed l.r.: "Boardman Robinson."
Published in the *Liberator*, December, 1920, p. 15 (half-page).

THE SYSTEM INVESTIGATES ITSELF *or* CAPITALISM IN-
VESTIGATING ITSELF   1920

Drawing. Lithograph crayon and pen and ink. 11½ ×15½ inches.
"Dedicated to the Lockwood Committee, the Whitman Commission, The Shipping Board Inquiry, The Investigation of the Meatpackers, and all other solemn attempts to find out if there is anything the matter." A grotesque figure in center scratches itself. At lower left center lies a bone; at far left, a skull.
Signed l.r.: "Boardman Robinson '20."
Collection of the artist.
Published in the *Liberator*, March, 1921, pp. 18–19 (double-page spread); listed in the *Comprehensive Exhibition Catalogue*, No. 99; reproduced in *Ninety-three Drawings*, Pl. 44.

A TYPICAL BOLSHEVIK ATROCITY   1920

Drawing.
Subtitle: "Five minutes after prisoners of war are brought into a Bolshevik camp they are served with bread and tea, and five minutes later they are given propaganda literature in their own language." At lower left a prisoner sits eating bread and drinking tea. Behind him, at center left, stands another, who drinks his glass of tea. At right, holding an enormous stack of leaflets, one of which he extends to seated prisoner, is a military figure in uniform with cap and high boots.
Signed l.r.: "Boardman Robinson."
Published in the *Liberator*, January, 1920, p. 4 (full page).

74. NUDE TORSO   About 1920

Ink wash drawing. 9½×7¼ inches.
Three-quarter-length female nude, arms clasped behind head. Strong, bold, thick brush lines, supported by thin brush strokes.
Signed l.r.: "Boardman Robinson."
Collection of the C. W. Kraushaar Art Galleries, New York.
Reproduced in *Ninety-three Drawings*, Pl. 80.

UNTITLED   1921

Drawing.
Sammy Gompers: "If we're not careful, this fellow will learn dangerous ideas from those foreigners." Gompers, at right, leading with his right hand the large figure of a laborer, labeled "A.F. of L.," carries in his left hand "Bill to Restrict Immigration," which he presents to "Congress" at left.
Signed l.l.: "Boardman Robinson."
Published in the *Liberator*, January, 1921, p. 22 (full page).

UNTITLED   1921

Drawing.
CITY CHILD: "Oh, Mama! Look at the poor bird, it hasn't got any cage." Back view of child in broad flat hat, who faces back at center, pointing to bird in tree at upper right. Plump female figure in flat hat and spectacles stands left, looking toward bird. Old male rustic figure at right looks down at child. Horse and landscape with house in center distance.
Signed l.r.: "Boardman Robinson."
Published in the *Liberator*, May, 1921, p. 23 (almost full page).

45A. THE SECOND COMING   1921

Drawing. 12×20¼ inches.
"The Bolsheviks are capturing the churches, says the 'Times.'" A strong, virile figure, apparently Christ's, directs the battering of a church door framed by a Gothic arch. Five male figures hold battering rams. A child stands beside the figure of Christ at left. In center distance a mass of indistinguishable heads.
Signed l.l.: "Boardman Robinson."
Collection of the artist.
Published in the *Liberator*, April, 1921, pp. 18–19 (double-page spread); reproduced in *Ninety-three Drawings*, Pl. 31, and in *Comprehensive Exhibition Catalogue*, p. 5; listed in *Comprehensive Exhibition Catalogue*, No. 97.

THE TAX GATHERER OF JERUSALEM *or* HE STIRRETH
UP THE PEOPLE   1921

Wash drawing. 19×15½ inches.
Seated male figure at right sits in judge's chair. At left an obese figure of an old bearded man gesticulates with sweeping arms. At center the figure of Christ stands simply, guarded by a centurion. Back of them are indistinct figures of a crowd of people.
Signed l.r.: "Boardman Robinson."
Collection of the artist.
Published in the *New York Call;* reproduced in *Ninety-three Drawings*, Pl. 30; listed in the *Comprehensive Exhibition Catalogue*, No. 107.

AN UNEMPLOYMENT CONFERENCE   1921

Drawing.
Two portly businessmen sit talking at table at right. At left in doorway the gaunt figure of a workingman looks on.
Signed l.c.l.: "Boardman Robinson."
Published in the *Liberator*, 1921; reproduced in *Ninety-three Drawings*, Pl. 43.

YOU CAN'T DO IT IN THESE CLOTHES, YOU KNOW
                                                  1921

Drawing.
"Communism," at right, dressed as bricklayer, barefooted, works with trowel and bricks to rebuild civilization. At left, "Capitalism," a female figure wearing

1921–22 high heels, a much beruffled, bustled, voluminous skirt, much jewelry, and a large hat, which is ornamented with two plumes—"Profit System" and "Parliaments" —attempts to help him.
Signed l.r.: "Boardman Robinson."
Published in the *Liberator*, August, 1921, pp. 18–19 (double-page spread).

SURVIVOR LIST   1921
Ink drawing. 15½×12 inches.
Man and woman reading list of those drowned on "Titanic." Three-quarter length.
Collection of Mrs. Spencer Penrose, Colorado Springs, Colorado.
Published in the *New York Tribune;* listed in the *Comprehensive Exhibition Catalogue*, No. 91.

DEMPSEY-CARPENTIER   1921
Ink drawing. 18½×16 inches.
Two boxers in ring. Figure on left stands, while figure at right plunges to floor, taking the count.
Signed l.r.: "Boardman Robinson."
Collection of the artist.
Listed in the *Comprehensive Exhibition Catalogue*, No. 46.

THE STRIKE   1921
Ink drawing. 12½×18¾ inches.
Street scene. People rioting.
Collection of the artist.
Published in the *New York Call;* listed in the *Comprehensive Exhibition Catalogue*, No. 109.

UNTITLED   1921
Drawing.
"My son, what are you reading? You should remember that your ancestors have been Americans ever since 1776." Boy sits in chair at left reading the *Liberator*, while father stands beside him at right. Yale pennant in background on wall at center.
Signed l.l.: "Boardman Robinson."
Published in the *Liberator*, September, 1921, p. 10 (full page).

BACK TO THE GOOD OLD TIMES   1921
Drawing.
"The Associated Press estimates the number of unemployed in the United States today at from 3,000,000 to 5,000,000" Long line of unemployed, containing fourteen figures, faces left. Sign at upper left: "Line Forms on This Side."
Signed l.r.: "Boardman Robinson."
Published in the *Liberator*, June, 1921, pp. 18–19 (double-page spread).

AMBASSADOR HARVEY—STUDY #1   1921
Black crayon with color. 19¼×13⅞ inches.
Signed l.r.: "Boardman Robinson."
Collection of the Whitney Museum of American Art, New York City.

AMBASSADOR HARVEY—STUDY #2   1921
Pen and ink. 23¾×7 inches.
Signed l.r.: "Boardman Robinson '21."
Collection of the Whitney Museum of American Art, New York City.

UNTITLED   1921
Drawing.
"We could not strike against the government.—L. E. SHEPPARD, head of the Conductors Union." "Big Business," excessively large figure in top hat, seated at right, holds tiny American flag on his paunch with right hand, index finger of which points to large button labeled "The Government," which bears Harding's picture. At left distance back of him, a male figure bows, hat in hands.
Signed l.l.: "Boardman Robinson."
Published in the *Liberator*, December, 1921, p. 13 (full page).

FEODOR CHALIAPIN   1921
Drawing.
Head of Chaliapin.
Signed u.r.: "Fyodor Chaliapin, New York, 1921"; l.r.: "Boardman Robinson '21."
Reproduced in *Ninety-three Drawings*, Pl. 6.

MARIANNE   1922
Crayon, pen, and ink.
Marianne (France) beats her thin cow, "Germany," with the milk stool. Male figure, "Bonar Law," raises a remonstrating hand.
Signed l.c.l.: "Boardman Robinson."
Collection of the artist.
Published in the *Outlook* (London); reproduced in *Ninety-three Drawings*, Pl. 42.

STRANGE MILLINERY   1922
Crayon drawing. 14×16 inches.
Marianne tries on a German hat, while Poincaré decks himself in Napoleon's costume.
Signed l.l.: "Boardman Robinson."
Collection of the artist.
Published in the *Outlook;* listed in the *Comprehensive Exhibition Catalogue*, No. 106.

STONEHENGE   1922
Wash drawing. 7¼×9½ inches.
Three great stones of the Stonehenge.
Collection of the artist.
Listed in *Comprehensive Exhibition Catalogue*, No. 15.

LENIN AT GENOA   1922
Drawing.
Lenin, a schoolmaster, stands left, points to board at center, on which is inscribed "F-A-C-T-S Facts Facts Facts." His class is composed of five male figures, who are apparently diplomats and leaders.
Signed l.c.l.: "Boardman Robinson."
Published in the *Liberator*, March, 1922, pp. 18–19 (double-page spread).

THE WITNESS   1922
Drawing. 16×21 inches.
Jury, in box at right, looks on at court-room scene containing a judge, upper center; a witness, at center right; and a table of lawyers. Four of them are seated; a fifth stands pointing at the witness.
Signed l.r.: "Boardman Robinson '22."
Collection of the artist.
Reproduced in *Ninety-three Drawings*, Pl. 35; listed in the *Comprehensive Exhibition Catalogue*, No. 95.

SIDNEY WEBB   1922
Drawing.
Head of Sidney Webb, looking downward. Wears pince-nez.
Signed l.l.: "London 1922"; l.r.: "Boardman Robinson."
Published in the *Outlook* (London); reproduced in *Ninety-three Drawings*, Pl. 3.

ROGER FRY   1922
Caricature drawing. 15×7 inches.
Head of Roger Fry. He wears formal clothes and eyeglasses.
Signed l.r.: "Boardman Robinson"; "B.R."
Collection of the artist.
Reproduced in *Ninety-three Drawings*, Pl. 8.

THE RING   1922
Lithograph (edition of 10). 6×5 inches.
"Honest, Ray, it's 14-karat gold!"
Male figure in overcoat and derby hat sits at left. Beside him sits female figure in coat and hat. They bend heads as they look at a piece of jewelry in their hands.
Signed l.r.: "Boardman Robinson."
Published in the *Liberator*, March, 1922, p. 17.

THE TREATY *or* SIGNING THE TREATY   1922
Drawing. 14×18 inches.
"Now, gentlemen, we have signed the treaty: let's go into the other room and make a gentlemen's agreement." Treaty lies on table at center. At left, one statesman escorts another out. At right, two other statesmen enter.
Signed l.c.l.: "Boardman Robinson."
Collection of the artist.
Published in the *Baltimore Sun;* reproduced in *Ninety-three Drawings*, Pl. 45; listed in the *Comprehensive Exhibition Catalogue*, No. 112.

POINCARÉ AND MUSSOLINI   1922
Drawing.
POINCARÉ: "Upon what meat doth this our Caesar feed—?"
Large mailed figure, "Mussolini," with sword, shield, and helmet, strides forward at center, followed by small aide in background, bearing fasces. At right stands Poincaré in French uniform.
Signed l.l.: "Boardman Robinson."
Published in the *Outlook* (London), 1922.
Reproduced in *Ninty-three Drawings*, Pl. 26.

MOUNT AIRY   1922
Drawing.
Small landscape shows scene of winding river, with tall trees at left, small trees at right, more distant, with hills beyond them.
Signed l.r.: "B.R." and "Boardman Robinson."
Published in the *Liberator*, May, 1922, p. 22.

A BRITISH ALLIANCE   1922
Drawing.
"France Doesn't Seem Cheered about a British Alliance." Large lion sits on edge of channel, holding a rope in his mouth. Across the channel stands small figure of Marianne (France), the other end of the rope attached to her neck.
Signed l.r.: "Boardman Robinson."
Reproduced in *Ninety-three Drawings*, Pl. 47.

HAIL, THE WORKER'S PARTY   1922
Drawing.
A mob of people, arms upraised, face front. In the distance a bridge and factories.
Signed l.r.: "Boardman Robinson."
Published in the *Liberator*, February, 1922, p. 26 (full page).

104. DE VALERA   About 1922
Drawing.
Head of Irish leader, wearing pince-nez.
Signed l.r.: "Boardman Robinson."

TREE   About 1922
Ink drawing. 9×5½ inches (approximately)
Signed u.r.: "Boardman Robinson."
Collection of Henry Schnakenberg, New York City.

SAMSON AND DELILAH   1923
Drawing. 15½×21 inches.
Huge figure of Samson lies sleeping on the pillow labeled "Europe." Creeping up behind him is the figure of Delilah (France), her shears poised for action. "R.F." on neck of her dress.
Signed l.l.: "Boardman Robinson."
Collection of the artist.
Published in the *Outlook* (London); reproduced in *Ninety-three Drawings*, Pl. 27; listed in the *Comprehensive Exhibition Catalogue*, No. 103.

104A. BERTRAND RUSSELL   1923
Drawing. 13½×9 inches.
Head of Bertrand Russell.
Signed l.c.r.: "Boardman Robinson, London '23."
Collection of the artist.
Reproduced in *Ninety-three Drawings*, Pl. 7; listed in the *Comprehensive Exhibition Catalogue*, No. 71.

103. HEAD OF SINCLAIR LEWIS   1923
Caricature drawing. 9¾×8¼ inches.
Hair and skin in red crayon. Tie and jacket in ink. Cigarette-holder in ink, cigarette in pencil. Eyeball

1923–26

outline in ink. Fingernail in pencil on middle finger. Profile view.
Signed l.r.: "Boardman Robinson."
The John de Leittre Memorial Collection, Minneapolis Institute of Arts, Minneapolis, Minnesota.

SINCLAIR LEWIS   1923
Pencil drawing.
Caricature of Lewis. Full-face view. He wears extremely dour expression.
Signed l.r.: "B.R." "Lewis in '23."

STATESMANSHIP   1923
Drawing. 13×18½ inches.
Collection of the artist.
Published in the *Outlook* (London); listed in the *Comprehensive Exhibition Catalogue*, No. 105.

MARIANNE CONSULTS THE SYBIL *or* MARIANNE HAS HER FORTUNE TOLD *or* MARIANNE CONSULTS THE ORACLE   1923
Drawing. 13¾×19½ inches.
A gnarled old gypsy, at round table covered with astronomical signs, tells a fortune with cards. On the table lie three cards, "Gt. Britain," "Italy," "France." In her hand she holds two others, "Germany," "Italy." Marianne (France) looks on from back of gypsy's chair at right. Raven sits at upper left.
Signed l.l.: "Boardman Robinson."
Collection of the artist.
Published in the *Outlook* (London), 1923; reproduced in *Ninety-three Drawings*, Pl. 20; listed in the *Comprehensive Exhibition Catalogue*, No. 104.

78. DRAPED NUDE   1923
Pencil with colored washes. 14×10 inches.
Signed l.r.: "Boardman Robinson '23."
Collection of the Whitney Museum of American Art, New York City.

DRAPED TORSO   1923
Pencil drawing. 13½×7 inches.
Signed l.r.: "Boardman Robinson '23."
Collection of the Philadelphia Museum of Art, Philadelphia, Pennsylvania.

39. STUDY FOR THE SERMON ON THE MOUNT   1923
Drawing—pencil, crayon, pen, and wash, heightened with white on white paper. 16⅝×20 inches.
Christ sits in the center, surrounded by a group of ten figures. His figure, with an upraised right arm, is silhouetted against the mountain in the background.
Signed l.r.: "Boardman Robinson '23."
Collection of the Fogg Museum of Art, Harvard University, Cambridge, Massachusetts.

SIGNOR BENITO MUSSOLINI   1923
Pen drawing.
Caricature-drawing of head and shoulders of the Italian leader.

Signed l.r.: "Boardman Robinson."
Published in the *Outlook* (London), June 30, 1923.

GIRLS WRESTLING *or* WRESTLERS   1924
Drawing. 15×11 inches.
Two women wrestle. They wear bathing suits, the one on the right a light suit, the one on the left a darker suit.
Signed l.r.: "Boardman Robinson."
Collection of the artist.
Reproduced in *Ninety-three Drawings*, Pl. 60; listed in the *Comprehensive Exhibition Catalogue*, No. 123.

THE PARTY ON THE CLIFFS   1924
Drawing in colored crayon. 14×12 inches.
Collection of Dr. S. W. Schaefer, New York City.

STANDING NUDE   About 1924
Drawing. 8×12 inches (approximately).
Signed: "Boardman Robinson."
Collection of Mrs. Malcolm L. McBride, Cleveland, Ohio.

79. NUDE   About 1924
Wash, pen, and crayon.
Three-quarter-length figure of female nude, left hand in back of head. Modeling strong with wash, supported by pen lines and crayon.
Signed l.l.: "Boardman Robinson."
Collection of the artist.
Reproduced in *Ninety-three Drawings*, Pl. 77.

STEEL WORKER, SKETCH 4   About 1925
Drawing. 8×12 inches (approximately).
Signed: "Boardman Robinson."
Collection of Mrs. Malcolm L. McBride, Cleveland, Ohio.

73. NUDE   1926
Drawing.
Full-length female nude. Long hair falls backward. Right arm to elbow is visible, left arm behind back.
Signed l.l.: "Boardman Robinson '26."
Reproduced in *Ninety-three Drawings*, Pl. 82.

THE TORRENT   About 1926
Ink drawing. 10×17½ inches.
Head of female figure in foreground before a suggestion of torrent and flood.
Collection of the artist.
Published in the *New Yorker*; listed in the *Comprehensive Exhibition Catalogue*, No. 130.

JUSTICE AND THE MURDERER   About 1926
Drawing. 12×13 inches.
Plump, matronly figure of Justice sits atop a stack of law tomes, while she shakes an admonishing finger at a murderer, who stands in front of her, his gun still smoking, over a recumbent figure. Her words are, "Naughty, naughty."
Signed l.r.: "Boardman Robinson."
Collection of the artist.

Published in the *New Yorker;* reproduced in *Ninety-three Drawings*, Pl. 40; listed in the *Comprehensive Exhibition Catalogue*, No. 111.

SOUTHERN PINES   1927
Pen and ink drawing. 7½×5¾ inches.
Line drawing of trees on French coast.
Signed l.l.: "Boardman Robinson"; l.r.: "Southern Pines.'
Collection of Agnes Barnes, Athens, Georgia.

SERMON ON THE MOUNT   1927
Red chalk and black drawing. 16×20 inches.
Study for fresco (Colorado Springs Fine Arts Center) of same name.
Signed: "Boardman Robinson."
Collection of Eugene Schoen, New York City.

MILLINERY DISTRICT   1927
Water color with crayon. 12½×16½ inches.
Semicaricature, with strong character content. There are three figures, two fully drawn and one abstracted, in the background.
Signed: "Boardman Robinson '27."
Collection of Walker Winslow, Palo Alto, California.

CONSTRUCTION   1928
Brush drawing. 10½×8 inches.
Bold drawing of a building construction. Girders at top, other buildings in background.
Signed l.r.: "Boardman Robinson '28."
Collection of the artist.

PARK SCENE—NEW YORK   1928
Pen drawing with wash. 11½×8½ inches.
Two trees dominate composition. At lower left, a street scene with figures on benches and others in street. Upper background filled with buildings. Shrubbery at lower right.
Signed l.r.: "Boardman Robinson '28."
Collection of the artist.

SALLY   1928
Pencil drawing. 10¾×7½ inches.
Full-face view. Head only.
Signed l.r.: "Boardman Robinson '28."
Collection of the artist.

PORTRAIT STUDY   1928
Pen drawing. 5×4 inches.
Sketch of a woman's head, on lined notebook paper.
Signed l.r.: "Boardman Robinson."
Collection of the artist.
Reproduced in *Ninety-three Drawings*, Pl. 16.

STREET WORKERS   1928
Ink drawing.
Workers repair street. Three figures in foreground. One at left bends toward right. A second at right swings pick from an upright position. A third crouches in center. Two indistinct figures in left background.
Signed l.r.: "Boardman Robinson."
Reproduced in *Ninety-three Drawings*, Pl. 67.

GIRL'S HEAD   1928
Drawing. 8½×6¾ inches.
Head of girl with short hair, shadow on left side.
Unsigned.
Collection of the artist.
Reproduced in *Ninety-three Drawings*. Pl. 17; listed in *Comprehensive Exhibition Catalogue*, No. 39.

84. SQUATTING FIGURE   1928
Ink drawing. 6⅝×4¾ inches.
Male figure facing front, knees bent out from body, left arm resting on leg and right arm stretched out. High-tasseled cap on head. Dark blue-green ink.
Signed l.r.: "Boardman Robinson '28."
Collection of the C. W. Kraushaar Art Galleries, New York City.

84A. CROUCHING FIGURE   1928
Black crayon drawing. 9¾×8½ inches.
Male figure seen from back; crouching with right knee drawn up and left knee on ground; head bent, back muscles emphasized.
Signed l.c.l.: "Boardman Robinson '28."
Collection of the C. W. Kraushaar Art Galleries, New York City.
Listed in the *Comprehensive Exhibition Catalogue*, No. 51.

118A. SKETCH FOR MURAL   1928
Pen and brush drawing.
Constructional preliminary study, with block figures for the panel, "Portuguese in India" in "A History of Commerce" mural.
Signed l.r.: "Boardman Robinson."

119A. FIGURE STUDIES FOR MURAL   1928
Charcoal and brush drawings.
Two male figure studies for two seamen in "Clipper Ship Era" panel in "A History of Commerce."
Signed l.l.: "Boardman Robinson."

120A. FIGURE STUDIES FOR MURAL   1928
Brush drawings.
Three figure studies for "The English in China" panel of "A History of Commerce."
Signed l.l.: "Boardman Robinson."

AMOS R. E. PINCHOT   1928
Pen and ink sketch. 2×4 inches.
Head of Amos R. E. Pinchot.
Collection of Ruth Pickering Pinchot (Mrs. Amos R. E. Pinchot), New York City.

76. DANCER   1929
Ink drawing. 10¼×6¼ inches.
Female nude figure stands with legs crossed, left hand resting on hip, right hand raised to back of head.
Signed l.r.: "Boardman Robinson '29."
Reproduced in *Ninety-three Drawings*, Pl. 93; listed in the *Comprehensive Exhibition Catalogue*, No. 49

1929–34

HEAD   1929
Drawing. 4×4½ inches.
Female head.
Collection of the artist.
Listed in the *Comprehensive Exhibition Catalogue*, No. 61.

PROSPECTOR   1930
Brush line, with some water color, on linen-textured paper. 8×6 inches.
Head of an old prospector, bearded, with large hat.
Signed l.r.: "Boardman Robinson."
Collection of Paul Parker, Des Moines, Iowa.

TOURISTS, NEW MEXICO   1931
Drawing, ink and colored pencil. 8×10 inches.
Depicts a group of tourists in an overloaded, broken-down automobile, ogling two stolid Indians.
Signed l.r.: "Boardman Robinson."
The Mr. and Mrs. William Preston Collection, Los Angeles County Museum, Los Angeles, California.

CENTRAL CITY   1932
Wash drawing. 9×7 inches.
Collection of Dr. S. W. Schaefer, New York City.
Listed in the *Comprehensive Exhibition Catalogue*, No. 34.

71. MIDNIGHT, CENTRAL CITY   1932
Lithograph (edition of 50). 11¾×15 inches.
Two houses and a telephone pole stand at upper left, silhouetted against the sky. From them a wooden stairway leads down to twisting street at lower right. Large telephone pole in foreground, steeple and buildings in background at right.
Signed l.l.: "Midnight, Central City"; l.r.: "Boardman Robinson '32."
Reproduced in *Ninety-three Drawings*, Pl. 68; listed in *Comprehensive Exhibition Catalogue*, No. 164.

75. BATHER *or* LEANING WOMAN *or* NUDE 4   1932
Pencil drawing. 8⅝×5⅞ inches.
Female nude, draped from waist down, bending forward. Her weight is supported by her right arm on solid form at left of composition. Her right leg is upraised, the foot directly in front of the left knee.
Signed l.c.r.: "Boardman Robinson '32."
Collection of the C. W. Kraushaar Art Galleries, New York City.
Reproduced in *Ninety-three Drawings*, Pl. 79; listed in *Comprehensive Exhibition Catalogue*, No. 178.

41. SAMSON AND DELILAH   About 1932
Wash drawing. 21×13½ inches.
Bold, powerful lines depict Samson, at right, and Delilah, at left, in embrace. Hills in lower half of background.
Signed l.r.: "Boardman Robinson."
Collection of Mrs. Meredith Hare, New York City.
Reproduced in *Ninety-three Drawings*, Pl. 54.

PORTRAIT OF A NEGRO MAN   About 1932
Pencil and wash. 14½×10⅝ inches.
Signed l.c.l.: "Boardman Robinson,"
Collection of Lieutenant George A. Cress, Athens, Georgia.

GARDEN OF THE GODS   1933
Conte crayon, pen and ink, wash. 10½×13¼ inches.
Rock formations.
Signed l.r.: "Boardman Robinson '33."
Collection of Lamar Dodd, Athens, Georgia.

COLORADO MINER *or* COLORADO GOLD MINER   1933
Ink wash and crayon. 15×9½ inches.
Two male figures, one on right, slightly in background, with glasses and beard. Other figure is miner, facing left—talking and gesturing with right hand out, left hand in pocket. Dressed in cap, breeches, and high laced boots.
Signed l.l.: "Boardman Robinson."
Collection of the C. W. Kraushaar Art Galleries, New York City.
Reproduced in *Ninety-three Drawings*, Pl. 70; listed in *Comprehensive Exhibition Catalogue*, No. 53.

THE LAND OF PLENTY   1933
Ink drawing. 15¾×11 inches.
Collection of the artist.
Listed in the *Comprehensive Exhibition Catalogue*, No. 88.

DUDE RANCHER   1933
Wash drawing—dark blue. 17⅜×11⅜ inches.
Stout figure, side view—ten-gallon hat, chaps, cigar —leading tiny horse by string.
Signed l.r.: "Boardman Robinson '33."
Collection of the C. W. Kraushaar Art Galleries, New York City.
Listed in the *Comprehensive Exhibition Catalogue*, No. 72.

WALTER HUSTON AS OTHELLO   1933
Pen and ink drawing. 9×6 inches.
Collection of Dr. S. W. Schaefer, New York City.

HEAD   1933
Wash drawing. 12×9½ inches.
Full-face head drawing.
Signed l.r.: "Boardman Robinson '33."
Collection of the University of Georgia, Athens, Georgia.

CHARLES HALTON IN *Othello*   1933
Pen and ink drawing. 9×6 inches.
Sketch of the actor in his dressing-room.
Collection of Dr. S. W. Schaefer, New York City.

COLORADO RIVER   1934
Blue and black ink. 9¼×13½ inches.
The canyon between the sheer rocky cliff on the right and the blue mountain on the left.
Signed: "Colorado River"; "Boardman Robinson '34."
Collection of Mrs. N. F. Galbraith, Colorado Springs, Colorado.

FIGURE   About 1934
   Drawing. $10\frac{1}{2} \times 6\frac{1}{4}$ inches.
   Male action figure, back view.
Signed l.r.: "Boardman Robinson."
Collection of Lieutenant George A. Cress, Athens,
   Georgia.

BANKER'S CREDIT AND REAL MONEY   1935
   Brush and pen and ink. $11 \times 8\frac{1}{2}$ inches.
   Overdressed and pompous figures, male and female,
staring in contempt at figure of girl in right back-
ground.
Signed l.r.: "Boardman Robinson."
Published in *New Democracy*, May 15, 1935, p. 101.

40. THE ENTOMBMENT   1935
   Wash and pencil, touched with white. $9\frac{1}{2} \times 13\frac{1}{2}$ inches.
   Bold, semiabstract handling of figures, moving pat-
tern of shapes. Two figures stand at either end of bier,
a woman bows over it in the center background. In left
foreground the kneeling figure of a woman.
Signed l.r.: "Boardman Robinson '35."
Collection of the Dallas Museum of Fine Arts, Dallas,
   Texas.
Reproduced in *Ninety-three Drawings*, Pl. 55.

SAMSON AND DELILAH   1935
   Lithograph (edition of 25). 10×6 inches.
Signed l.r.: "Boardman Robinson."
Listed in the *Comprehensive Exhibition Catalogue*, No. 160.

NUDE   1935
   Pen and wash (black). 17×11 inches.
Signed l.c.r.: "Boardman Robinson"; l.r.: "For Oscar
   Ogg, Nov. '38."
Collection of Margaret and Oscar Ogg, Alexandria,
   Virginia.

COSTUME STUDY   About 1935
   Dry brush, pen and ink, conte crayon, wash. $10\frac{1}{2} \times 8$
inches.
   Woman's back. She wears heavy coat with full lines
and a hat. Right arm upraised.
Signed l.c.r.: "Boardman Robinson."
Collection of Lamar Dodd, Athens, Georgia.
Reproduced in *Ninety-three Drawings*, Pl. 73.

DANCING FIGURE   1935
   Pen and ink and wash. $9\frac{1}{2} \times 7$ inches.
   The figure is very freely drawn and, in conjunction
with the swirling draperies, forms a beautiful spiral de-
sign, suggestive of the movements of dancing.
Signed l.r.: "Boardman Robinson."
Collection of Edgar Britton, Colorado Springs, Colo-
   rado.

COWBOY MOUNTING HIS PONY   About 1935
   Black and white ink drawing. 10×8 inches.
Collection of Dr. S. W. Schaefer, New York City.

101. PRIZE FIGHT *or* BOXERS   About 1935
   Wash drawing on paper. $18\frac{3}{4} \times 13\frac{3}{4}$ inches.
   Figures of two fighters, one standing over the other,
who is recumbent.

Signed l.r.: "Boardman Robinson."
Collection of the Museum of Cranbrook Academy of
   Art, Bloomfield Hills, Michigan.
Reproduced in *Ninety-three Drawings*, Pl. 61.

COLORADO MOUNTAINS   About 1935
   Drawing. 11×15 inches.
Collection of Mrs. Elliot D. Blumenthal, Jr.

NUDE   1936
   Pencil drawing. $10\frac{1}{2} \times 7$ inches.
Collection of Dr. S. W. Schaefer, New York City.

MURAL STUDY   1936
   Drawing. 24×16 inches.
   One figure, apparently Egyptian, sits facing right.
He wears headdress.
Signed l.l.: "Boardman Robinson '36."
Collection of the artist.
Reproduced in *Ninety-three Drawings*, Pl. 72.

MOUNTAINS   About 1936
   Pen, blue ink, on cream paper.
Collection of Margaret and Oscar Ogg, Alexandria,
   Virginia.

MOUNTAIN RHYTHMS   1936
   Pen drawing. $11\frac{3}{4} \times 8\frac{3}{4}$ inches.
   A study of mountains, inscribed at l.l.: "I've rear-
ranged the mountains at my pleasure." One of the pen
drawings in which the pen is held flat-back to paper,
giving brushlike effects.
Collection of Thomas H. Ferrill, Denver, Colorado.
Reproduced in *Ninety-three Drawings*, Pl. 65; listed in
   the *Comprehensive Exhibition Catalogue*, No. 27.

NUDE   1936
   Pen and ink drawing. 9×12 inches.
Collection of Dr. S. W. Schaefer, New York City.

LIFE-STUDY—FEMALE   About 1936
   Drawing.
Collection of Margaret and Oscar Ogg, Alexandria,
   Virginia.

ROCKY MOUNTAINS   About 1936
   Lithograph (edition of 10). $8\frac{1}{2} \times 11$ inches.
Listed in the *Comprehensive Exhibition Catalogue*, No.
   166.

116A. STUDY—HANDS OF HAMMURABI   1937
   Drawing. 18×6 inches.
   Two hands. Draped hand at lower left supports el-
bow, forearm, and hand, pointing up, at right. Detail of
Hammurabi in mural, "Great Figures in the History
of The Law."
Signed l.r.: "Boardman Robinson '37."
Collection of Eugene Schoen, New York City.
Reproduced in *Ninety-three Drawings*, Pl. 85.

1937–38

St. Thomas Aquinas   1937
Charcoal drawing. $17\frac{3}{4} \times 14\frac{3}{4}$ inches.
Large head and shoulders.
Collection of the artist.
Listed in the *Comprehensive Exhibition Catalogue*, No. 174.

10. Socrates   1937
Wash drawing. Study. 14×11 inches.
Head of Socrates, sepia washes supported by dark-brown brush strokes.
Signed l.r.: "Boardman Robinson."
Collection of the artist.
Reproduced in *Ninety-three Drawings*, Pl. 4; listed in the *Comprehensive Exhibition Catalogue*, No. 43.

Portrait of S. W. Schaefer   1937
Pen and ink drawing. 10×7 inches.
Collection of Dr. S. W. Schaefer, New York City.

Portrait of the Son of Dr. S. W. Schaefer   1937
Pen and ink drawing. 10×17 inches.
Collection of Dr. S. W. Schaefer, New York City.

90. Head   1937
Ink drawing (brown). $10 \times 6\frac{1}{2}$ inches.
Sketch for a mural.
Signed l.r.: "Boardman Robinson '37."
Collection of the artist.
Listed in the *Comprehensive Exhibition Catalogue*, No. 50.

Ford Madox Ford   1937
Wash drawing. $12\frac{1}{2} \times 16\frac{1}{2}$ inches.
Caricature of the English author (profile).
Signed: "Boardman Robinson '37."
Collection of Farnsworth Crowder, Palo Alto, California.

Head of Moses   1937
Pen and wash (sepia). 14×10 inches.
Study for murals in Department of Justice Building, Washington, D.C.
Signed l.l.: "Boardman Robinson."
Collection of Margaret and Oscar Ogg, Alexandria, Virginia.
Reproduced in *Ninety-three Drawings*, Pl. 10.

116. Menes, Moses, Hammurabi   1937
Wash drawing.
Studies for three panels in murals, "Great Figures in the History of the Law," Department of Justice Building, Washington, D.C.
Collection of the artist.

83. Kneeling Scribe   1937
Brush drawing.
Preliminary study for detail of the Moses panel in Department of Justice mural, "Great Figures in the History of the Law."

Portrait of Daughter of S. W. Schaefer   1937
Drawing, pen and ink. 10×17 inches.
Collection of Dr. S. W. Schaefer, New York City.

105A. George Biddle   1937
Pen drawing. 9×6 inches.
Profile view of head.
Signed l.r.: "B.R."; l.c.: "George Biddle '37."
Collection of the artist.

102. Jo Davidson   1937
Wash drawing. $14 \times 10\frac{1}{4}$ inches.
Caricature head of the sculptor, in soft wash, with strong brush accentuations about the eyes and mouth. Monochrome.
Signed l.r.: "Boardman Robinson C.S. '37."
Collection of the C. W. Kraushaar Art Galleries, New York City.

91. Study for Christ   1937
Wash drawing on paper.
Study for head of Christ to be used in "Great Figures in the History of the Law," Department of Justice murals, Washington, D.C.
Signed l.r.: "Boardman Robinson."
Collection of the artist.

Mother and Child   About 1937
Wash, pen and ink. $12\frac{7}{8} \times 8\frac{1}{8}$ inches.
Nude, holding child.
Signed l.r.: "Boardman Robinson."
Collection of Lamar Dodd, Athens, Georgia.

Untitled   About 1937
Brown ink, wash.
Group of four figures with drapes.
Signed l.c.r.: "Boardman Robinson."
Collection of Lieutenant George S. Cress, Athens, Georgia.

Au Revestel, Pine   1938
Wash drawing. 10×10 inches.
Drawing of Boushde de Rhune. Foliage with small house.
Collection of the artist.
Listed in the *Comprehensive Exhibition Catalogue*, No. 17.

Moses   1938
Pen and ink. $12 \times 8\frac{1}{2}$ inches.
Sketch for a mural.
Signed: "Boardman Robinson."
Collection of Mrs. Jewett Campbell, Richmond, Virginia.

Nude   1938
Pen and wash (black). 17×11 inches.
Dedicated l.r.: "For Oscar Ogg, Nov. '38"; signed l.c.r.: "Boardman Robinson."
Collection of Margaret and Oscar Ogg, Alexandria, Virginia.

Head of Christ   1938
Sanguine chalk with reddish wash drawing. $14 \times 12\frac{1}{2}$ inches (approximately).

Study for mural in Department of Justice Building, Washington, D.C. Gray mantle on shoulders. Outstretched hands.
Signed l.r.: "Boardman Robinson."
Collection of Henry Schnakenberg, New York City.

82. Women of the Loire   1938
Wash drawing.
Three peasant women carry large, heavy loads on their heads and shoulders. Two on left face forward; the third at right walks toward left.
Signed l.r.: "B.R."; "On the Loire '38."

A Cleric   About 1938
Wash drawing. 14×12 inches.
Study of head of a bishop.
Signed l.r.: (in ink) "Boardman Robinson."
Collection of the Museum of Cranbrook Academy of Art, Bloomfield Hills, Michigan.
Reproduced in *Magazine of Art*, June–July, 1941, p. 321.

Egyptian   About 1938
Drawing, pen and wash.
Male head. Study for figure in Department of Justice mural.
Signed l.r.: "Boardman Robinson."
Reproduced in *Ninety-three Drawings*, Pl. 15.

Frozen Vineyard   1939
Drawing.
Collection of Miss Gillespie, Stanbury Road, Columbus, Ohio.

Standing Nude   1939
Drawing. 14×8¾ inches.
Full-length female nude.
Signed l.r.: "Boardman Robinson."
Reproduced in *Ninety-three Drawings*, Pl. 81; listed in the *Comprehensive Exhibition Catalogue*, No. 40.

Cowboy Head   1939
Pencil drawing. 12½×10½ inches.
An old cowboy with lined face. Wears hat.
Signed l.l.: "Boardman Robinson '39."
Collection of Dr. A. M. Mullett, Colorado Springs, Colorado.

Sally   1939
Pencil drawing.
Head and shoulders. Full-face view. Her eyes are closed.
Signed l.l.: "Apr. 16, '39."

121A. Study of Cowboy Head   1939
Ink and brush drawing.
Head of cowboy wearing hat. Detail for mural in Englewood Post Office.

92. Laughing Cowboys   1939
Wash drawing and pencil.
Two cowboy heads, wearing large hats. One at left, front view; the right in profile, facing left.
Signed l.r.: "Boardman Robinson."

95. Antonio and Gratiano for *Merchant of Venice*   About 1939
Pen drawing, supported with crayon. 12×9 inches.
Full-length, standing figures. Design for Antonio seen from back. He wears white doublet with red sleeves. Gratiano seen from front. His costume is green and yellow, with brown sleeves and hose. Both hatted.
Unsigned.
Collection of Alexander Campbell, Colorado Springs, Colorado.

94. Cothurnos for *Aria da Capo*   About 1939
Wash drawing. 14½×9¼ inches.
Design for a character for the Edna St. Vincent Millay play. Robed and hooded figure, standing. Sketched figure of Pierrot at upper right. Theatrical mask at lower right.
Signed l.r.: "B.R."
Collection of Alexander Campbell, Colorado Springs, Colorado.

Nude   1940
Crayon drawing.
Female nude. Left hand at top of head; right arm reaching back of head. Contour lines strong and distinct, supported in the inner structure by crayon tones.
Signed l.c.r.: "Boardman Robinson."
Collection of the artist.
Reproduced in *Ninety-three Drawings*, Pl. 78.

Nude   1940
Pencil and brush drawing in sepia, on paper. 6¾×10½ inches.
Female standing nude figure, one foot relaxed.
Signed l.c.r.: "Boardman Robinson, Aug. '40."
Collection of Otis Dozier, Dallas, Texas.

Old Woman   1940
Ink drawing. 10×8 inches.
Owner unknown.
Listed in the *Comprehensive Exhibition Catalogue*, No. 47.

98. Reading His Mouth   1940
Lithograph (edition of 200). 8×12 inches.
Inspecting a horse's mouth at a horse auction.
Signed l.r.: "Boardman Robinson."
Listed in the *Comprehensive Exhibition Catalogue*, No. 168.

112. Triad   About 1940
Drawing. 13¼×6 inches.
Nude male and female figures hold child upon their shoulders: male on left reaches above head to clasp woman's upraised left hand. Gray wash tones supported by strong brush lines.
Signed l.c.l.: "Boardman Robinson."
Collection of the artist.

1941–44

RECLINING NUDE 1941
    Ink drawing. $7\frac{3}{4} \times 13\frac{1}{4}$ inches.
Listed in the *Comprehensive Exhibition Catalogue*, No. 66.

PEAKS 1941
    Wash drawing. $12\frac{1}{2} \times 16$ inches.
Listed in the *Comprehensive Exhibition Catalogue*, No. 35.

A HORSE TRADE 1941
    Pencil drawing. $9\frac{1}{8} \times 11$ inches.
    Four male figures—two on left with ten-gallon hats, cowboy boots, hands in pockets, are inspecting horse. Rump of horse shows in right of picture.
Signed l.r.: "Boardman Robinson '41."
Collection of the C. W. Kraushaar Art Galleries, New York City.

72. WALKING NUDE 1941
    Drawing. $12 \times 6\frac{1}{2}$ inches.
    Full-length nude female figure, walking forward with head turned to left. Left arm lifted out toward front; right arm hanging at side.
Signed l.r.: "Boardman Robinson '41."
Collection of the C. W. Kraushaar Art Galleries, New York City.

ROCKS 1941
    Wash drawing. $12\frac{3}{4} \times 15\frac{1}{2}$ inches.
Listed in the *Comprehensive Exhibition Catalogue*, No. 20.

45. RELEASE 1941
    Wash drawing. 13×19 inches.
    Fantastic image of faces and figures in an oval composition, to the left of which hangs a figure on a cross.
Signed l.r.: "Boardman Robinson '41."
Collection of the artist.
Listed in the *Comprehensive Exhibition Catalogue*, No. 169.

STUDY FOR "POLLY" 1941
    Drawing. 12×16 inches.
    Portrait study.
Collection of Polly Duncan.
Listed in the *Comprehensive Exhibition Catalogue*, No. 44.

68A. CHALK CREEK 1942
    Wash drawing. $12 \times 15\frac{3}{4}$ inches.
    Brush drawing of mountainside, with two trees in lower left foreground. Cloud formation in upper right.
Signed l.l.: "Chalk Creek '42"; l.r.: "Boardman Robinson."
Collection of the artist.

70. THE GULCH 1942
    Lithograph. 16×11 inches.
    Large, dark pine tree contrasts with white background at lower right. Two fallen logs and stump at lower left. In center distance and beyond, dark powerfully drawn mountains rise above the gulch to touch clouds above.
Signed l.r.: "Boardman Robinson '42."
Listed in the *Comprehensive Exhibition Catalogue*, No. 156.

92A. ROUGH CHARACTER 1942
    Wash drawing. 13×9 inches.
    Ink in heavy line. Male head with hat.
Signed l.r.: "Boardman Robinson '42."
Collection of the artist.
Listed in the *Comprehensive Exhibition Catalogue*, No. 41.

89. NEGRO GIRL 1942
    Wash drawing. $12\frac{3}{4} \times 10$ inches.
    Head and shoulders of Negro girl, wearing hat.
Collection of the artist.
Listed in the *Comprehensive Exhibition Catalogue*, No. 38.

68. IN THE ROCKIES 1943
    Wash and pen drawing. $9\frac{1}{2} \times 13\frac{1}{4}$ inches.
    Rocky Mountain range, bold and heavy at peak in upper left. Rain-cloud formation in upper center right. Spindly trees suggested along lower left border, at the base of which is a ranch house.
Signed l.l.: "In the Rockies"; l.r.: "Boardman Robinson '43."
Collection of the artist.

SELF-PORTRAIT 1944
    Pen drawing. $12\frac{1}{2} \times 10\frac{1}{2}$ inches.
    Full-face sketch from sketchbook.
Signed l.r.: "Oct. '44."
Collection of the artist.

NUDE SEATED Date unknown
Collection of Lawrence R. McCoy, Worcester, Massachusetts.

COLORADO COW PERSONS Date unknown
    Pen and wash.
    Two cowboys face each other. Figure at left with hands in hip pockets, as he leans forward with left foot on stump.
Signed l.r.: "Boardman Robinson."
Collection of William Elmsley, Washington, D.C.
Reproduced in *Ninety-three Drawings*, Pl. 64.

SKETCH Date unknown
    Brush and pen drawing.
    Sketch of short, rotund Mexican peon figure, wearing sombrero. Brush lines fat and bold.
Signed l.r.: "Boardman Robinson."
Collection of the artist.
Reproduced in *Ninety-three Drawings*, Pl. 74.

TWO FROGS Date unknown
    Pencil drawing. $4\frac{3}{4} \times 2\frac{3}{4}$ inches (approximately).
    Two studies of bullfrogs, one above the other.
Signed l.l.: "Boardman Robinson."
Collection of Henry Schnakenberg, New York City.

COLORADO CRAG   Date unknown
    Wash drawing.
Collection of the American Academy of Arts and Let-
    ters, New York City.

MAN'S BACK   Date unknown
    Dry brush, lithograph pencil, pen and ink. $9\frac{1}{2}\times7\frac{3}{8}$
inches.
    A study.
Signed l.l.: "Boardman Robinson."
Collection of Lamar Dodd, Athens, Georgia.

ENTOMBMENT   Date unknown
    Wash drawing. $9\frac{1}{2}\times13\frac{1}{2}$ inches.
    Five figures lowering body into grave; three mourn-
ing figures. Broad strokes indicate weight of body and
emotion of the mourners.
Signed l.r.: "Boardman Robinson."
Collection of the Denver Art Museum, Denver, Colo-
    rado.

NUDE   Date unknown
    Crayon drawing. 14×10 inches.
    Female nude. Seated back.
Signed: "Boardman Robinson."
Collection of Mr. F. Martin Brown, Colorado Springs,
    Colorado.

CHINESE LAUNDRY   Date unknown
    Drawing. $26\frac{1}{2}\times21\frac{1}{2}$ inches.
Signed: "Boardman Robinson."
Collection of Eugene Boissevain, Austerlitz, New York.

SUSIE   Date unknown
    Pencil and conte drawing. $13\frac{1}{2}\times7\frac{3}{4}$ inches.
    Classic nude, seated, back view.
Collection of the Dallas Museum of Fine Arts, Dallas,
    Texas.

RECLINING NUDE   Date unknown
    Conte drawing. $8\times10\frac{1}{2}$ inches.
    Designed figure, back view.
Collection of the Dallas Museum of Fine Arts, Dallas,
    Texas.

TOM BENTON   Date unknown
    Ink drawing. $10\times7\frac{3}{4}$ inches.
    Side view of Benton reading.
Collection of the Dallas Museum of Fine Arts, Dallas,
    Texas.

MURALS AND FRESCOES

115. EXCAVATION   1926
    Fresco on plaster. 24×30 inches.
    Four workmen in a building-excavation pit, two saw-
ing a heavy timber, one moving a timber into place, another handling a large pipe. Color remains subservient
to strength of line and bulk of mass.
Signed l.l.: "Boardman Robinson '26."
Collection of the Denver Art Museum, Denver, Colo-
    rado.

SERMON ON THE MOUNT   1928
    Fresco in plaster of Paris, in a wooden tray. $59\frac{3}{4}\times$
$71\frac{3}{4}$ inches.
    Composition with thirteen figures, Jesus in the cen-
ter. An arbitrary use of color distribution, predominantly in low intensities of all hues, with one figure,
seated before Jesus, in high-value, medium-intensity
red. A formal arrangement of clouds and floral forms in
the high background. An experimental problem.
Signed l.r.: "Boardman Robinson."
Collection of the artist.
Listed in the *Comprehensive Exhibition Catalogue*, No.
    147.

A HISTORY OF COMMERCE   Completed 1929
    Murals in the Kaufmann Department Store, Pitts-
burgh, Pennsylvania.
    Oil.
    Ten murals:
    1. The Persians and the Arabs—before the Chris-
       tian Era.
    2. The Carthaginians on the Mediterranean—
       Dawn of the Christian Era.
    3. Venetians in the Levant—End of the Middle
       Ages.
    4. The Portuguese in India—the Fifteenth Cen-
       tury.
    5. The Dutch in the Baltic—the Sixteenth Century.
    6. The English in China—the Seventeenth Cen-
       tury.
    7. Slave Traders in America—the Eighteenth Cen-
       tury.
119. 8. The Clipper-Ship Era—the First Half of the
       Nineteenth Century.
120. 9. Commerce on the Mississippi—the Nineteenth
       Century.
    10. Trade and Commerce in the United States—the
       Twentieth Century.

117. QUIXOTE AND SANCHO   1931
    Oil on canvas glued to pressed wood. $45\times70\frac{3}{4}$
inches.
    A formal composition of armored Don Quixote on
horseback, with Sancho following on donkey. Rock
structure in left of painting balanced by tree formation
on right. Patterned mountains in background. Highly
stylized clouds. Hues predominately in gray-reds, relieved by blue sky and green foliage.
Signed l.r.: "Boardman Robinson '31."
Collection of Mr. Donald Gilpin, Colorado Springs,
    Colorado.

MURALS AT FOUNTAIN VALLEY SCHOOL Completed 1931
    Colorado Springs, Colorado.
    Dry pigment in wet plaster.
    Two frescoes, 13 feet 1 inch $\times$ 5 feet $7\frac{1}{2}$ inches each.

1931–40

114.
1. Mountain scene with horses and riders.
2. Highly stylized mountain scene.
Both unsigned.

114A. FRESCO IN PORTAL OF FIRST HOUSE
Completed 1931
Fountain Valley School, Colorado Springs, Colorado.
Fresco.
A group of five workmen, with shovels, stand (one sits) in front of mountain scene.

MURAL AT RADIO CITY Completed 1932
Rockefeller Center, New York City.
Egg tempera upon canvas on plaster.
Allegorical subject matter of all the machinery of material progress compared with man's fundamental needs.

THE FIVE ARTS Completed 1936
Colorado Springs Fine Arts Center, Colorado.
Five frescoes—dry color in plaster. 43¼×61¼ inches each.
The five arts represent the arts of the Fine Arts Center: (left to right) sculpture, drama, dance, music, painting. Predominant colors: burnt sienna, yellow ocher, and black.

GREAT FIGURES IN THE HISTORY OF THE LAW
Completed 1937
Murals for the Department of Justice Building, Washington, D.C.
Tempera base with oil glazes on canvas over plaster.
Separate panel portraits of: Holmes, Blackstone, Solon, Hammurabi, Thomas Aquinas, Grotius, Menes, Moses, Socrates, Christ, Vittoria, Coke, Kent, Marshall, Papinian, and Justinian. Two panels: Magna Carta, The Signing of the Constitution.

121. COLORADO HORSE SALE Completed 1940
Mural for Englewood Post Office, Englewood, Colorado. 6½ feet × 13 feet.
Tempera base with oil glazes on canvas on plaster.
A group of ranchers in attendance at an auction. People seated on bleachers, at left and right of composition. Auctioneer in center. Two ranchers at right seated on a bench; two under bleachers; two standing at left, in conversation.

WATER COLORS AND PAINTINGS

BARBARA 1907
Oil on canvas. 16×14 inches.
Portrait of a small child, Barbara Robinson, half-length. Black headdress and muff. Flesh tones in clear, light red and yellow. Coat of medium-value gray ocher; background in darker value of the same hue.
Signed l.r.: "Boardman Robinson 1907."
Collection of the artist.
Listed in the *Comprehensive Exhibition Catalogue*, No. 5.

CHRIST AND THE WOMAN OF SAMARIA About 1910
Water color. 12×14 inches (approximately).
Figure of Christ is seated. Female figure stands at a New England well sweep.
Collection of Mr. and Mrs. Whitney Shepherdson, New York City.

CARL RUGGLES About 1914
Oil. 22×14 inches (approximately).
Male figure at piano. Head in profile. Small female figure in background.
Collection of Carl Ruggles, Arlington, Vermont.

SERBIAN SOLDIERS 1915
Water color on brown paper. 10×12¾ inches.
Tired soldiers sit on ground, leaning against a white building. Guard stands at left.
Collection of the Colorado Springs Fine Arts Center, Colorado.
Listed in the *Comprehensive Exhibition Catalogue*, No. 139.

RUSSIAN COLONEL 1915
Gouache sketch. 20×16 inches.
Head of Russian officer in uniform. Very dark, frowning features.
Collection of the artist.
Listed in the *Comprehensive Exhibition Catalogue*, No. 142.

55. EVENING, THE CLIFFS 1917
Tempera. 28×35 inches (approximately).
Female figure sitting, male figure reclining, with head in her lap. Martha's Vineyard landscape.
Signed l.l.: "Boardman Robinson."
Collection of Harlan Miller, Arlington, Vermont.

53. ZULOAGA AT KNOEDLER'S 1916
Gouache. 13½×17¾ inches.
Scene of an exhibition at Knoedler's Gallery. Twelve figures in composition; a painting of the nude female in center. Colors of low intensity. High-value contrast between nude in painting and the background.
Signed l.l.: "Boardman Robinson '16."
Collection of the artist.
Listed in the *Comprehensive Exhibition Catalogue*, No. 76.

FALL OF THE HOUSE OF USHER 1917
Water color supported by gouache, on paper. 19½×13½ inches.
White-clad figure, falling into arms of second figure. Loosely drawn. High-value contrasts in center. Colors in low value of brown and red. White in center.
Signed l.r.: "Boardman Robinson '17."
Collection of the artist.
Reproduced in *Ninety-three Drawings*, Pl. 91; listed in the *Comprehensive Exhibition Catalogue*, No. 114.

52. THE CLUB 1917
Oil and lithograph crayon on paper. 13×8¼ inches.
Eight male figures. Three seated in foreground of composition, waiter attending to one at left. Four

standing figures in background. At upper left a modeled head looks down upon table at lower left.
Signed l.r.: "Boardman Robinson '17."
Collection of the Whitney Museum of American Art, New York City.
Reproduced in *Ninety-three Drawings*, Pl. 92.

LOT'S WIFE   1918
Water color. $14\frac{1}{2} \times 8$ inches.
Full female figure of strong blue and white stands at center left of composition, facing left, with arm upraised and horrified expression on her face. Mountain ridges in blues, whites, and blacks show in distance behind her. Right third of composition is composed of crag with tree on top. Three shrouded figures in center right march away from the scene.
Signed: "Boardman Robinson."
Collection of L. V. Pulsifer, Mountainville, New York.
Published in the *Liberator*, May, 1918, p. 26 (two-thirds page).

SOUTH SHORE, MARTHA'S VINEYARD   1918
Pencil drawing, supported by water color. $12\frac{1}{2} \times 14\frac{1}{2}$ inches.
Red cliffs against the black of distant ocean. Distinguishing feature is the value of the black and reddish-brown pencil shading superimposed upon water color.
Signed u.l.: "Boardman Robinson"; l.r.: "Boardman Robinson."
Collection of Mrs. N. F. Galbraith, Colorado Springs, Colorado.

CROTON-ON-THE-HUDSON   1918
Oil. 22×29 inches.
View of the Hudson River from the Croton Hills. Colors in brilliant autumn reds, complementing blue river. For many years this painting hung in the living-room of the artist's home.
Unsigned.
Collection of Dr. S. W. Schaefer, New York City.

46. EXPULSION   1920
Ink, water color, and crayon. $10\frac{3}{4} \times 8$ inches.
Adam, with head bowed, precedes Eve, who looks backward as they walk toward left. A study for a painting.
Signed l.l.: "Boardman Robinson '20."
The Mr. and Mrs. Frank M. Hall Collection, University of Nebraska Art Galleries, Lincoln, Nebraska.
Reproduced in *Ninety-three Drawings*, Pl. 59.

HUDSON RIVER   1920
Oil. 23×29 inches.
Scene on Hudson River. Shining blue mountains, the river a luminous green. In the foreground bare trees, a dock, and small buildings are shown in dark brown and greens.
Signed: "B.R. '20."
Collection of Scott R. Bond, North Plainfield, New Jersey.

ACROBATS   1921
Gouache. 13×11 inches (approximately).
Male and female figure standing side by side; trapeze suggested in background. Colors in light reds and grays.
Signed l.r.: "Boardman Robinson."
Collection of Henry Schnakenberg, New York City.

SOUTH SHORE—MARTHA'S VINEYARD   1921
Oil. 14×10 inches (approximately).
Moors terminate in clay cliff. Ocean beyond.
Signed: "Boardman Robinson."
Collection of Dr. Frederic H. Bartlett, New York City.

TREE AND HOUSE   1921
Water color. $14 \times 9\frac{1}{2}$ inches.
Pattern of large trees against façade of old Colonial house. Predominating colors are green, brown, and black, strengthened by the reds in the bricks of the house.
Signed l.r.: "Boardman Robinson."
Collection of Morton R. Goldsmith, Scarsdale, New York.

PRIVATE BAR, LONDON   1922
Water color with gouache on thin illustration board. 13×15 inches.
Two figures, half-length, male and female, drinking at a bar. Gray water-color hues of red and dark green. Background of warm tones behind hatted female head and head of male figure.
Signed: "Boardman Robinson, London, '22."
Collection of the artist.
Listed in the *Comprehensive Exhibition Catalogue*, No. 75.

SERMON ON THE MOUNT   1924
Water color, supported by gouache upon cardboard. $12\frac{1}{2} \times 16$ inches.
Color sketch with eleven figures, Jesus in center. right arm upraised. Trees on left counterbalance three standing figures on right of composition. Warm tones of graded reds in flesh tones and in drapes, relieved by blue and blue-greens of ground and sky. Floral forms and clouds highly formalized. (A sketch for the large fresco of the same title.)
Signed l.r.: "Boardman Robinson '24."
Collection of the artist.

SKIN AND SEA   1924
Oil sketch. 12×16 inches.
One figure in rosy hue, another tan—three-quarter length. Ocean in background.
Collection of the artist.
Listed in the *Comprehensive Exhibition Catalogue*, No. 170.

1924–27

SEA CLIFFS AND FIGURES—CHILMARK   1924
    Oil. 24×30 inches.
    Three seminude, female figures form a triangular mass at the left of composition; cliffs in background open for a view of the sea on the right.
    Signed l.c.: "Boardman Robinson '24."
    Collection of L. V. Pulsifer, Mountainville, New York.

W. H. PITKIN   1924
    Oil on canvas. 28×22 inches.
    Unfinished portrait of W. H. Pitkin, New York City. Half-length. Left hand holding a book. Brown suit upon background of blue and violet.
    Signed l.c.: "Boardman Robinson '24."
    Collection of the artist.
    Listed in the *Comprehensive Exhibition Catalogue*, No. 6.

SKETCH IN COLOR   1924
    Oil on canvas board. 11¾×15¾ inches.
    Two male figures draped below torsos; background of beach, ocean, and sky. One figure in pronouncedly red hue, the other in yellow ocher. Blue-green beach; light-blue sky and ocean.
    Signed l.r.: "B.R."
    Collection of the artist.

UNTITLED   1924
    Water color. 18½×14 inches.
    One seminude figure in foreground. At right, nude draped with flowing cloth. Nude seated at left of composition. Cliffs and sea in background.
    Signed l.l.: "B.R."
    Collection of Mr. and Mrs. Bartlett Robinson, New York City.

36. CLIFF PARTY   1924
    Oil on wood panel. 12×15 inches.
    Seven figures, picnicking on cliffs.
    Signed l.r.: "Boardman Robinson '24, for O. O."
    Collection of Margaret and Oscar Ogg, Alexandria, Virginia.
    Listed in the *Comprehensive Exhibition Catalogue*, No. 172; reproduced in *Ninety-three Drawings*, Pl. 63.

96. ONE-STEP   1924
    Wash drawing with Chinese white on green paper. 12×9 inches.
    Male and female figures dance the one-step. Male on right, female on left. His left hand clasps her right.
    Signed l.l.: "Boardman Robinson '24."
    Collection of Edgar Britton, Colorado Springs, Colorado.

WOMEN WRESTLING   1925
    Oil. 24×18 inches (approximately).
    Two women in bathing suits, one in red, the other in black, struggling on ocean beach. Figures are promi-nent in foreground. Red bathing cap on head of one figure. Background of cliffs and sea in grey and greens.
    Signed: "Boardman Robinson '25."
    Collection of Ruth Pickering Pinchot, New York City.

MOORS AND SEA—CHILMARK   1925
    Oil on wood panel. 21½×27½ inches.
    Yellow-green moors, extending from the right of the composition almost to the center. Cliffs drop off to sea.
    Signed l.l.: "Boardman Robinson '25."
    Collection of L. V. Pulsifer, Mountainville, New York.

97. TWO-STEP   1925
    Water color and Chinese white on dark-brown paper. 11¼×9¼ inches.
    Male and female figures dance the two-step. Right arm of male figure upraised. Female dancer's head and right hand resting upon male dancer's left shoulder.
    Signed l.c.: "Boardman Robinson '25."
    Collection of Connie Zachritz, Colorado Springs, Colorado.
    Reproduced in *Ninety-three Drawings*, Pl. 84.

PORTRAIT OF A YOUNG WOMAN   1926
    Oil. 30×24 inches (approximately).
    Young woman sits at a stand, talking over an old-fashioned candlestick telephone.
    Collection of Wolcott H. Pitkin, New York City.

47. ADAM AND EVE   1926
    Oil. 42×36 inches.
    Expulsion from Paradise. Eve looks defiantly backward, while Adam hides his head. Soft gray-green and warm browns in background, a woodland path.
    Unsigned.
    Collection of Eugene Schoen, New York City.

37. BATHERS   About 1926
    Gouache. 15¼×21 inches.
    Four figures grouped on rocks. Central figure stands with arms upraised, holding towel over head. Water and clouds show in upper right corner.
    Signed l.l.: "Boardman Robinson."
    Collection of the artist.
    Listed in the *Comprehensive Exhibition Catalogue*, No. 67.

JULIAN WILLIAM MACK   About 1926
    Oil. 31½×24½ inches.
    Half-length, seated figure of Judge Mack, turned to left. Left hand rests on table.
    Collection of the United States Circuit Judges, Langdell Hall, Harvard University, Cambridge, Massachusetts.

STREET SCENE   1927
    Gouache and wash.
    A construction scene. Two male figures, upper right, atop sidewalk scaffolding, load a truck at left. Three pedestrians walk under scaffolding at lower right.

Signed l.c.: "Boardman Robinson '27."
Collection of the artist.
Reproduced in *Ninety-three Drawings*, Pl. 66.

81. SUSAN *or* NUDE I   1927
     Gouache on toned paper. $18 \times 15\frac{1}{2}$ inches.
     Female nude figure, three-quarter length. Warm tones of graded red in light flesh tones; cool tones of graded green in shadows. Figure against silvery-white background.
Signed l.l.: "Boardman Robinson '27."
Collection of the artist.
Reproduced in *Ninety-three Drawings*, Pl. 76; listed in the *Comprehensive Exhibition Catalogue*, No. 57.

MOANA OF THE SOUTH SEAS   1928
     Gouache and crayon on toned paper. $11 \times 17\frac{1}{2}$ inches.
     Two figures of South Sea natives, in landscape of palm trees and tropical flora upon shore of ocean-island. Colors in graded green, red, and blue, with strong areas of black washes. High-intensity hues superimposed with crayon. An impression of a moving picture.
Signed l.c.l.: "Boardman Robinson."
Collection of the artist.
Published in the *New Yorker*; listed in the *Comprehensive Exhibition Catalogue*, No. 129.

MANIKIN   1928
     Oil on plywood. 15×11 inches.
     A study of red drape upon manikin, against a grayed green background. This is a study for the Kaufman murals.
Signed l.l.: "Boardman Robinson '28."
Collection of the artist.
Listed in *Comprehensive Exhibition Catalogue*, No. 179.

APPLE   1928
     Oil upon wood. $7\frac{1}{4} \times 6$ inches.
     Study of an apple upon table surface. Apple in high intensities of red, green, and yellow, surrounded by graded brown and violet tones.
Signed l.r.: "B.R."
Collection of Mr. and Mrs. Roy Harris, Colorado Springs, Colorado.
Listed in the *Comprehensive Exhibition Catalogue*, No. 180.

118. A HISTORY OF COMMERCE   1928
     Water color and pen and ink. $9\frac{1}{2} \times 15\frac{3}{4}$ inches.
     Sketch for the mural panel, "The Portuguese in India," one of the series of paintings executed in the Kaufmann Department Store, Pittsburgh. Composition contains eight figures. Colors predominantly cool blue with warm tones.
Signed l.r.: "Boardman Robinson 1928."
Collection of the artist.
Reproduced in *Ninety-three Drawings*, Pl. 62; listed in the *Comprehensive Exhibition Catalogue*, No. 152.

A HISTORY OF COMMERCE   1928
     Oil on cardboard. $8 \times 15\frac{3}{4}$ inches.
     Three sketches for a mural study, plans for the panels entitled "Arabs and Persians" (2) and "Romans and Carthaginians," which were carried out fully in the above-named sections of the Kaufmann murals.
Unsigned.
Collection of the artist.
Listed in the *Comprehensive Exhibition Catalogue*, No. 148.

38. ROAD TO EMMAUS   1928
     Water color. $13\frac{7}{8} \times 21\frac{1}{2}$ inches.
     Six figures: Christ, in white robe, seated on stone at left center, talking to two laboring men. A well-dressed man of the world walks away at left. Two female figures stand at right. Background of trees. Dominant colors are dull violets and oranges. Sketch for a mural.
Unsigned.
Collection of the Newark Museum, Newark, New Jersey.

FIGURE STUDY   1928
     Oil. 16×12 inches.
Listed in the *Comprehensive Exhibition Catalogue*, No. 54.

STUDY FOR KAUFMANN MURALS   1928
     Lacquer on composition board. $15\frac{1}{2} \times 12$ inches.
     A female figure, three-quarter length. Warm burnt sienna and yellow hues in drape, with left breast of figure revealed. Background of cool grays. Drawing of arms in pen lines.
Signed l.r.: "B.R."
Collection of the artist.

STUDY OF CAST   1929
     Oil on thick cardboard. 16×12 inches.
     An almost monochromatic painting of a male nude figure, lying upon a drape. The background has been toned with graded green. A study from Greco-Roman cast.
Signed: "Boardman Robinson '29."
Collection of the artist.
Listed in the *Comprehensive Exhibition Catalogue*, No. 171.

OLD MODEL   1929
     Gouache. $12\frac{1}{4} \times 9\frac{1}{4}$ inches.
     Drawing of head and shoulders of bearded old man.
Unsigned.
Collection of the artist.
Listed in the *Comprehensive Exhibition Catalogue*, No. 42.

ON THE RIO GRANDE   1930
     Water color. $13\frac{1}{2} \times 9$ inches.
     Two trees on the bank of a river. Two figures lie

under tree on right. Crayon color supports dark ink brush lines.
Signed l.r.: "Boardman Robinson '30."
Collection of the artist.

65. HIGH VALLEY *or* ROCKY MOUNTAINS 1930
Water color. 8¾×11 inches.
Strong black linear pattern of mountains, supported by dark-gray areas and tints of red and green. Weathered tree stands in first plane at lower right.
Signed l.l.: "Boardman Robinson '30."
Collection of Dr. and Mrs. N. M. Nesset, Palatine, Illinois.
Reproduced in *Ninety-three Drawings*, Pl. 71.

MOUNTAINS 1930
Water color. 9×11 inches.
Collection of Mrs. Malcolm L. McBride, Cleveland, Ohio.
Listed in the *Comprehensive Exhibition Catalogue*, No. 31.

LINCOLN STEFFENS 1932
Water color. 11×8 inches.
Portrait of Lincoln Steffens, in profile. Black tie, white jacket.
Signed l.r.: "Boardman Robinson '32."
Collection of the artist.
Listed in the *Comprehensive Exhibition Catalogue*, No. 64.

SKETCH FOR A MURAL 1932
Oil. 18×29 inches (approximately).
Sketch for a mural in Rockefeller Center. At left, figures of man, woman, and child, half-draped, stand overlooking a city of skyscrapers. Huge guns at lower right corner.
Collection of John W. Robinson, Oxnard, California.

DON QUIXOTE 1932
Oil. 12×16 inches.
Mounted figure of Don Quixote, carrying shield and sword, climbs crest of a hill. A tree at right. He is followed by figure of Sancho, also mounted, who rides with hands upraised. Mountainous background. Sketch for a mural panel.
Signed l.r.: "Boardman Robinson."
Collection of the artist.
Listed in *Comprehensive Exhibition Catalogue*, No. 149; reproduced in *Ninety-three Drawings*, Pl. 69.

56A. MOUNTAIN STUDY 1933
Water color. 7¼×10¾ inches.
Mountain ranges with snow-topped peaks in distance. Fields and trees in foreground valley. Dark values in lower half of composition relieved by areas of greens and spots suggesting trees and forms of floral life.

Signed l.r.: "Boardman Robinson."
Collection of the artist.

THE PORTAL 1935
Water color. 7¾×10¾ inches.
Five rather indistinct female figures, gathered around the dark portal of a tomb in the side of a mountain. Mountain peaks rise in the distance.
Signed l.c.: "Boardman Robinson"; l.r.: "Boardman Robinson."
Collection of the artist.
Reproduced in *Ninety-three Drawings*, Pl. 57; listed in the *Comprehensive Exhibition Catalogue*, No. 26.

COWBOYS 1936
Water color.
Collection of Margaret and Oscar Ogg, Alexandria, Virginia.

MARSHALL 1936
Casein on cardboard. 17¾×7 inches.
Single male figure, wearing robe and holding papers in right hand. Escutcheon in rear of head. Plan for a mural, Department of Justice Building, "Great Figures in the History of the Law."
Unsigned.
Collection of the artist.

KENT 1936
Casein on cardboard. 17¾×6 inches.
Single male figure, wearing dark robe, with paper in right hand. Graded violet areas in background. Plan for a mural, Department of Justice Building, "Great Figures in the History of the Law."
Unsigned.
Collection of the artist.

COKE 1936
Casein on cardboard. 17¾×6 inches.
Single male figure with academic headdress, in cloak and red gown. Plan for a mural, Department of Justice Building, "Great Figures in the History of the Law."
Unsigned.
Collection of the artist.

CONSTITUTION 1936
Casein on cardboard. 17¾×15½ inches.
Nine male figures, two seated at a table, at the signing of the Constitution. Colonial flag in upper left of picture. Sketch for a mural, Department of Justice Building, "Great Figures in the History of the Law."
Unsigned.
Collection of the artist.

UNTITLED 1936
Ink, water color, and crayon. 9×13¾ inches.
Two trees prominent in foreground of composition. Distant view of hills. Fence and grass create a connecting line between trees and mountains. The mountains are dominant.
Signed l.r.: "For Helen—Boardman Robinson."
Collection of Helen Sherbon, Philadelphia, Pennsylvania.

64. HILL AND CLOUD   1936
Water color. 12×9 inches.
Heavy black brush lines inclose the areas of mountains. Areas are tinted with grayed warm and cool tones. Suggestion of forest of pine trees in immediate foreground at lower right.
Signed l.r.: "Boardman Robinson '36."
Collection of the artist.
Listed in the *Comprehensive Exhibition Catalogue*, No. 19.

MAGNA CARTA   1936
Casein on cardboard. 17¾×15½ inches.
Eight male figures, with king in center of composition. Self-portrait in extreme lower right corner. Sketch for a mural, Department of Justice Building, "Great Figures in the History of the Law."
Collection of the artist.

SIGNING OF THE CONSTITUTION   1937
Gouache. 19×34½ inches.
Three studies for the Department of Justice murals, "Great Figures in the History of the Law."
Signed l.r.: "Boardman Robinson."
Collection of Fine Arts Section, Treasury Department, Washington, D.C.
Listed in the *Comprehensive Exhibition Catalogue*, No. 153.

THE MAGNA CARTA   1937
Gouache. 19×34½ inches.
Three studies for the Department of Justice murals, "Great Figures in the History of the Law."
Signed l.r.: "Boardman Robinson."
Collection of Fine Arts Section, Treasury Department, Washington, D.C.
Listed in the *Comprehensive Exhibition Catalogue*, No. 154.

11. SOLON   1937
Gouache. 15¼×11¼ inches.
Head of Greek lawgiver. Strong value contrasts, bold lines. Limited warm hues, supported by black. Sketch for a mural, Department of Justice Building, "Great Figures in the History of the Law."
Signed l.r.: "Boardman Robinson '37."
Collection of the artist.
Listed in the *Comprehensive Exhibition Catalogue*, No. 175.

66. EROSION   1937
Water color. 13×19¾ inches.
Two low mountains, the one in the background a light purple. The other, stretching from center to right of the composition, is strong in value contrasts. Pale road or gully stretches across the foreground.
Signed u.r.: "Boardman Robinson '37"; l.r.: "Boardman Robinson '37".
Collection of the C. W. Kraushaar Art Galleries, New York City.

BATHERS, KEY WEST   1938
Water color and ink. 15¾×10¾ inches.
Two bathers, man on left about to descend ladder into water. Female figure on right in the water. Large seagull flying in upper right of composition. Light and warm colors.
Signed l.c.: "Boardman Robinson '38."
Collection of the C. W. Kraushaar Art Galleries, New York City.

CASSIS   1938
Water color. 10½×8¼ inches.
Pines on the Mediterranean.
Signed l.r.: "Boardman Robinson."
Collection of the artist.
Listed in the *Comprehensive Exhibition Catalogue*, No. 32.

COW PEOPLE   1938
Water color and tempera. 12×10 inches.
Signed: "Boardman Robinson."
Collection of Margaret and Oscar Ogg, Alexandria, Virginia.

106. PORTRAIT: PERCY HAGERMAN   1939
Mixed medium on canvas. 32×25 inches.
Portrait of Percy Hagerman, Colorado Springs. Half-length, seated. Head in gray-reds, greens in hair. Red necktie, cool gray suit. Cigarette in right hand. Painted without commission.
Signed l.r.: "Boardman Robinson '39."
Collection of the Colorado Springs Fine Arts Center, Colorado.
Listed in the *Comprehensive Exhibition Catalogue*, No. 2.

COLORADO IRRIGATION   1939
Water color and gouache. 14½×9 inches.
Figure of portly female in dull blue-green dress, holding grayish umbrella over her head, watering a clump of bushes. Blue, cool background.
Signed l.r.: "Boardman Robinson '39."
Collection of the C. W. Kraushaar Art Galleries, New York City.
Listed in the *Comprehensive Exhibition Catalogue*, No. 74.

CASSIS SUR MER   1939
Ink and water color. 11×9 inches.
Strong sunlight shining through lines of trees bordering each side of composition. House at end of lawn, in center background.
Signed l.r.: "Boardman Robinson."
Collection of the C. W. Kraushaar Art Galleries, New York City.
Listed in the *Comprehensive Exhibition Catalogue*, No. 16.

1939–40

COWBOY STUDY   1939
Water color. 11½×8½ inches.
Head of cowboy.
Listed in the *Comprehensive Exhibition Catalogue*, No. 37.

BATHING FIGURES   1939
Pen line and water color. 7¾×13½ inches.
Eight figures in bathing suits in foreground beach, lolling about in amusing attitudes. Three figures on pier extending out in right middle distance. Blue-green ocean.
Signed l.l.: "Boardman Robinson, Key West '39"; l.r.: "For Madelene and Paul."
Collection of Paul Parker, Des Moines, Iowa.

95A. STAGE DESIGN—*Love's Labours Lost*   About 1939
Water color.
Male and female figures stand at left, in front of elaborate gate. Castle in background. A third figure at right in foreground.
Unsigned.
Collection of Alexander Campbell, Colorado Springs, Colorado.

67. FOOT OF THE RANGE   1940
Water color. 11½×17 inches.
Almost monochromatic, in greens, with supporting black lines. Left background shows high peaks of mountain range, a bit of blue sky, and some clouds in center background. Dark boulders in right foreground. Small gully in center foreground, with some foliage at left.
Signed l.r.: "Boardman Robinson '40."
Collection of the C. W. Kraushaar Art Galleries, New York City.

ROCKY MOUNTAIN LANDSCAPE   1940
Oil. 32×25 inches.
Listed in the *Comprehensive Exhibition Catalogue*, No. 24.

SELF-PORTRAIT   1940
Mixed medium. 30×24 inches.
Head and shoulders, with pipe. Wearing a smock. Three-quarter view, facing left.
Signed l.r.: "Boardman Robinson '40."
Collection of the Colorado Springs Fine Arts Center, Colorado.
Reproduced in the *Pacific Art Review*, 1944, p. 40.

113. TRIAD   1940
Gouache on paper. 15×6½ inches.
Three figures, male, female, and child, in close arrangement, with child held aloft between the two parent-figures. Colors in subtle gradations of cool reds. Forms contained in black lines.
Signed l.r.: "Boardman Robinson."
Collection of Mr. and Mrs. Roy Harris, Colorado Springs, Colorado.

Listed in the *Comprehensive Exhibition Catalogue*, No. 70.

THE RODEO   1940
Gouache. 9½×20½ inches.
Spectators—a group composed of tourists, cowboys, dude-ranch guests—gather for a rodeo. Predominant colors of group in grayed blues, which form the mountains also. Sharp color contrasts in foreground, with deep orange, bright pinks, and other warm colors in spectator's clothes and cowboy's shirts.
Signed l.l.: "Boardman Robinson."
Collection of Mr. and Mrs. Jack Jungmeyer, California.
Reproduced in the *Comprehensive Exhibition Catalogue*, p. 11, and listed, No. 150.

62A. MOUNTAIN RODEO (SKETCH)   1940
Gouache. 9½×20½ inches.
The original sketch for the Jungmeyer "Rodeo." Identical in composition.
Signed l.l.: "Boardman Robinson '40"; l.r.: "Mountain Rodeo."
Collection of the artist.

AT THE HORSE SALE   1940
Gouache. 16×12¾ inches.
Figures of man, woman, and child, seated on bleachers. Three-quarter view.
Signed l.r.: "Boardman Robinson."
Collection of the artist.
Listed in the *Comprehensive Exhibition Catalogue*, No. 73.

POLLY   1940
Mixed medium on gesso on pressed wood. 27½×23 inches.
Portrait of young woman, seated. Long blond hair, falling on yellow jacket. Flesh tones yellow; neckerchief in varied hues; blue blouse.
Signed l.l.: "Boardman Robinson '40."
Collection of the artist.
Listed in the *Comprehensive Exhibition Catalogue*, No. 10.

COLORADO MILL   1940
Mixed medium on gesso on plywood. 32×25 inches.
A Colorado mountain scene, with a mill in the lower right corner. First plane contains a cool, yellow-green eroded hill. In the valley of the second plane, which contains the red mill, the hues are light and extremely grayed. The next series of planes, going into higher elevation, have strong contrasts of cool and warm colors. The sky is gray-green, with a few accents of white, toned with yellow.
Signed l.r.: "Boardman Robinson '40."
Collection of Mrs. E. Cribbs, Florence, Colorado.

125. THE MAN-EATING STATE   1940
Water color. 18×12¾ inches.
Cartoon shows enormous male figure, with dome-shaped hat, atop of which a flag flies. Napkin tucked around collar. He eats small figures of men, who lie

flat in platter on table in front of him. He is in the act of popping one into his mouth.
Signed l.c.r.: "Boardman Robinson."
Collection of the artist.
Listed in the *Comprehensive Exhibition Catalogue*, No. 87.

PORTRAIT OF OSCAR OGG   1941
  Oil on gesso board. 16×12 inches.
  A portrait of Ogg, painted from memory.
Signed l.c.l.: "B.R."
Collection of Margaret and Oscar Ogg, Alexandria, Virginia.

58. MOUNTAIN LANDSCAPE   1941
  Oil. 30×24 inches.
  Foreground of pines, in green, with a tone of warm-colored rocks in frontal plane. Blues and violets in rearing crags in background.
Signed l.r.: "Boardman Robinson."
Collection of the International Business Machines Corporation.
Reproduced in *Contemporary Art of the Western Hemisphere*, Pl. 56.

87. GIRL'S HEAD   1941
  Water color on paper. 9¾×10¼ inches.
  Head of young girl, in monochrome, relieved by one area of light-value grayed yellow in hair. Face in low-value contrasts.
Signed l.c.r.: "Boardman Robinson '41."
Collection of Mitchell A. Wilder, Colorado Springs, Colorado.

NORTH OF BERTHOUD   1941
  Water color. 13½×19 inches.
  Mountain near Denver. Dramatic water color, with distant rugged blue crags.
Signed l.r.: "Boardman Robinson '41."
Collection of Dr. A. M. Mullett, Colorado Springs, Colorado.
Listed in the *Comprehensive Exhibition Catalogue*, No. 21.

THE BACHELOR   1941
  Gouache. 10×8 inches.
  Head.
Collection of the artist.
Listed in the *Comprehensive Exhibition Catalogue*, No. 52.

NEAR LOVELAND   1941
  Water color. 15½×20 inches.
  Rocky crags in background. Green foreground with mountain road.
Signed l.r.: "Boardman Robinson '41."
Collection of the artist.
Listed in the *Comprehensive Exhibition Catalogue*, No. 25.

COWBOY   1941
  Gouache. 12½×8½ inches.
  Head with hat.
Unsigned.

Collection of the artist.
Listed in the *Comprehensive Exhibition Catalogue*, No. 48.

32A. MOUNTAIN CRAGS   1941
  Water color. 16×21 inches.
  Loosely drawn, rugged mountain landscape. Indistinct figures of horse and rider in lower right.
Signed l.r.: "Boardman Robinson."
Listed in the *Comprehensive Exhibition Catalogue*, No. 33.

FAYE   1941
  Oil. 15×12 inches.
  Study for portrait of Robinson's daughter-in-law. Head and shoulders of a young woman, boldly brushed with free and spontaneous strokes. Dark-brown hair is strongest color note; dress in light red; background in gray, with yellow accent in lower right corner.
Signed l.r.: "Boardman Robinson."
Collection of Daniel R. Fitzpatrick, St. Louis, Missouri.

31A. MOUNTAIN   1941
  Water color. 10×15 inches.
  Somber mountain scene. Dark and cloudy effect.
Signed l.r.: "Boardman Robinson '41."
Collection of Dr. A. M. Mullett, Colorado Springs, Colorado.

DEDICATION   1941
  Pen and brush and water color. 8×13 inches.
  Seven figures on a stage, including Mrs. Spencer Penrose, ex-Governor Carr of Colorado, and two church dignitaries in brilliant red robes. Carr and one of the bishops are exchanging comments in an amusing manner.
Signed l.r.: "Boardman Robinson"; titled in lower corner: "A Dedication, Apr. '41, Colorado Springs."
Collection of Paul Parker, Des Moines, Iowa.

CHALK CREEK   1942
  Mixed medium on gesso on pressed wood. 12×16 inches.
  The white-yellow formations of Chalk Creek, Colorado. Floral forms in the foreground in low intensities, warm hues of yellow and gray-reds. In upper right center an oblong-shaped cloud of dark-medium value, of gray color, is designed forcefully against a pale gray-blue sky in high value.
Signed l.r.: "Boardman Robinson."
Collection of the artist.

56. PIKES PEAK UNDER SNOW *or* PIKES PEAK   1942
  Mixed medium on gesso on pressed wood. 14×19 inches.
  Scene of snow-capped Pikes Peak. First plane in warm tones of yellow gradations and red; second plane in gray, cold blue; third plane in cold white and light

1942

blue; sky area in blue-gray, relieved with tones of gray and yellow. A roadway runs down and into the center of the picture.
Signed l.r.: "B. R. '42."
Collection of the artist.
Reproduced in the *Comprehensive Exhibition Catalogue*, p. 4; and listed, No. 11.

109. PORTRAIT 1942
Mixed medium.
Female, head and shoulders. She holds her hands clasped to support the right side of her face. Elbows rest on table, which cannot be seen at bottom of composition.
Signed l.r.: "Boardman Robinson."
Collection of the artist.

HITCHHIKERS OF THE DEPRESSION 1942
Oil. 19×14 inches.
Male and female figures walk on road. Rocks in background. Man carries suitcase, woman carries baby. Gray, greens, rusts.
Signed l.r.: "Boardman Robinson."
Collection of the artist.
Listed in the *Comprehensive Exhibition Catalogue*, No. 81.

NUDE 1942
Water color. 12½×9 inches.
Listed in the *Comprehensive Exhibition Catalogue*, No. 58.

CHALK CREEK 1942
Mixed medium. 21×11½ inches.
White cliffs in foreground, with mountains behind a diagonal pine. Sky in light values, with series of white clouds.
Signed l.l.: "Boardman Robinson."
Collection of Mr. and Mrs. Bartlett Robinson, New York City.

GULCH 1942
Oil. 16×12 inches.
Deep gulch in foreground, with snow-clad peak in distance.
Listed in the *Comprehensive Exhibition Catalogue*, No. 22.

THE LAY PREACHER 1942
Water color and gouache. 14½×12 inches.
Head.
Signed: "Boardman Robinson."
Collection of Mrs. Jewett Campbell, Richmond, Virginia.

OLD TIMER 1942
Water color. 11×8 inches.
Head of a thin old man.
Unsigned.

Collection of Paul Parker, Des Moines, Iowa.
Listed in the *Comprehensive Exhibition Catalogue*, No. 63.

111. SOCIETY DAME 1942
Water color. 10×7¼ inches.
Seated female figure in blue and brown. Staid and dignified in severe evening dress. Evening wrap with white collar over left shoulder. Right arm crossed on lap.
Signed l.r.: "Boardman Robinson."
Collection of the C. W. Kraushaar Art Galleries, New York City.

SOCIETY DAME 1942
Mixed medium on canvas board. 16×12 inches.
Unfinished portrait of female figure, three-quarters length. Red formal dress, surrounded by a dark cape. Blue background, relieved with gray tones.
Signed l.r.: "Boardman Robinson '42."
Collection of the artist.
Listed in the *Comprehensive Exhibition Catalogue*, No. 80.

DR. GERALD H. WEBB 1942
Mixed medium on canvas on stretcher. 30×24 inches.
Portrait of Dr. Webb, half-length. Warm red and pink flesh tones, gray hair, blue suit with flower in lapel. Watch chain across vest. Not commissioned.
Signed l.l.: "Boardman Robinson."
Collection of the artist.
Listed in the *Comprehensive Exhibition Catalogue*, No. 9.

CATTLE MEN 1942
Mixed medium on canvas on stretcher. 17×17 inches.
Two male heads, wearing western, large-brimmed hats. Warm yellow and graded red tones in faces, one in light and the other in shadow, against a light-blue, thin background.
Signed l.l.: "Boardman Robinson '42."
Collection of the artist.
Listed in the *Comprehensive Exhibition Catalogue*, No. 68.

RANCH IN WINTER 1942
Oil. 11½×15½ inches.
Collection of the artist.
Listed in the *Comprehensive Exhibition Catalogue*, No. 13.

COLORADO CLIFF 1942
Mixed medium on gesso on pressed wood. 19×14 inches.
Mountain scene with female figure in foreground. Colors in high-intensity blue, green, and yellow ocher. Palette-knife technique.
Signed l.r.: "Boardman Robinson '42."
Collection of the artist.
Listed in the *Comprehensive Exhibition Catalogue*, No. 23.

63. WINTRY PEAK   1942
   Mixed medium.
   Mountain scene with peak in center distance. Two-pronged fallen tree limb in lower foreground.
   Signed l.r.: "Boardman Robinson '42."
   Collection of Lieutenant Colonel Edward G. Nichols, Colorado Springs, Colorado.

62. ROCKY MOUNTAINS IN SNOW   1942
   Oil on compo board. $11\frac{1}{4} \times 15\frac{3}{8}$ inches.
   Snow-covered mountains dominate composition. In lower foreground a road winds from lower right to center left.
   Signed l.l.: "Boardman Robinson '42."
   Collection of the Cleveland Museum of Art, Cleveland, Ohio.

MOUNTAINS No. 2   About 1942
   Water color. $13\frac{1}{2} \times 8\frac{3}{4}$ inches.
   Color predominantly in dark blue-green, supported by heavy black outlines of mountains. High, round hill in center background. Hills on each side, with deep valley in middle center, front plane. Tall thin rock at right of composition.
   Signed l.r.: "Boardman Robinson"; l.l.: "Boardman Robinson."
   Collection of the C. W. Kraushaar Art Galleries, New York City.

CHRIST   1943
   Mixed medium. 60×48 inches, plus triangular shape at top; over-all height, 8 feet (approximately).
   One of three separate altarpieces for the 117th Airborne Division of the A.U.S. (This piece was for Protestant sects; the other two were made by other artists for the Catholic and the Jewish faiths.) Painting represents a three-quarter figure of Jesus with his hands outstretched. Rose-colored mantle.
   Signed l.l.: "Boardman Robinson."
   Collection of the 117th Air-borne Division, Army of the United States.

COLLEGIATE RANGE   1943
   Water color. 11×15 inches.
   Mountain scene of Harvard, Yale, and Princeton Mountains, Colorado.
   Collection of the artist.
   Listed in the *Comprehensive Exhibition Catalogue*, No. 18.

ROCKY MOUNTAINS   1943
   Oil. 12×16 inches.
   Background mountains are massive, blue-gray, and white. The ravine in the foreground is painted in warm reds and browns.
   Signed l.r.: "Boardman Robinson."
   Collection of Mr. and Mrs. Max W. Foresman, Lincoln, Nebraska.
   Listed in the *Comprehensive Exhibition Catalogue*, No. 14.

THE MOUNTAIN   1943
   Oil. 16×20 inches.
   Listed in the *Comprehensive Exhibition Catalogue*, No. 36.

88. LAUGHING GIRL *or* GIRL'S HEAD   1943
   Gouache. $8\frac{1}{2} \times 7$ inches.
   Smiling girl's head. Warm flesh tones.
   Signed l.l.: "B.R." "43" (in pencil); l.r.: "Boardman Robinson."
   Collection of the artist.
   Listed in the *Comprehensive Exhibition Catalogue*, No. 60.

SNOWY RIDGE   1943
   Oil. 12×16 inches.
   Snowy crags in background, blue hills in middle distance, brown foreground.
   Signed l.r.: "Boardman Robinson."
   Collection of the artist.
   Listed in the *Comprehensive Exhibition Catalogue*, No. 30.

SPENCER PENROSE   1943
   Tempera and oil. 32×54 inches.
   Commissioned portrait. Penrose wears white chef's hat and apron. In his right hand he holds a glass; his left is empty, slightly extended.
   Signed l.l.: "Boardman Robinson '43."
   Collection of the Cooking Club, Colorado Springs, Colorado.

MOUNTAIN LANDSCAPE   1943
   Oil. 12×14 inches.
   Collection of the artist.
   Listed in the *Comprehensive Exhibition Catalogue*, No. 28.

107. DR. CHARLES W. ELIOT AT NINETY   1943
   Mixed medium on canvas on stretcher. 30×24 inches.
   Portrait of the former president of Harvard University, head and shoulders. Extremely gray color in face; white hair, blue tie, and blue-green suit against a warm background relieved with touches of green. Started in 1924; completed, 1943.
   Signed l.r.: "Boardman Robinson."
   Collection of the artist.
   Reproduced in the *Comprehensive Exhibition Catalogue*, p. 6, and listed, No. 8.

CHALK CREEK GULCH   1943
   Oil. 22×18 inches.
   Listed in the *Comprehensive Exhibition Catalogue*, No. 12.

1943

GLORIA   1943
Mixed medium on pressed wood. 20×16 inches.
Portrait of a woman. Gray, warm flesh tones on
background of blue-green. Yellow drape held in the
crook of the left arm.
Signed l.r.: "Boardman Robinson."
Collection of the artist.
Listed in the *Comprehensive Exhibition Catalogue*, No.
62.

34. SOLDIER AND GIRL   1943
Mixed medium on gesso on pressed wood. 12×16
inches.
Two heads, male and female. Thinly glazed flesh
tones of graded red in the faces. Yellow ocher and
burnt sienna hues in woman's hair and headdress. Male
with soldier's cap.
Signed l.l.: "Boardman Robinson."
Collection of the Colorado Springs Fine Arts Center,
Colorado.
Listed in the *Comprehensive Exhibition Catalogue*, No.
79.

PORTRAIT OF A COWBOY   1943
Mixed medium on canvas on stretcher. 30×24 inches.
Portrait of a cowhand, half-length. Large Stetson
hat, sheep-lined jacket, in warm tones of yellow and
gray. Blue shirt. Head of horse in middle right of pic-
ture. Background in dark value, warm hues of violet.
Signed l.r.: "Boardman Robinson '43."
Collection of the Colorado Springs National Bank,
Colorado.
Reproduced in the *Comprehensive Exhibition Catalogue*,
p. 3, and listed, No. 7.

FRANCIS FROELICHER   1943
Mixed medium on canvas on stretcher. 30×25
inches.
Portrait of the headmaster of the Fountain Valley
School for Boys, half-length. Warm red and yellow
hues in the face, light-yellow hair, red necktie, gray
suit. Right hand holding a pen; pipe in lower right
corner.
Signed l.l.: "B.R."
Collection of the artist.
Listed in the *Comprehensive Exhibition Catalogue*, No. 1.

Frontispiece. SELF-PORTRAIT   1943
Mixed medium on plywood. 19×14 inches.
Head-and-shoulder portrait of the artist. Warm yel-
low and red flesh tones against background of varied
brown and green gradations.
Signed l.r.: "Boardman Robinson '43."
Collection of Mr. and Mrs. Albert Christ-Janer,
Bloomfield Hills, Michigan.
Reproduced in the *Comprehensive Exhibition Catalogue*,
p. 1, and listed, No. 3.

GEORGE IVANOVITCH GOURDJIEFF   1943
Mixed medium on canvas on stretcher. 17×17
inches.
Portrait of Gourdjieff, head and shoulders, in profile.
Begun in 1929, actually completed in 1943.
Signed l.r.: "B.R. '43."
Collection of the artist.
Listed in the *Comprehensive Exhibition Catalogue*, No. 4.

8. TARTAR OFFICER   1943
Mixed medium on gesso on pressed wood. 14×
11¾ inches.
Portrait of fur-capped, moustached Russian officer
of czarist regime. Head only. Warm tones of yellow
ocher, umbers, and low-intensity violets, against cool
blue background. Slight point of high-intensity red on
left shoulder strap. (From an old drawing of 1915.)
Signed l.l.: "Boardman Robinson '43."
Collection of the artist.
Listed in the *Comprehensive Exhibition Catalogue*, No.
144.

ONE-ARMED POLKOVNIK   1943
Mixed medium on gesso board. 20×16 inches.
Central figure of sideburned Russian officer. A helmeted Cossack rider on horse in lower right. Color of
officer's uniform is warm tan; the coat of the rider is
red; the horse, white. White used extensively in the
sky, supported by areas of blue, loosely drawn.
Signed l.r.: "Boardman Robinson '43 from sketch made
in 1915."
Collection of the C. W. Kraushaar Art Galleries, New
York City.

RUSSIAN CABDRIVER *or* RUSSIAN CABBY   1943
Mixed medium on pressed wood.
Portrait of bearded, black-hatted, Russian figure.
Head only. Simple color scheme of warm-toned gray
and black upon warm gray background. (From an old
sketch of 1915.)
Signed l.l.: "Boardman Robinson."
Collection of the artist.
Listed in the *Comprehensive Exhibition Catalogue*, No.
69.

35. NAVAL FAMILY   1943
Mixed medium on gesso board. 15¾×14 inches.
Three figures. Female on left, child in center, male
on right. High-intensity hues, bright light red on wom-
an's slacks, violet in child's dress, sailor in off-whites.
Signed l.r.: "Boardman Robinson '43."
Collection of the C. W. Kraushaar Art Galleries, New
York City.

31. PORTALS OF THE CAÑON   1943
Mixed medium on gesso board. 12×16 inches.
Mountains. Foreground plane in low-intensity green;
second plane in light value; third plane in dark, cool
hues.
Signed l.l.: "B.R."; l.l.: "Boardman Robinson '43" (in
ink).

Collection of the C. W. Kraushaar Art Galleries, New York City.
Listed in the *Comprehensive Exhibition Catalogue*, No. 29.

OLD SOLDIER, SERBIA   1943
Oil. 12×16 inches.
Portrait of an old soldier. Mountain background.
Signed l.r.: "Boardman Robinson 1943."
Collection of F. Martin Brown, Colorado Springs, Colorado.
Listed in the *Comprehensive Exhibition Catalogue*, No. 145.

9. CZARIST OFFICER   1943
Mixed medium on gesso on pressed wood. 16×12 inches.
Portrait of a uniformed, heavy-jowled officer of czarist army. Head and shoulders. He wears visored cap, with small red insignia in front. Officer's cap in brown tones, lighter than the same hue in the background. Touch of warm red color in shoulder straps. (From an old drawing of 1915.)
Signed l.r.: "Boardman Robinson '43."
Collection of the C. W. Kraushaar Art Galleries, New York City.
Reproduced in the *Comprehensive Exhibition Catalogue*, p. 9, and listed, No. 143.

TURKOMAN   1943
Mixed medium on gesso on pressed wood. 14×12 inches.
Portrait of fur-capped soldier of czarist regime, with small silhouette of mosque spire in distance at right side of face. Hat in brown tone, accented with black. High-intensity red on left shoulder in lower right corner. Background of cool, light gray. (From an old drawing of 1915.)
Signed l.l.: "Boardman Robinson '43."
Collection of the Museum of New Britain Art Institute, New Britain, Connecticut.
Listed in the *Comprehensive Exhibition Catalogue*, No. 146.

108. MARY McLANE   1943
Mixed medium on gesso on pressed wood. 30×25¼ inches.
Portrait of Mary McLane, commissioned by the Rev. J. L. McLane. Half-length seated figure. Graded umber flesh tones; large red hat, full impasto on rim. Cool green blouse, high value. Orange-red book in lower right corner.
Signed l.r.: "Boardman Robinson '43."
Collection of the Rev. J. L. McLane, Colorado Springs, Colorado.

MOUNTAIN VALLEY   1943
Mixed medium. 11¾×13¼ inches.
Large rocky mesa on left, with valley in the foreground and snow-covered peaks in the background. Distinguishing features: the terra-cotta outline and accent

of the mountains is the underpainting showing through the light overpainting.
Signed l.l.: "Boardman Robinson" (green paint); l.l.: " '43" (in ink).
Collection of Mrs. M. F. Galbraith, Colorado Springs, Colorado.

60. MOUNTAIN LANDSCAPE   About 1943
Mixed medium.
Mountain scene, dominated by one large peak in left distance. Foothills and trees in lower foreground.
Collection of Gertrude Riechke, New York City.

32. CHALK CREEK CANYON, MIDDAY   1944
Oil on panel. 11½×15½ inches.
High cliff at left background, with group of small trees on right. Two small figures in left foreground. White cloud in center of background sky.
Signed l.r.: "Boardman Robinson."
Collection of the C. W. Kraushaar Art Galleries, New York City.

33. MOUNTAIN ANATOMY   1944
Mixed medium. 20¾×26½ inches.
Monumental mountains, with accents upon their basic structure. Yellowish, warm foreground. Broadly indicated mountains in grays, light red in the middle distance, and gray-blue in the background.
Signed l.r.: "Boardman Robinson '44."
Collection of the C. W. Kraushaar Art Galleries, New York City.

VIEW OF THE ROCKY MOUNTAINS   1944
Oil. 11½×15½ inches.
In the foreground a road leads across pale-green fields, past a haystack to a small farm. Beyond the farm rises a range of hills. In the last plane towers a large snow-covered mountain.
Signed: "Boardman Robinson '44."
Collection of Alice P. Doyle.

ROCKY MOUNTAINS   1944
Mixed medium on gesso on pressed wood. 22¼×28 inches.
Mountain scene, with warm frontal plane against cool gray-green background mountains. Two small buildings in lower center. Two small dark umber clouds in top right of sky, under a line of white clouds at top frame edge.
Signed l.r.: "Boardman Robinson '44."
Collection of the artist.

WE LOVE HIM FOR THE ENEMIES HE HAS MADE 1944
Gouache. 15×19 inches.
Ten heads: Hitler, labeled "Fascist"; fat-jowled, frowning head with moustache, labeled "Monopolist"; head with large black hat, labeled "Hearst"; bull-necked head with cigar in mouth, labeled "Rugged Individualist"; scrawny, red-nosed old man with white

1944-45

moustache, labeled "Nigger Hater"; gray-haired man with weak moustache, labeled "McCormick"; gray, weak-faced head, labeled "Defeatist"; glowering face, labeled "Labor Hater"; bellowing, red-faced man, labeled "Jew Hater"; buck-toothed, skinny female head, labeled "America Firster."
Signed: "B.R."
Collection of the C. W. Kraushaar Art Galleries, New York City.

61. SPRING SNOW   1944
Oil. 19×28 inches (approximately).
Harsh mountainous background, contrasted with gay skiing figures in snow in foreground. Snow contrasts with dull rock. Tundra is warm in color, contrasting with cool of mountains. Sky contains large white clouds.
Signed l.r.: "Boardman Robinson '44."
Collection of Mr. and Mrs. Anders S. Lunde, Woodstock, Vermont.

MT. YALE   1944
Oil on panel. 20×26 inches.
Green slope in the foreground, male and female figures in left foreground. Woman points toward the mountains. High, craggy peaks cover background. Two small clouds in sky at left.
Signed l.r.: "Boardman Robinson '44."
Collection of the C. W. Kraushaar Art Galleries, New York City.

ROCKY MOUNTAINS, EARLY FALL   1944
Oil on canvas. 23½×29½ inches.
Seated male and female figures lean against rock formation in right foreground. Small green hills and valleys interweave back to large blue snow-capped mountain in background.
Signed l.r.: "Boardman Robinson '44."
Collection of the C. W. Kraushaar Art Galleries, New York City.

57. COLORADO LANDSCAPE   1944
Oil on panel. 21½×27½ inches.
Sharp, craggy, sunlit mountain rises in left foreground. Very small blue mountain in far right background. Patches of trees and grass through middle ground. Slight rise in right foreground with short, twisted tree in center.
Signed l.r.: "Boardman Robinson '44."
Collection of the C. W. Kraushaar Art Galleries, New York City.

59. MOUNTAIN MINE   1944
Mixed medium on gesso plywood.
Rocky mountain landscape, with deep-purple haze covering background hills. Foreground contains a road

in extreme lower left. In lower right the composition is balanced by a mill, painted in red hues.
Signed l.r.: "Boardman Robinson '44."
Collection of the artist.

48. JESUS AND JUDAS   1945
Oil on gesso board. 18×13¼ inches.
Jesus and his disciple stand beneath an arch. Jesus' gown is white, a red mantle is thrown over his shoulders. The disciple at right is dressed in a green robe.
Signed l.r.: "Boardman Robinson '45."
Collection of the artist.

ILLUSTRATIONS

The War in Eastern Europe[1]

HALF-SAVAGE GIANTS   Frontispiece
Pen drawing with washes. 15×10 inches.
At right a Cossack in uniform leans against a doorway; at left, in interior, a barefooted chambermaid stands.
Signed l.r.: "Boardman Robinson Cholm"; l.l.: "Cholm, Poland 1915."
Collection of the artist.

OLYMPUS AND SALONIKA   Facing p. 4
Pen drawings; sketches.
Four drawings on one page:
1. Bird's-eye view of Salonika. Minarets in distance, the harbor and mountains in background.
Signed l.l.: "B.R. Salonika."
2. Street scene. Narrow street, overhanging building. Three figures discernible.
Signed l.l.: "B.R. Salonika."
3. Sketch of man and woman. He stands at left; she walks behind him at right.
Signed l.r.: "B.R. Salonika."
4. The French correspondent and Bulgarian diplomat. Two men on deck of ship. One at left, at railing, has fieldglass in hand; other holds lorgnette.
Signed l.r.: "B.R."
Collection of the artist.

REFUGEE PRIESTS, SALONIKA   Facing p. 18
Pen drawing. 6×10 inches.
Port scene. Group of priests, two men, and a horse at left of picture. In center foreground is a squatting figure. At right, many and various figures.
Signed l.r.: "B.R. Salonika, Apr. '15."
Collection of the artist.

THE SEVEN JOLLY CARPENTERS (SALONIKA)
                                                            Facing p. 20
Pen drawing. 9×14 inches.
Four men sit at table, which extends from center to right. Two men dance together in center. Two seated onlookers at left.
Signed l.r.: "Boardman Robinson '15."
Collection of the artist.

[1] John Reed and Boardman Robinson, *The War in Eastern Europe* (New York: Charles Scribner's Sons, 1916).

PRECAUTIONS AGAINST TYPHUS (NISH) Facing p. 30
Pen drawing. 10×14 inches (approximately).
    A group of men sit on ground in the curve of a road,
applying ointments to their bodies and hunting lice. A
sentry stands at left. A yoke of oxen attached to wagon
approach at right, with driver. Mountains in right distance.
Signed l.r.: "Boardman Robinson Nish '15."
Collection of the artist.

SERBIA—NISH Facing p. 32
    Sketches:
    1. Groves along the Vardar. Valley scene filled with
        crosses marking graves in the foreground. Moun-
        tains in the distance.
    Signed l.r.: "B.R. Serbia."
    2. An old soldier with turbaned head.
    Signed on shoulder at right: "B.R. Nish."
    3. Refugees. Male figure carries heavy rucksack.
        Hooded female also carries belongings. Child in
        front. Group walking toward right.
    Signed r.: "B.R."
    4. Peasant soldiers; two male figures face each
        other.
    Unsigned.
Collection of the artist.

THE CHEECHA *or* THE SENTRY Facing p. 34
    Water color. 13½×10½ inches.
    A Serbian soldier, wearing hood and carrying gun,
stands guard. Mountains in background.
Signed l.r.: "Boardman Robinson, on the Vardar,
Serbia '15."
Collection of the Colorado Springs Fine Arts Center,
Colorado.
Reproduced in *Ninety-three Drawings*, Pl. 52; listed in
the *Comprehensive Exhibition Catalogue*, No. 136.

THE GOVERNMENT SENDS THE SOLDIERS ALL OVER
    SERBIA TO HELP WITH THE PLOWING Facing p. 36
    Drawing. 12×17 inches (approximately).
    Hooded woman leads oxen on brow of hill. They
pull a plow, which is held in furrow by the stooping
figure of a man. Sentry stands at right.
Signed l.r.: "Boardman Robinson, Serbia '15."
Collection of the artist.

DISCHARGED FROM A TYPHUS HOSPITAL Facing p. 44
    Drawing. 12×8 inches (approximately).
    Three emaciated male figures in uniform proceed
down a street. Two of them support the limp third soldier between them.
Signed l.r.: "Boardman Robinson, Nish Apr. '15."
Collection of the artist.

AUSTRIAN PRISONERS IN UNIFORM Facing p. 46
    Drawing. 12×8 inches.
    Wounded prisoners in uniform walk toward left.
Rooftops in the background.
Signed l.l.: "Boardman Robinson, Nish '15."
Collection of the artist.

A HOSPITAL AT NISH Facing p. 48
    Drawing. 14×7 inches (approximately).
    Many recumbent figures on floor. Some half-raised
on arms, with bowed heads, showing defeat. At far
right a man raises arms, throws head back. Lantern suspended in center distance.
Signed l.r.: "Boardman Robinson, Nish."
Collection of the artist.

ALONG THE ROAD Facing p. 52
    Pen and ink.
    Sketches:
    1. Sketched from the saddle. Rear view of two sol-
        diers on horseback.
    Signed r.: "B.R."
    2. Old peasants, man with stick walks toward
        right. Back of barefooted woman at right.
    Signed l.c.: "B.R."
    3. Sick refugees, lying in the road. Woman at left
        bends over a prostrate figure. Indistinct oxen and
        wagon in distance. At right a figure crouches on
        roadside.
    Signed l.r.: "B.R."
    4. Serbian officers. Profile view of officer left. Full-
        face view of officer at right.
    Signed l.: "B.R."
Collection of the artist.

A LITTLE AVENGER OF KOSSOVO Facing p. 54
    Drawing. 12×8 inches.
    A hooded figure with child. Head of two oxen in
lower left distance.
Signed l.r.: "Boardman Robinson."
Collection of the artist.

TROOP TRAINS MOVING NORTH *or* SERBIAN TROOP
    TRAIN Facing p. 60
    Drawing. 14×10¾ inches.
    Open cars moving wounded troops through a region
of high, rolling hills.
Signed l.r.: "Boardman Robinson, Serbia '15."
Collection of the Colorado Springs Fine Arts Center,
    Colorado.
Listed in the *Comprehensive Exhibition Catalogue*, No.
    141.

LOOKING TOWARD AUSTRIA Facing p. 66
    Drawing. 14×7 inches.
    Serbian soldier in uniform stands with his hands on
his gun, the butt of which rests on the ground. Distant
hills.
Signed l.r.: "Boardman Robinson."
Collection of the artist.

IN THE SERB TRENCHES ON THE SAVE *or* "TRENCHES
    IN THE SAVE" Facing p. 70
    Drawing. 14×10 inches.
    River in foreground. Visible at right, half of a boat,
containing one soldier. One soldier kneels beside river

1916

bank at center, another stands. At right, a soldier peers out over top of a high trench. Tree at far left.
Signed l.r.: "Boardman Robinson."
Collection of the Colorado Springs Fine Arts Center, Colorado.
Listed in the *Comprehensive Exhibition Catalogue*, No. 140.

DODGING SHRAPNEL ON THE SAVE   Facing p. 72
Drawing. 8×12 inches
Boat containing six male figures and the boatman, who stands at bow. A building explodes at far right. Other buildings beside river bank in center.
Unsigned.
Collection of the artist.

THE NIGHT RIDE TO SHABATZ   Facing p. 82
Drawing. 14×8 inches.
Moon shines from upper right on scene, which shows horses and carriage containing two figures at left, two armed horsemen in center, hooded carriage driven by one driver and drawn by two horses, at right.
Signed l.r.: "Boardman Robinson."
Collection of the artist.

CHURCH AT SHABATZ   Facing p. 84
Drawing. 12×8 inches.
White church with one tower dominates scene at center. Roof is completely destroyed. At left, a group of people, horses, and oxen. At right, stands a soldier.
Signed l.r.: "Boardman Robinson."
Collection of the artist.

THE WOMAN OF GOUTCHEVO MOUNTAIN *or* SERBIAN
GYPSY   Facing p. 96
Drawing. 10×9 inches.
Barefooted woman strides toward right, carrying violin in left hand, gun and balanced bags slung over her right shoulder. Indistinct house in background.
Signed l.r.: "Boardman Robinson."
Collection of the artist.

122. THE UNBURIED DEAD (GOUTCHEVO) *or* GUCHEVO
Facing p. 98
Water color. 10¾×13¾ inches.
Unburied dead lie on rounded curve of hill. Three tree stumps, a half-starved dog, and broken wagon in background. Another dog, white, in right foreground.
Collection of the Colorado Springs Fine Arts Center, Colorado.
Listed in the *Comprehensive Exhibition Catalogue*, No. 137.

HIT BY A BURSTING SHELL   Facing p. 100
Drawing. 12×8 inches (approximately).
A soldier with cap carries wounded soldier over his shoulder. Two indistinct figures in lower left background.
Signed l.r.: "Boardman Robinson June '15."
Collection of the artist.

RIDING BEHIND VOYVODA MICHITCH AND KING PETER
Facing p. 102
Drawing. 8×12 inches.
Covered wagon, drawn by horses, goes down a rocky hill.
Signed l.r.: "Boardman Robinson May '15."
Collection of the artist.

SERBIA, MY DEAR MOTHER   Facing p. 104
Wash drawing. 8×12 inches (approximately).
Serbian soldier, leaning on rifle, stands on platform facing left, gazing toward the far distance: "How is it with thee, O Serbia, my dear mother?"
Signed l.r.: "B.R. Valievo, Serbia."
Collection of Mrs. Malcolm L. McBride, Cleveland, Ohio.

CROSSING THE PRUTH IN A FLAT-BOTTOMED SCOW
Facing p. 110
Drawing. 8×12 inches.
Three male figures sit in flatboat, while a fourth stands, pulling the boat by grasping a rope stretched across the river.
Signed l.l.: "Boardman Robinson '15."
Collection of the artist.

PONTOONS FOR THE PRUTH   Facing p. 112
Drawing. 6×14 inches (approximately).
A team of four horses, aided by many men pushing, pulls the pontoon as it ascends from a valley. In lower right distance another load follows. Trees at left. Mountains in distance at center and right.
Signed l.r.: "Boardman Robinson '15."
Collection of the artist.

TURCOMANS FROM BEYOND THE CASPIAN *or* TURKOMAN
CAMP   Facing p. 114
Water color. 11½×15½ inches.
At right, two figures, standing. Both wear tall fur hats. In center a hatless figure is seated. At right two others squat, one hatted, one hatless. Blanketed horse stands in center middle ground. Many indistinct figures of men and horses in all parts of the composition.
Signed l.r.: "Boardman Robinson."
Collection of John W. Robinson, Oxnard, California.
Listed in the *Comprehensive Exhibition Catalogue*, No. 117.

MADJI INDICATED HER WITH HIS HAND   Facing p. 116
Drawing. 6×12 inches (approximately).
Fat woman smoking cigarette sits at table at left. At corner of table, in center, stands plump, moustached man. At right sits officer with goatee.
Unsigned.
Collection of the artist.

TURKOMAN   Facing p. 118
Wash drawing. 12½×11½ inches.
Striking head of Turkoman or Kurd tribesman, with enormous white shako framing the face and a high red collar around the throat. Features Mongolian, small moustache, slanted eyes.
Signed: "Boardman Robinson—Nova Sielitza—1915."
Collection of Dorothy Kenyon, New York City.
Reproduced in *Ninety-three Drawings*, Pl. 14.

NOVA SIELITZA   Facing p. 122
Two sketches:
1. Ivan the Horrible. Head of short-bearded Russian wearing cap.
Signed: "B.R. Nova Sielitza '15."
2. An aged Jew, black-robed, black-capped, with beard, sits at table reading a book by candle-light.
Signed l.r.: "B.R. Nova Sielitza."
Collection of the artist.

GUN POSITIONS IN BUCOVINA   Facing p. 130
Drawing. 15×6 inches (approximately).
A peasant, with two oxen, plows a field on the crest of a hill. Mountains in the distance.
Signed l.r.: "Boardman Robinson."
Collection of the artist.

PEASANT CARTS JOLTED BY WITH FAINTLY GROANING HEAPS OF ARMS AND LEGS (BUCOVINA)
           Facing p. 132
Drawing. 6×14 inches (approximately).
Large, broad wagon, containing many men, goes toward left. House and standing male figures in right background.
Signed l.r.: "Boardman Robinson."
Collection of the artist.

DIGGING TRENCHES NEAR ZASTEVNA   Facing p. 134
Drawing. 6×14 inches (approximately).
Peasants work in long trench, supervised by officer, who stands with arms folded. At far left a peasant woman stands with large bundle on her head. Mountains in background.
Signed l.r.: "Boardman Robinson."
Collection of the artist.

THE STATION AT TARNOPOL   Facing p. 146
Drawing. 6×14 inches (approximately).
Scene contains many figures: in foreground, a group of peasants; at right, a hatted, long-coated figure; in background, a boxcar, out of which pour soldiers and wounded.
Signed l.r.: "Boardman Robinson, Tarnopol, '15."
Collection of the artist.

REFUGEES   Facing p. 148
Drawing. 6×14 inches (approximately).
Refugees stand and sit in many positions. Old, white-bearded man in right foreground. Prostrate figure on floor at center. At left, in background, a group of soldiers marches in formation, with guns.
Signed l.r.: "Boardman Robinson."
Collection of the artist.

BLIND FOR LIFE (KOVEL)   Facing p. 150
Gouache painting. 12×5 inches (approximately).
Bearded soldier in uniform leads another soldier, who has bandaged eyes and left hand in a sling.
Signed l.r.: "Boardman Robinson, Poland, June '15."
Collection of the artist.

A SOLDIER ON DUTY   Facing p. 154
Drawing. 12×7 inches (approximately).
Russian soldier stands on street corner, gazing across street at two American figures. Buildings in background. Many people on walks in background.
Signed l.l.: "Boardman Robinson, Tarnopol '15."
Collection of the artist.

CHANTING LEGIONS (LEMBERG)   Facing p. 164
Drawing. 6×14 inches (approximately).
Russian soldiers in formation march with guns and packs, singing and swinging in stride.
Signed l.r.: "Boardman Robinson, Tarnopol '15."
Collection of the artist.

ON THE WAY TO LEMBERG   Facing p. 166
Sketches.
Five sketches, showing types of officers; hatted, long-coated man leading girl; skeptical colonel; a pope; Austrian figures, prisoners.
All signed.
Collection of the artist.

CHOLM   Facing p. 172
Sketches.
Five sketches showing tall, thin Russian soldier; Russian officer; Cossack; soldier's head; head of a Cossack in black fur cap.
All signed.
Collection of the artist.

EVERY MAN LOOKED UP AND GRINNED AND SALUTED
           Facing p. 188
Drawing. 6×14 inches (approximately).
Courtyard scene. Six figures of civilians in lower right. A Cossack soldier stands on roof at center right. A figure sits in window at upper right. In street, at left, many Cossacks on horses raise hands in salute.
Signed l.l.: "Boardman Robinson '15, Cholm."
Collection of the artist.

RUSSIAN COSSACK   Facing p. 190
Water-color drawing. 15×11 inches.
Russian Cossack in tall black cap and red coat, astride a black horse. Russian village in background.
Signed: "Boardman Robinson, Cholm '15."
Collection of Connie Zachritz, Colorado Springs, Colorado.

A TRAGIC LITTLE PROCESSION   Facing p. 194
Drawing. 5×12 inches (approximately).
Soldier, carrying gun on shoulder, marches at right, leading two prisoners in black, followed by soldier at

1916

left with gun in right hand. A woman passes them in front of a high wall with buildings in upper left.
Signed l.r.: "Boardman Robinson, Cholm, June '15."
Collection of the artist.

CIVIL AND POLITICAL PRISONERS AT A STATION
                                            Facing p. 216
  Gouache on toned paper, pasted on cardboard, 16×19 inches.
  Chained prisoners in white stand in center, attended by guards with swords. They all face right. Monochromatic, with strong value contrasts.
Signed l.r.: "Boardman Robinson, Poland, '15."
Collection of the artist.
Listed in the *Comprehensive Exhibition Catalogue*, No. 116.

THE CALEA VICTORIEI IN BUCAREST   Facing p. 300
  Drawing. 8×14 inches (approximately).
  Street scene of much color and gaiety, containing women dressed with much style, officers in fancy dress. In center background, an ornate building with striking sculpture.
Signed l.r.: "Boardman Robinson, Bucarest, '15."
Collection of the artist.

A GLIMPSE OF THE SERBIAN RETREAT   Facing p. 320
  Drawing. 12×16 inches (approximately).
  Peasant figures retreat toward right in foreground, many of them looking backward over their shoulders. Mountains in the distance. Center background with soldiers retreating in the same direction.
Signed l.r.: "Boardman Robinson, '15."
Collection of the artist.

THE SERB   Facing p. 332
  Drawing. 6×4 inches (approximately).
  Head of Serb soldier.
Signed l.l.: "B.R. Boardman Robinson, Serbia, '15."
Collection of New York University, New York City.

THE SENTRY IN THE BALKANS   Facing p. 324
  India-ink wash drawing. $10\frac{3}{4} \times 14\frac{1}{2}$ inches.
  Sentry stands on right, high on a mountainside overlooking an encampment below. In middle foreground are distinguishable a broken wheel, a shoe, and a bone. In background rise vast and rugged mountains.
Signed l.c.l.: "Boardman Robinson May '15."
Collection of L. V. Pulsifer, Mountainville, New York.

The Brothers Karamazov[2]

7. OLD MAN KARAMAZOV   Title-page, Book I
  Wash drawing on thin paper, strengthened with crayon and ink. $12 \times 10\frac{7}{8}$ inches.
  Large head of Father Karamazov, full-front view.

  [2] Feodor Dostoevski, *The Brothers Karamazov* (New York: Random House, 1933).

Signed l.r.: "Boardman Robinson."
Collection of Warren Chappell, New York City.
Listed in the *Comprehensive Exhibition Catalogue*, No. 126.

AN UNFORTUNATE GATHERING Title-page, Book II, p. 31
  Wash drawing.
  Courtyard scene within two arches. Black-robed figure at the left talks to female figure in white. Eight other figures in the composition, some seated, some standing.
Signed l.r.: "B.R."

A SCANDALOUS SCENE   Facing p. 84
  Wash drawing. 14×12 inches.
  Four figures in a room. Black-robed figure bows before a male figure in double-breasted coat. Another man faces them at back left. Head of a fourth is at far right. Top hat and cane lie on the floor in lower right foreground.
Signed l.l.: "Boardman Robinson."
Collection of the artist.

LIZAVETA   P. 93
  Wash drawing. 7×15 inches.
  Figure of child putting on boots in doorway.
Signed l.r.: "B.R."
Collection of the artist.

KATERINA IVANOVNA   Facing p. 106
  Wash drawing. $14 \times 11\frac{1}{2}$ inches.
  Two persons stand in room—female figure at left in coat and hat, male figure in uniform. He bows to her at the door. Table with officers' cap in left foreground.
Signed l.r.: "Boardman Robinson."
Collection of the artist.

KARAMAZOV AND THE BOYS   Book III, facing p. 138
  Wash drawing.
  Three male figures, who stand in center background, look at seated male figure, who bows head held in his hands. Most prominent standing figure is turning to leave, left arm upflung, partly obstructing view of picture on back wall.
Signed l.r.: "Boardman Robinson."
Collection of the artist.

THE GRAND INQUISITOR Title-page, Book IV, p. 167
  Wash drawing.
  Candle glows on table at center, lighting up silhouettes of two figures—a monk, who stands at left with left hand on table, and a robed figure (Christ) at right, who wears halo around head and shoulders. Vaulted ceiling.
Signed l.r.: "Boardman Robinson."
Collection of the artist.
Reproduced in *Ninety-three Drawings*, Pl. 90; listed in the *Comprehensive Exhibition Catalogue*, No. 128.

SMERDYAKOV   Title-page, Book V, p. 219
  Wash drawing.
  Male figure sits at center left, playing a guitar be-

side a tree at far left. At right, back view of female figure stands in listening attitude.
Signed l.l.: "Boardman Robinson"; l.r.: "Boardman Robinson."
Reproduced in *Ninety-three Drawings*, Pl. 88.

THE CAPTAIN   Book V, facing p. 224
Wash drawing. 13¾×11½ inches.
Five figures in a room. Female figure sits at left. Male figure stands at right, with hands stretched toward her. Another female figure, with shawled head, sits directly behind them at center. Indistinct figure seated at far left; indistinct head in right background. Icon on wall high at far right.
Signed l.r.: "Boardman Robinson."
Collection of the C. W. Kraushaar Art Galleries, New York City.

110. MADAME HOHLAKOV   Book V, facing p. 280
Wash drawing. 16¼×10¾ inches.
Three-quarter-length view of female figure, facing right with hands clasped, waist-high. Sharp nose, hair frizzed over forehead and tied with ribbon. Narrow black band around throat.
Signed l.r.: "Boardman Robinson."
Collection of the C. W. Kraushaar Art Galleries, New York City.

FATHER ZOSSIMA'S BIOGRAPHY
             Title-page, Book VI, p. 293
Wash drawing. 8½×13½ inches.
Two male figures sitting at a table, figure at left in profile, hands folded in front of him. Figure at right almost faces front. Icon on center wall, in background, and oval picture on left.
Collection of Clifford B. West, Bloomfield Hills, Michigan.

THE ANGEL   Title-page, Book VII, p. 341
Wash drawing. 11×13 inches.
Angel with great wings hovers over scene of anguish, containing many figures in flaming region. They all reach up. One central figure, who has mounted higher than the others, grasps at something the angel holds.
Signed l.c.: "Boardman Robinson."
Collection of the artist.

THE MAD MONK   Book VII, facing p. 366
Wash drawing
Mad monk at center, both arms upraised over head, faces front. Head of another figure appears at center left, watching him. Three icons on wall in background.
Signed l.r.: "Boardman Robinson '33"; inscribed l.l.:
     "For W. C.
       1936
       Colorado Springs"
Collection of Warren Chappell, New York City.
Reproduced in *Ninety-three Drawings*, Pl. 86.

KUZMA KUZMITCH   P. 383
Wash drawing.
Four male figures, one lying down at lower right, one in cap holding a candle, as he looks at the reclining fig-

ure. The other two watch from left. Table with samovar and cups in left foreground.

DELIRIUM   Facing p. 456
Wash drawing.
A physical struggle between two male figures at center, in front of table holding bottle and playing cards. Female figure at right looks on, helpless. Heads of three others look on from background.
Signed l.r.: "Boardman Robinson."

RUSSIAN OFFICIALS   Title-page, Book IX, p. 471
Wash drawing.
Street scene containing many men in uniform. Wagon (back view) stands at left. Two doorways in background.
Signed l.r.: "B.R."

THE LAST OF KARAMAZOV   Book IX, facing p. 500
Wash drawing.
Male figure lies supine on the floor. A face peers in at the window at left. Candle burns on the table at far right.
Signed l.r.: "Boardman Robinson."
Collection of the artist.

MITYA AND THE PEASANTS   Book IX, facing p. 512
Wash drawing.
Half-nude male figure sits at left, facing man with beard at right. In upper center stands third male figure.
Signed l.r.: "B.R."
Collection of the artist.

KOLYA   Title-page, Book X, p. 543
Wash drawing.
Male figure in tall fur hat, at center right, talks to boy in fur hat at center left. Bust of woman in lower foreground. Head and forepart of horse in center background. Figures, houses, and tree at left make up background.

AT GRUSHENKA'S   Title-page, Book XI, p. 595
Wash drawing. 10×15 inches.
Three figures in prison cell. Male figure at left bends forward in gesture of violence. Female figure at right raises hand toward him. Male figure back of her stands looking left with hat in hand.
Signed l.r.: "Boardman Robinson."
Collection of the artist.

IVAN AND SMERDYAKOV   Book XI, facing p. 666
Wash drawing. 13×11 inches.
Two male figures—one, seated at left, faces the other, who stands talking to him. Seated figure is removing his hose.
Signed l.l.: "B.R."
Collection of the artist.

1935

THE POOR RELATION   Book XI, facing p. 670
Wash drawing. 13 × 10½ inches.
Two male figures in room—one in dressing gown stands at left; the other, holding hat and cane, sits at right, facing him. Chair at lower right. Samovar and glasses on dresser in center right background.
Signed l.r.: "B.R."
Collection of the artist.
Listed in the *Comprehensive Exhibition Catalogue*, No. 127.

THE PROSECUTOR   Book XII, facing p. 700
Wash drawing.
Male figure gesticulates with right hand to a group of people, who are sitting in jury box. He leans across composition diagonally from l.r. to u.l. Other figures stand at right in distance.
Signed l.r.: "Boardman Robinson."
Collection of Dr. S. W. Schaefer, New York City.

THE TROIKA   Title-page, Epilogue, p. 799
Wash drawing.
Russian three-horse carriage and two occupants. One, the driver, sits above and in front of the other.
Signed l.r.: "Boardman Robinson."
Collection of Otis Dozier, Dallas, Texas.
Reproduced in the *Comprehensive Exhibition Catalogue*, p. 2, and listed, No. 125.

ILUSHA'S FUNERAL   Endpiece, facing p. 822
Wash drawing. 8½ × 14 inches.
Children carry a coffin. Other figures precede and follow them. Building and tree in background.
Signed l.r.: "B.R."
Collection of the artist.

The Idiot[3]

THE TRIAL   Frontispiece
Pen and wash on eggshell-surfaced paper. 15¼ × 11⅛ inches.
Constellation of five heads. Four of the five characters are shown almost three-quarter length.
Signed l.r.: "Boardman Robinson"; l.l.: "Affectionately inscribed to Warren Chappell, Colorado Springs, Aug. '36."
Collection of Warren Chappell, New York City.

NASTASYA   P. 10
Drawing. 5 × 14 inches.
Female figure in horse-drawn carriage, being driven by fat driver with whip, bows to male figure, who greets her from left at the side of the street. Head of male figure on the other side of the street, directly back of her, lifts top hat.
Signed l.r.: "B.R."
Collection of the artist.

[3] Feodor Dostoevski, *The Idiot* (New York: Random House, 1935).

THE EXECUTION   P. 59
Pen drawing. 5 × 12 inches.
Male figure on gallows bows forward as priest blesses him from lower right. Hangman stands behind him at left. Indistinct spectators and buildings around them.
Signed l.r.: "B.R."
Collection of the artist.

THE PARTY, NASTASYA AND THE GENERAL
       Facing p. 100
Ink wash drawing.
Eight figures in a room. Young woman seated at left faces two male figures, who bend over to talk to her at right. Others stand in background. The old gentleman with whiskers is burning a paper in his hand. Table and chair at lower right.
Collection of Helen Sherbon, Philadelphia, Pennsylvania.

THE STORY   P. 140
Pen drawing. 6 × 10 inches.
Soldier scolds an old woman who is huddled in a corner at left. Pitcher stands beside her.
Signed l.c.l.: "B.R."
Collection of the artist.

NASTASYA BURNS THE MONEY   Facing p. 162
Ink wash drawing. 11 × 15½ inches.
Many figures in a room, all in violent action. Central figure is a woman, pointing her finger toward the left. Others look shocked. Chair stands in left corner.
Signed l.l.: "Boardman Robinson."
Collection of the artist.

THE BLESSING OF MYSHKIN   P. 210
Pen drawing. 5 × 10 inches.
Four figures in room, two old women seated at right. The other two are men, who stand talking to them. At left, chair, and samovar on table.
Signed l.r.: "B.R."

STABBING ON THE STAIRWAY   Facing p. 222
Ink wash drawing. 15¾ × 11½ inches.
Man falls downstairs backward toward left. Arm with knife at right points toward him.
Signed l.r.: "Boardman Robinson."
Listed in *Comprehensive Exhibition Catalogue*, No. 118.

NASTASYA WIELDS THE WHIP   Facing p. 334
Ink wash drawing. 15½ × 11 inches.
Fashionably dressed female figure, at center, stands at head of stairs, swinging whip. Officer in uniform stands behind and below her at lower right. Other figures stand in front of her, man with moustaches and wearing top hat being the most prominent.
Signed l.r.: "Boardman Robinson."
Collection of the artist.
Reproduced in *Ninety-three Drawings*, Pl. 89.

FINDING THE POCKETBOOK   P. 378
Pen drawing. 5 × 12 inches.
Three male figures, one walking along the sidewalk

toward left, the other two stoop down to pick up fallen object. Street lamp at left.
Signed l.r.: "B.R."
Collection of the artist.

THE GARDEN—MYSHKIN AND AGLAIA   Facing p. 402
Ink wash drawing. 16×11 inches.
Man talks with a lady, who is dressed in flowing coat and small hat. They sit on a bench in a garden, beneath a large tree at left in background.
Signed l.c.r.: "Boardman Robinson."
Collection of Mrs. Jewett Campbell, Richmond, Virginia.
Listed in the *Comprehensive Exhibition Catalogue*, No. 119.

THE IDEA WAS NAPOLEON'S   P. 478
Pen drawing.
Napoleon sits at table at left, opposite a small boy, who sits facing him. Ink bottle with quill stands on table between them.
Signed l.r.: "B.R."

MYSHKIN TUMBLES THE VASE   Facing p. 522
Ink wash drawing. 11×15½ inches.
Room filled with many figures. Doorway in center background. Oval picture on wall at right. Large vase totters toward floor at left.
Signed l.r. (outside oval): "Boardman Robinson."
Collection of the artist.

THE DEATHBED   Facing p. 582
Ink wash drawing. 11×15½ inches.
Female corpse lies on bed at right. Male figure is seated at left foreground, another male figure leans over him. Glass and playing cards on table at lower left. Half-glimpse of icon on wall in left background.
Signed l.l.: "Boardman Robinson."
Collection of the artist.
Reproduced in *Ninety-three Drawings*, Pl. 87; listed in *Comprehensive Exhibition Catalogue*, No. 120.

King Lear[4]

15. LEAR   Frontispiece
Ink and opaque whites. 10×6 inches.
Head of Lear, full-face view. He wears a full white beard and has white hair.
Signed l.r.: "Boardman Robinson '38."
Collection of the artist.
Listed in the *Comprehensive Exhibition Catalogue*, No. 135.

12. LEAR WITH HIS DAUGHTERS, AND THE FOOL
    Facing p. 4
Wash drawing. 15¾×9½ inches.
Lear sits at left with the Fool at his feet. At right stands Cordelia with her sisters. Heads of two male figures indicated beyond them in background.
Signed l.l.: "Boardman Robinson '38."

[4] William Shakespeare, *King Lear* (New York: Limited Editions Club, 1939).

Collection of the artist.
Listed in the *Comprehensive Exhibition Catalogue*, No. 131.

LEAR AND KENT   Facing p. 44
Wash drawing. 15¾×9½ inches.
Lear stands at center; Kent sits at lower left, with left hand half-opened. Lear makes gesture toward him.
Signed l.l.: "Boardman Robinson '38."
Collection of the artist.
Listed in the *Comprehensive Exhibition Catalogue*, No. 132.

LEAR AND THE FOOL ON THE HEATH   Facing p. 58
Wash drawing. 15¾×9½ inches.
Massive figure of Lear faces left in center. Arms are half-raised. Tremendous wind blows toward right. Small figure of the Fool looks upward at lower right.
Signed l.l.: "Boardman Robinson '38."
Collection of the artist.
Listed in the *Comprehensive Exhibition Catalogue*, No. 133.

14. GLOUCESTER AND EDGAR ON THE CLIFFS
    Facing p. 78
Wash drawing. 15¾×9½ inches.
Two figures, Gloucester and Edgar, in the first plane of the composition, supported by a background of sea and cliffs. Gloucester, hands spread out before his blind eyes, is being led by his companion.
Signed l.r.: "Boardman Robinson, '38."
Collection of the artist.
Listed in the *Comprehensive Exhibition Catalogue*, No. 134.

13. LEAR CARRYING THE BODY OF CORDELIA
    Facing p. 118
Wash drawing.
Lear walks forward, holding the limp figure of Cordelia in his arms.
Signed l.l.: "Boardman Robinson '38."
Collection of the artist.

Spoon River Anthology[5]

FLETCHER McGEE   Facing p. 6
Heavy opaque water color on gesso board. 16×12 inches.
Large female head in center left. Male seated figure in lower right, horrified at vision. Middle values, with thick impasto of casein opaque. Colors low graded.
Signed l.r.: "B.R."
Collection of the C. W. Kraushaar Art Galleries, New York City.

[5] Edgar Lee Masters, *Spoon River Anthology* (New York: Limited Editions Club, 1942).

1942

CASSIUS HEUFFER — Facing p. 16
Water color on paper. 12×9½ inches.
Male figure in graveyard, left hand on tombstone. Background of grave monuments. Values dark; colors in dark, cool greens.
Signed l.r.: "B.R."
Collection of the C. W. Kraushaar Art Galleries, New York City.

1. SEREPTA MASON — Facing p. 22
Mixed medium on gesso board. 14½×11½ inches.
Portrait of Serepta Mason, her head turned to her right, hand resting on form in lower foreground. Colors varied, combinations of low intensity; cools in background and warms in center. Free drawing. Rich texture qualities.
Signed l.r.: "Boardman Robinson."
Collection of the Museum of Cranbrook Academy of Art, Bloomfield Hills, Michigan.

2. DAISY FRASER — Facing p. 28
Opaque water color on gesso board. 16×12 inches.
Female figure covers left side of composition, with cab, horse, and figures in distant right-center. Loosely drawn design, gesso white supporting colors in all white areas. Light-value contrasts.
Signed l.r.: "B.R."
Collection of the C. W. Kraushaar Art Galleries, New York City.

"INDIGNATION" JONES — Facing p. 38
Wash drawing on gesso.
Bowed, bearded old man, wearing a hat and carrying a cane, walks toward left. Indistinct stairway and storefront in background.
Signed l.l.: "Boardman Robinson."
Collection of Nelson Goodman, Boston, Massachusetts.

DOC HILL — Facing p. 44
Casein tempera, with some pencil lines. 15¼×13¼ inches.
Female figure, lower left, in mourning. Graveyard scene in background reveals figures attending funeral. Trees, shrubs, and grave monuments surround one large tree in center left of composition. Colors graded, mostly cool, with supporting warm hues.
Signed l.r.: "B.R."
The Mr. and Mrs. F. M. Hall Collection, University of Nebraska Art Galleries, Lincoln, Nebraska.
Reproduced in the Art Institute of Chicago's catalogue of *The Twenty-second International Exhibition of Water Colors*, Pl. II.

MARGARET FULLER SLACK — Facing p. 62
Opaque water color on gesso board. 10×13¾ inches.
Portrait of Margaret Fuller Slack, who occupies central position in oval composition. Distant castle upon a hill in right area. Light values. Light-blue tone in sky.

Freely drawn in umbers.
Signed l.r.: "B.R."
Collection of the C. W. Kraushaar Art Galleries, New York City.

LOIS SPEARS — Facing p. 80
Tempera on illustration board. 11½×14 inches.
Portrait of a blind woman, who holds small object in both hands in front of her.
Signed l.r.: "B.R."
The Roland P. Murdock Collection, Wichita Art Museum, Wichita, Kansas.

4. LUCIUS ATHERTON — Facing p. 86
Mixed medium on gesso panel. 15×11¾ inches.
Head of man against white-tone background. Hat in background. Middle value. Gray-green background wash. Gesso white used in white areas of head. Drawing supported with pen and ink.
Signed l.r.: "B.R."
Collection of the C. W. Kraushaar Art Galleries, New York City.

A. D. BLOOD — Facing p. 96
Opaque water color on illustration board. 12½×10 inches.
Male and female figures lying upon mound of grave. Tombstone in center right of picture; trees in left. Dark values. Colors in cool grays and blacks.
Signed l.r.: "B.R."
Collection of the C. W. Kraushaar Art Galleries, New York City.

RUSSIAN SONIA — Facing p. 106
Mixed medium on gesso board. 16×12 inches.
Two figures, head and shoulders, male and female. Graded cool tones in background. High-intensity warm colors (red) in woman's gown. She wears a yellow headdress.
Signed l.r.: "B.R."
Collection of Mrs. Everett Angle, Lincoln, Nebraska.

3. THOMAS RHODES — Facing p. 116
Opaque water color on gesso board. 14×11¾ inches.
Figure of a man with heavy sideburns. Hands on chest, thumbs in vest. Light values, warm tones, light-red in face.
Signed l.r.: "B.R."
Collection of the C. W. Kraushaar Art Galleries, New York City.

PENNIWIT, THE ARTIST — Facing p. 124
A photographer, with cloth-shrouded camera, stands at left, ready to take a photograph of posed man with grim face, hand carefully placed inside vest, who sits in front of large draped window at right. At his right stands small table with vase.
Signed l.c.: "B.R."
Collection of the Art Institute of Chicago.

ELSA WERTMAN   Facing p. 138
    Casein tempera on gesso-sized pressed wood. 15×11 inches.
    Rough male figure in vest and shirt sleeves embraces peasant female figure, who is sitting at table with a dish in front of her.
Signed l.c.: "Boardman Robinson '40."
Collection of the Whitney Museum of American Art, New York City.

5. WILLIAM LLOYD GARRISON STANDARD
                      Facing p. 160
    Mixed medium on gesso. 15×11½ inches.
    Portrait in monochrome. Sharp value contrasts in head, against middle-value background. No predominant color.
Signed l.l.: "Boardman Robinson."
Collection of the C. W. Kraushaar Art Galleries, New York City.

ROSIE ROBERTS   Facing p. 174
    Mixed medium on gesso board. 12×16 inches.
    Two figures, male and female. Male figure, right, peering under bed. Woman in great agitation. Warm tones, middle values.
Signed l.c.l.: "B.R."
Collection of the C. W. Kraushaar Art Galleries, New York City.

BATTERTON DOBYNS   Facing p. 180
    Water color on water-color paper. 13½×11 inches.
    Figure of hatted woman, dining in presence of figure in coffin. Oval composition. Colors gray; loose drawing in details with pen and ink.
Signed l.r.: "B.R."
Collection of the C. W. Kraushaar Art Galleries, New York City.

SEARCY FOOTE   Facing p. 186
    Water color on gesso board. 14½×11 inches.
    Two figures, one with book, *Proudhon*. Male figure standing. Monochrome. Drawing in umbers.
Signed l.r.: "B.R."
Collection of the C. W. Kraushaar Art Galleries, New York City.

HORTENSE ROBBINS   Facing p. 192
    Water color on illustration board. 10×12½ inches.
    Seated female figure looking out of window at distant church. Colors in greens and graded yellows. Freely drawn.
Signed l.r.: "B.R."
Collection of the C. W. Kraushaar Art Galleries, New York City.

PELEG POAGUE   Facing p. 198
    Opaque water color on gesso. 8¼×15¼ inches.
    Runaway horse, drawing cart, in which man stands, clutching the reins. Figure in lower left. Freely drawn in sepia. Warm colors, graded. Middle values.
Signed l.r.: "B.R."
Collection of the C. W. Kraushaar Art Galleries, New York City.

RICHARD BONE   Facing p. 204
    Tempera. 15⅝×13¾ inches.
    In lower left, bearded old man with spectacles, in shirt sleeves and apron, carving a gravestone. At right stands woman in widow's black and veil. Colors are black, white, grays; the only color is in face and hands of man.
Signed l.r.: "B.R."
Collection of the Art Institute of Chicago.

ARCHIBALD HIGBIE   Facing p. 218
    Gouache on cardboard. 15¼×13½ inches.
    Sculptor sits brooding in lower right. Behind him on a table stands a modeled head. Looking at it are three male figures—figure at left, bearded and hatted; center figure, moustached and top-hatted; right figure, stoop-shouldered, white-haired, in slouch hat. At far left in background, a window; at upper right a piece of figure sculpture, seated position.
Signed l.r.: "B.R."
Collection of the Museum of Cranbrook Academy of Art, Bloomfield Hills, Michigan.

126. HENRY C. CALHOUN   Facing p. 226
    Gouache on cardboard. 12¾×10 inches.
    Shows the three Fates. Shrouded figure at left holds shears; one at right kneels while holding thread. Third figure stands, spinning.
Signed l.r. (in ink): "Boardman Robinson '40."
Collection of the Museum of Cranbrook Academy of Art, Bloomfield Hills, Michigan.

ELMER KARR   Facing p. 236
    Opaque water color on paper. 13¼×10¼ inches.
    Male figure, striding to right, leaving prostrate figure at bottom left. Lamp hanging in upper left. Values dark. Colors cool, with accents of reds.
Signed l.r.: "B.R."
Collection of the C. W. Kraushaar Art Galleries, New York City.

HARRY WILMANS   Facing p. 244
    Water color on gesso. 10½×11¾ inches.
    Male figure in bowed position. Loosely drawn in monochrome; umber. Distant figure of soldier in lower right. Dark-blue sky.
Signed l.r.: "B.R."
Collection of the C. W. Kraushaar Art Galleries, New York City.

HANNAH ARMSTRONG   Facing p. 258
    Gouache. 9¾×12½ inches.
    Figures of Abraham Lincoln on right and Hannah Armstrong on left. Color in cool gray background, medium value; figures dressed in black, warm gray features, white in shirt front of Lincoln's costume.
Signed l.r.: "B.R."
Collection of the University of Arizona, Gallery of Modern American Painting, Tucson, Arizona.

1943

86. LUCINDA MATLOCK   Facing p. 278
Opaque water color on gesso panel. 16×12 inches.
Head and shoulder of female figure. Light values. Colors in light green, blue, and red. Opaque white glazed-over areas surrounding head of woman.
Signed l.r.: "B.R."
Collection of the C. W. Kraushaar Art Galleries, New York City.

ZILPHA MARSH   Facing p. 296
Opaque water color on gesso board. 10¼×12¾ inches.
Seven figures. Lamp in lower right corner. Page of inscription on border of bottom center. Middle values, colors subdued, varied.
Signed l.r.: "B.R."
Collection of the C. W. Kraushaar Art Galleries, New York City.

JUDSON STODDARD   Facing p. 302
Gouache. 14⅝×11⅞ inches.
Predominantly cool grays, with warm yellow-gray and dark-green contrasts. Figure against a background of mountains is strongest contrast.
Signed l.r.: "B.R."
Collection of the University of Arizona, Gallery of Modern American Painting, Tucson, Arizona.

ELIJAH BROWNING   Facing p. 312
Nude male figure faces left in half-kneeling position, right arm raised high, head thrown back, left arm half-raised. Light streams down in shaft behind him to disclose mountain peaks in the distance at lower right.
Signed l.r.: "B.R."
Collection of Mrs. George Martin, Cleveland, Ohio.

Moby Dick[6]

AT THE SPOUTER INN   Facing p. 15
Gouache on tempered masonite. 12×16 inches.
Two male figures sit together on wooden seat. One at left wears broad-brimmed hat, holds right hand behind head, crosses right foot over left knee. Old bearded man on right carves with a large knife.
Signed l.r.: "B.R."
Collection of the Museum of Cranbrook Academy of Art, Bloomfield Hills, Michigan.

CONVERSATION IN THE SPOUTER INN   Facing p. 22
Ink wash. 12×16 inches.
Young, rugged male figure stands at left. Seated at tables in foreground are five men in hats, talking. Ones at far left and far right smoke pipes. Center figure, who faces right, has right hand upraised. In background two figures at a bar.
Unsigned.
Collection of the artist.

[6] Herman Melville, *Moby Dick* (New York: Limited Editions Club, 1943). The paging in this Catalogue is based on the edition published by the Heritage Press (1943).

THE SERMON   Facing p. 46
Mixed medium on gesso board. 16×12 inches.
The preacher, in pulpit with ship's figure at front, looks out over figures congregated below. Colors graded. Low values with warm supporting hues in center of interest.
Signed l.r.: "B.R."
Collection of T. E. Hanley, Bradford, Pennsylvania.

6. AHAB   Facing p. 55
Mixed medium. 16×12 inches.
Head of Captain Ahab. Bronzed captain with white head, wearing short-brimmed hat, fills composition. Gray tone. Stern expression—the "mad" Ahab.
Signed l.r.: "Boardman Robinson."
Collection of Mr. and Mrs. Bartlett Robinson, New York City.

BILDAD AND PELEG   Facing p. 78
Mixed medium. 12×16 inches.
Two old, white-haired men, half-figure, glower at each other. Front view of left figure shows him sitting with open book in hands. Figure at right stoops so that their eyes are on a level.
Signed l.r.: "B.R."
Collection of the Art Institute of Chicago.

THE RAMADAN   Facing p. 87
Mixed medium on gesso board. 12×16 inches.
Three figures, left seminude, are seated cross-legged. Two on right staring in amazement. Colors varied, low intensities, with spot of Indian red in shape in lower right. Written in white area on lower right corner. "The Ramadan."
Signed l.r.: "B.R."
Collection of the C. W. Kraushaar Art Galleries, New York City.

THE PROPHET   Facing p. 95
Mixed medium on gesso board. 12×16 inches—oval.
Three figures, one on right pointing and gesturing. Houses in background. Colors are black and white with warm and cool tones.
Signed c.r. (edge of oval): "B.R."
Collection of the C. W. Kraushaar Art Galleries, New York City.

STUBB AND STARBUCK   Facing p. 102
Mixed medium. 12×16 inches.
Heads of two male figures, both in caps. One at left smokes a pipe and looks over shoulder of the head at right.
Signed l.l.: "Stubb and Starbuck"; l.l.: "Boardman Robinson."
Collection of Mrs. George Martin, Cleveland, Ohio.

THE MASTHEAD   Facing p. 174
Mixed medium. 12×16 inches.
Male figure stands, shouting, on masthead in rigging facing right, pointing with his right hand.
Signed l.r.: "B.R."
Collection of Mrs. George Martin, Cleveland, Ohio.

DRINK AND PASS   Facing p. 183
    Oil on tempered masonite. 12×16 inches.
    Ahab, with hat on, stands at left, his left hand up-
raised, his right hand holding a tankard at lower center.
Three figures face him, grasping in their hands, at upper center, their three harpoons.
    Signed: "B.R."
    Collection of the Museum of Cranbrook Academy of
        Art, Bloomfield Hills, Michigan.

THE BRAWL   Facing p. 187
    Mixed medium on gesso board. 12×16 inches.
    Ten figures, two in center in struggle. Violent ac-
tion. Colors cool in background, with yellow ocher
and raw sienna tones for support. Dark values.
    Signed l.r.: "B.R."
    Collection of Lieutenant and Mrs. George Capps, An-
        napolis, Maryland.

MOBY DICK   Facing p. 202
    Mixed medium on gesso board. 12×16 inches.
    Huge head of whale, rearing out of sea, in center.
Small lifeboat in lower right. Colors cool; low intensities. Dark values. Warm sienna in lifeboat and figures.
    Signed l.r.: "B.R."
    Collection of the C. W. Kraushaar Art Galleries, New
        York City.

29. HARK!   Facing p. 207
    Water color on gesso board. 16×12 inches.
    Two figures in listening pose, one kneeling, the other
standing. Free drawing in black upon white. No color.
    Signed l.c.l.: "B.R."
    Collection of the C. W. Kraushaar Art Galleries, New
        York City.

PASSION AND VANITY   Facing p. 214
    Opaque water color on composition board. 14¾×10½
inches.
    Two dominant figures in center, one upon shoulders
of the other. Distant lifeboats with figures, one distinct
in lower left. Colors in cool grays, with warm tones in
center.
    Signed l.l.: "B.R."
    Collection of the C. W. Kraushaar Art Galleries, New
        York City.

THE HARPOONER   Facing p. 239
    Mixed medium. 12×16 inches.
    In foreground, amid large waves, rides a small boat
containing four figures. Figure at left stands in end of
boat, aiming harpoon. At right in background a white-
rigged sailing vessel.
    Signed l.r.: "B.R."
    Collection of the Art Institute of Chicago.

THE FLOGGING   Facing p. 266
    Mixed medium. 16×12 inches.
    Almost nude male figure, half-suspended at right,
being flogged by man below him. Indistinct heads in
background at left.

Signed l.r.: "B.R"; l.l.: "The rope was once more   1943–44
    drawn back for the stroke."
Collection of the Art Institute of Chicago.

FEDALLAH   Facing p. 246
    Mixed medium. 12×16 inches.
    Head of a grim-looking, half-savage man, with high
cheek bones. Hands grasp the hilt of a knife. In background a dark head.
    Signed l.r.: "B.R."
    Collection of Mrs. George Martin, Cleveland, Ohio.

THE ALBATROSS   Facing p. 251
    Mixed medium on gesso board. 16×12 inches.
    Two figures in lower right corner, upon deck of ship,
watching "Ghost Ship" in distance. Values dark. Colors, blue-grays with accents of warm tones in figures.
    Signed l.l.: "B.R."
    Collection of the C. W. Kraushaar Art Galleries, New
        York City.

28. MONSTROUS PICTURES OF WHALES   Facing p. 282
    Opaque water color on gesso board. 16×12 inches.
    Monstrous whale, rearing and blowing. Rugged cliffs
in background. Black and white, with delicate tones of
cool and warm in background and waves. Lifeboat and
figures suggested in lower right.
    Signed l.r.: "B.R."
    Collection of the C. W. Kraushaar Art Galleries, New
        York City.

30. THE FLUKES   Facing p. 299
    Oil on tempered masonite. 16×12 inches.
    Five figures in small boat in foreground row desper-
ately. At left a sixth figure stands at end of boat, aiming
harpoon at body of whale that fills background.
    Signed l.r. (in white paint): "B.R."
    Collection of the Museum of Cranbrook Academy of
        Art, Bloomfield Hills, Michigan.

FLEECE ADDRESSING THE SHARKS   Facing p. 314
    Wash drawing. 16×12 inches.
    Colored man, with white beard and in pointed cap,
holds lantern in left hand as he bends over the side of the
boat. Male figure stands in background watching him.
    Signed l.l.: "Boardman Robinson."
    Collection of the C. W. Kraushaar Art Galleries, New
        York City.

GABRIEL OF THE "JEROBOAM"   Facing p. 331
    Opaque water color on gesso. 16×12 inches.
    Three figures in violent action in overwhelming
ocean. Dark value with accents upon uppermost figure.
Colors, black, umbers, with blue-green in waves.
    Signed l.r.: "B.R."
    Collection of the Museum of the Cranbrook Academy
        of Art, Bloomfield Hills, Michigan.

1944

AHAB ON HIS QUARTERDECK   Facing p. 431
Mixed medium. 12×16 inches.
Full figure of Ahab faces right. Background of rigging, water, and spray. One male figure stands below him in background.
Signed l.c.r.: "B.R."
Collection of Mrs. George Martin, Cleveland, Ohio.

CAPTAIN OF THE "BOUTON ROSE"   Facing p. 438
Water color on gesso panel. 16×12 inches.
Three hatted male figures, standing. One at right wears beard. Color, warm gray, black, and white. Free handling. Sketchy in parts.
Signed l.r.: "B.R."
Collection of the American Institute of Arts and Letters, New York City.

ON BOARD THE "SAMUEL ENDERBY"   Facing p. 474
Mixed medium on gesso. 12×16 inches.
Three figures, two dominating, one with only head in lower left. Colors, subdued grays, cool, with warm tones in faces. Suggestion of distant ship in center.
Signed l.l.: "B.R."; l.r.: "B.R."
Collection of the C. W. Kraushaar Art Galleries, New York City.

THE CARPENTER   Facing p. 491
Mixed medium. 12×16 inches.
Half-figure of bearded carpenter in shirt sleeves, working on oblong boards with hammer and nails.
Signed l.l.: "B.R."
Collection of the Art Institute of Chicago.

QUEEQUAG IN HIS COFFIN   Facing p. 511
Mixed medium on gesso board. 12×16 inches.
Figure lying in coffin, Negro boy examining it with horror. Profile head of bearded man in upper right. Black and white ochers in center. Textures rough and varied in central figure.
Signed l.l.: "B.R."
Collection of the C. W. Kraushaar Art Galleries, New York City.

BOUND 'ROUND THE WORLD   Facing p. 518
Mixed medium. 13×11 inches.
Oval-shaped painting of a full-rigged sailing vessel. Calm sea, clouds.
Signed l.r.: "B.R." (in oval); l.l.: "Bound 'round the World" (just outside the oval).
Collection of Mrs. George Martin, Cleveland, Ohio.

THE CANDLES   Facing p. 539
Mixed medium. 12×16 inches.
Figure of a burly man, high at right, silhouetted against light.
Signed l.l.: "The Candles"; l.r.: "B.R."
Collection of Mrs. George Martin, Cleveland, Ohio.

AHAB AND PIP   Facing p. 554
Mixed medium on gesso. 13¾×17½ inches.
Two male heads, the larger head silhouetted against the lighter sky; the smaller head located in lower right corner. Low-value contrasts in foreground and heads, against sky and water. Color, low-intensity blue-green predominant.
Signed l.l.: "B.R."; l.r.: "B.R."
Collection of Alfred Holbrook, New York City.

FLAG AND HAWK   Facing p. 614
Water color on gesso board. 16×12 inches.
Figure of Tashtego, body submerged in water, nailing to mast a flag in which a hawk is caught. Middle values with whites in center area. Color in cool grays. Warm tones in flag, wing of hawk, and figure.
Signed l.r.: "B.R."
Collection of the C. W. Kraushaar Art Galleries, New York City.

Leaves of Grass[7]

17. WALT WHITMAN   Frontispiece
Mixed medium on gesso on pressed wood. 20×15¾ inches.
Head of the poet. Sharp value contrast of white in hair and beard against warm-tone background. Drawing supported by visible pen lines.
Signed l.r.: "B.R."; l.c.: "Boardman Robinson '44."
Collection of the C. W. Kraushaar Art Galleries, New York City.

WHITMAN AT THE FUNERAL   P. 14
Mixed medium on gesso on pressed wood. 20×12 inches.
The poet and a girl looking into head of coffin. Picture on wall in background immediately to left of Whitman's head. Flower pattern in foreground.
Signed l.r.: "Boardman Robinson '44."
Collection of the C. W. Kraushaar Art Galleries, New York City.

THE RED-FACED GIRL   P. 30
Mixed medium on gesso on pressed wood. 11½×14¾ inches.
Male and female, head and shoulders. Male holding female figure in embrace with right arm. Flower pattern in foreground and right background. Oval composition.
Signed l.l. (edge of oval): "Boardman Robinson."
Collection of the C. W. Kraushaar Art Galleries, New York City.

THE FAMILY   P. 44
Mixed medium on gesso on pressed wood. 16×11¾ inches.
Male and female nudes, holding nude child. Tree at right-center background.
Signed l.r.: "B.R." and "Boardman Robinson '44."
Collection of the C. W. Kraushaar Art Galleries, New York City.

[7] Walt Whitman, *Leaves of Grass* ("Illustrated Modern Library" ed. [New York: Random House, 1944]).

SEA SHORE   P. 94
Mixed medium on gesso on pressed wood. 11¾×16 inches.

Rock cliff and boulder against water and moody sky. Tree in foreground. Cool colors in low-value contrasts.
Signed l.r.: "Boardman Robinson '44."
Collection of the C. W. Kraushaar Art Galleries, New York City.

18. NUDE   P. 106
Mixed medium on gesso on pressed wood. 16×12 inches.

Bathing female nude figure, seated, with towel draped over right leg. Green-tree form in right background. Colors in low intensities. Pen lines obvious in drawing of the tree.
Signed l.r.: "Boardman Robinson '44."
Collection of the C. W. Kraushaar Art Galleries, New York City.

24. THE CROWD   P. 124
Mixed medium on gesso on cardboard. 11¾×16 inches.

Heads of twelve figures, others indistinct in the background, filling the composition.
Signed l.r.: "Boardman Robinson '44."
Collection of the C. W. Kraushaar Art Galleries, New York City.

TWO HEADS   P. 138
Mixed medium on gesso on pressed wood. 15½×12 inches.

Male and female heads. Male bearded, with hat. Female in profile, with hat.
Signed l.r.: "B.R." and "Boardman Robinson '44."
Collection of the C. W. Kraushaar Art Galleries, New York City.

THE OPEN ROAD   P. 166
Mixed medium on gesso on pressed wood. 16×11¾ inches.

Youthful figure in lower left foreground is striding forward on open road, which winds through center of composition. Stake-and-rider fence in lower left. Tree formations and fields and buildings in center planes of picture.
Signed l.c.: "B.R." and "Boardman Robinson '44."
Collection of the C. W. Kraushaar Art Galleries, New York City.

26. BROOKLYN FERRY, 1865   P. 180
Mixed medium on gesso on pressed wood. 15¾×12 inches.

City towers in distance; multicolored sky, against which patterns of seagulls are arranged. Foreground of five figures, others indistinct behind them.
Signed l.r.: "Boardman Robinson '44."
Collection of the C. W. Kraushaar Art Galleries, New York City.

69. THE BARN-DOOR   P. 200
Mixed medium on gesso on pressed wood. 16×12 inches.

Fields with cattle; expanse of blue sky, framed by

barn door. Three chickens in foreground. Green hues in fields; graded blue in sky, relieved by series of white clouds; umber on border. Sharp value contrast between doorway and sky.
Signed l.r.: "Boardman Robinson '44."
Collection of the C. W. Kraushaar Art Galleries, New York City.

EUROPEAN HEADSMAN   P. 218
Mixed medium on gesso on pressed wood. 15¾×12 inches.

Male figure, half-masked, torso nude, holding ax. Castle tower with flag in lower right corner. Expanse of sky behind figure.
Signed l.l.: "B.R."; u.r.: "Boardman Robinson."
Collection of the C. W. Kraushaar Art Galleries, New York City.

49. CHRIST AND THE MONEY-CHANGERS   P. 224
Mixed medium on gesso on pressed wood. 16×11½ inches.

Figure of Jesus, with whip, driving money-changers, represented by two figures, from the temple. Freely drawn. Left figure in blue, right in warm red tones.
Signed l.r.: "Boardman Robinson '44."
Collection of the C. W. Kraushaar Art Galleries, New York City.

THE BLACKSMITH   P. 242
Mixed medium on gesso on pressed wood. 12½×12¼ inches.

Hatted, bearded blacksmith with hammer, at anvil. White horse in background gloom of the shop.
Signed l.r.: "Boardman Robinson '44."
Collection of the C. W. Kraushaar Art Galleries, New York City.

19. VISION   P. 254
Mixed medium on gesso on pressed wood. 15¾×12 inches.

Two nude figures, male and female. Flowers in red, yellow, and green in foreground. Figures in warm tones, surrounded by graded blue of sky and flowers at base.
Signed l.r.: "Boardman Robinson '44."
Collection of the C. W. Kraushaar Art Galleries, New York City.

SONG OF THE ROLLING EARTH   P. 256
Mixed medium on gesso on pressed wood. 11½×15 inches.

Nude female and male figures. Female in pose of action, reaching out toward upper left of composition. Male figure reclining at right center of picture. Oval composition.
Signed l.r. (right edge of oval): "Boardman Robinson '44."
Collection of the C. W. Kraushaar Art Galleries, New York City.

1944

21. PIONEERS! O PIONEERS! P. 262
Mixed medium on gesso on pressed wood. 15¾×11¾ inches.
Female, male, and child figures striding toward left. Above and at top of composition is a directing angel. Fallen figure at bottom, center. Drawing supported by heavy black lines.
Signed l.r.: "B.R."; u.r.: "Boardman Robinson '44."
Collection of the C. W. Kraushaar Art Galleries, New York City.

25. THE IMMIGRANTS P. 282
Mixed medium on gesso on pressed wood.
Immigrants on board ship, gazing with wonderment at the Statue of Liberty and, in the distance, New York.
Signed u.r.: "Boardman Robinson '44."
Collection of the C. W. Kraushaar Art Galleries, New York City.

TWO AND A HALF NUDES P. 284
Mixed medium on gesso on pressed wood. 16×12 inches.
Two outstanding nude figures, head to knee length, with third figure only partly visible. Central figure most prominent. Colors of bodies in brown flesh tones. Background of gray-blue.
Signed l.l.: "B.R."; l.r.: "Boardman Robinson '44."
Collection of the C. W. Kraushaar Art Galleries, New York City.

22. THE SHIP P. 300
Mixed medium on gesso on pressed wood. 15½×12 inches.
Ship, with sails, in heavy sea. Two bird shapes against clouds in upper half of composition. Large white-capped wave in lower right. Oval composition.
Signed l.r.: "Boardman Robinson '44."
Collection of the C. W. Kraushaar Art Galleries, New York City.

27. PARADE OF THE OLD SOLDIERS P. 302
Mixed medium on gesso on pressed wood. 11¾×16 inches.
Figures of five old soldiers, marching to right in foreground. Head and flags in background. Soldiers in costumes of Revolutionary War.
Signed l.r.: "B.R." and "Boardman Robinson '44."
Collection of the C. W. Kraushaar Art Galleries, New York City.

BEAUTIFUL WOMEN P. 312
Mixed medium on gesso on pressed wood. 15¾×12 inches.
Four female heads, one elderly, the others youthful. Elderly head in central position, surrounded with two heads at top center and one in lower right corner. Oval composition.

Signed l.l. (edge of oval): "B.R."; l.r.: "Boardman Robinson '44."
Collection of the C. W. Kraushaar Art Galleries, New York City.

THE MASK P. 314
Mixed medium on gesso on pressed wood. 16×11¾ inches.
Masked female figure, with black gloves and fan. Male head in right background.
Signed u.r.: "Boardman Robinson '44."
Collection of the C. W. Kraushaar Art Galleries, New York City.

23. DEFEAT P. 336
Mixed medium on gesso on pressed wood. 16×12 inches.
Fantastic figure, crawling up mountainous incline toward jagged peaks, which indistinctly reveal faces. Turbulent sky in upper left.
Signed l.r.: "B.R." and "Boardman Robinson."
Collection of the C. W. Kraushaar Art Galleries, New York City.

COME UP FROM THE FIELDS, FATHER P. 342
Mixed medium on paper mounted on cardboard. 15½×11¾ inches.
Female figure in center, holding letter, which she has removed from the mailbox. House and tree in background. Mailbox and picket fence in foreground.
Signed l.r.: "Boardman Robinson '44."
Collection of the C. W. Kraushaar Art Galleries, New York City.

ETHIOPIA SALUTING THE COLORS P. 366
Mixed medium on pressed wood. 19¾×15¾ inches.
Negro woman, aproned and wearing kerchief, saluting. Doorway in right center background. Two figures in lower left.
Signed l.r.: "Boardman Robinson '44."
Collection of Harry N. Abrams, New York City.

20. WHEN LILACS LAST IN THE DOORYARD BLOOMED P. 374
Mixed medium on gesso on pressed wood. 16×12 inches.
Head of the dead Lincoln, flowers in foreground, gable of house in background right.
Signed l.l.: "Boardman Robinson '44."
Collection of the C. W. Kraushaar Art Galleries, New York City.

PORTENT P. 386
Mixed medium on gesso on pressed wood. 15¾×12 inches.
Head and left hand of Lincoln in sky; foreground with figure reclining, left hand reaching toward the vision.
Signed l.r.: "B.R." and "Boardman Robinson."
Collection of the C. W. Kraushaar Art Galleries, New York City.

INDEX

[PRINTED
IN U·S·A]

ILLUSTRATIONS

SEREPTA MASON (1)

(2) DAISY FRASER

THOMAS RHODES (3)

(4) LUCIUS ATHERTON

WILLIAM LLOYD GARRISON STANDARD (5)

(6) AHAB

OLD MAN KARAMAZOV (7)

(8) TARTAR OFFICER

CZARIST OFFICER (9)

(10) SOCRATES

Boardman Robinson '37

SOLON (11)

(12) LEAR WITH HIS DAUGHTERS, AND THE FOOL

LEAR CARRYING THE BODY OF CORDELIA (13)

(14) GLOUCESTER AND EDGAR

KING LEAR (15)

(16) LINCOLN, NUMBER 2

WALT WHITMAN (17)

(18) NUDE

VISION (19)

(20) WHEN LILACS LAST IN THE DOORYARD BLOOMED

PIONEERS! O PIONEERS! (21)

(22) THE SHIP

DEFEAT (23)

(24) THE CROWD

THE IMMIGRANTS (25)

(26) BROOKLYN FERRY IN 1865

PARADE OF THE OLD SOLDIERS (27)

(28) MONSTROUS PICTURES OF WHALES

HARK! (29)

(30) THE FLUKES

PORTALS OF THE CANYON (31)

MOUNTAINS (31A)

(32) CHALK CREEK CANYON, MIDDAY

(32A) MOUNTAIN CRAGS

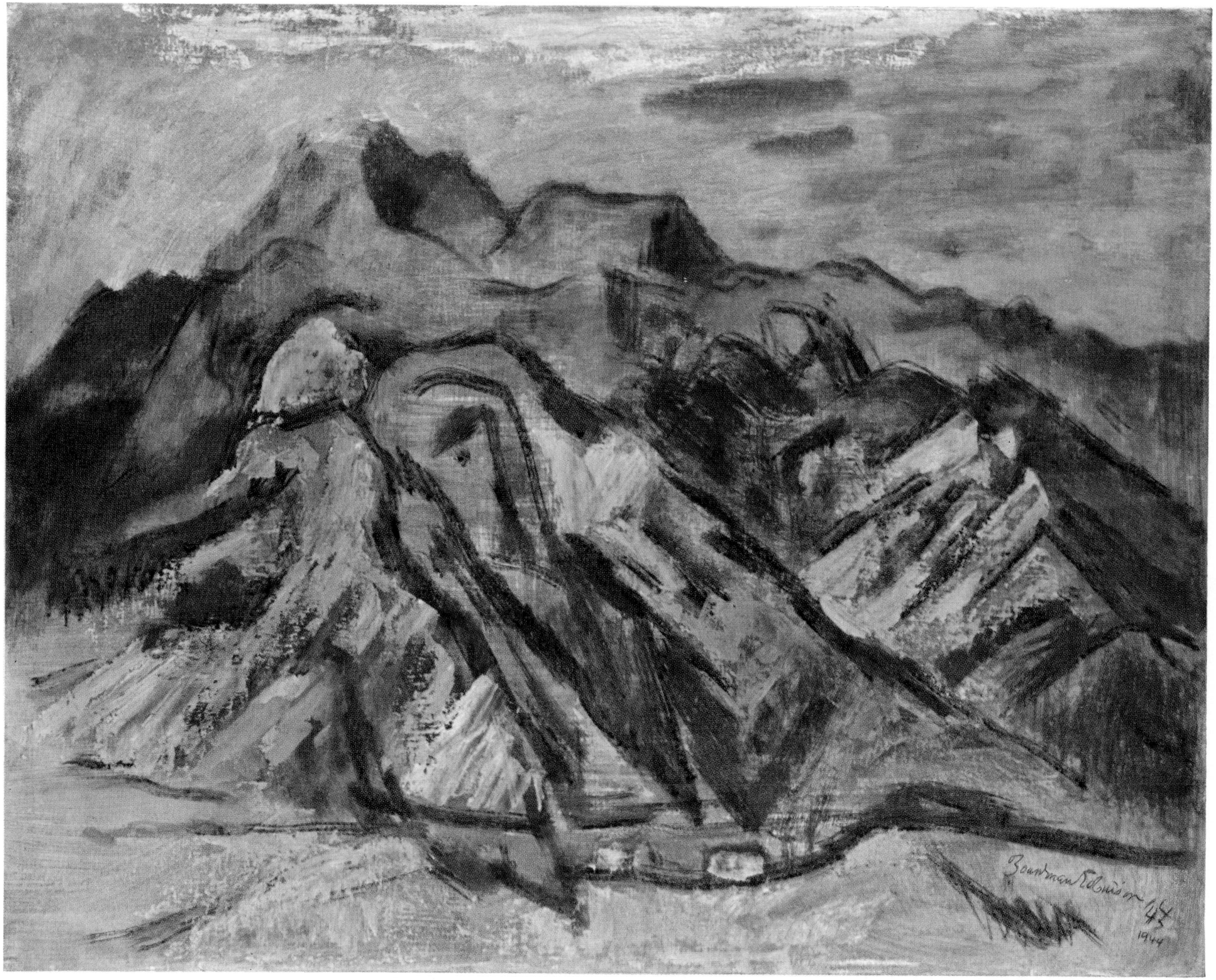

MOUNTAIN ANATOMY (33)

(34) SOLDIER AND GIRL

NAVAL FAMILY (35)

(36) CLIFF PARTY

BATHERS (37)

SUZANNAH AND THE ELDERS (37A)

(38) THE ROAD TO EMMAUS

STUDY FOR THE SERMON ON THE MOUNT (39)

(40) ENTOMBMENT

SAMSON AND DELILAH (41)

(42) JESUS TO A CERTAIN RICH MAN

THE PRODIGAL SON (43)

(44) HANDS OF MOSES

RELEASE (45)

THE SECOND COMING (45A)

(46) EXPULSION

ADAM AND EVE (47)

(48) JESUS AND JUDAS

CHRIST AND THE MONEY-CHANGERS (49)

(50) THE BREAD LINE

ADOPTED CHILDREN (51)

(52) THE CLUB

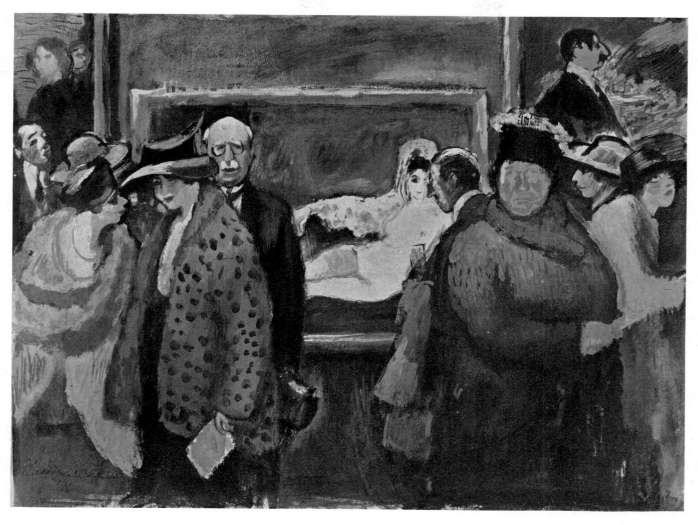

ZULOAGA AT KNOEDLER'S (53)

(54) STATEN ISLAND FERRY

EVENING, THE CLIFFS (55)

(56) PIKES PEAK UNDER SNOW

(56A) MOUNTAIN STUDY

COLORADO LANDSCAPE (57)

(58) MOUNTAIN LANDSCAPE

MOUNTAIN MINE (59)

(60) MOUNTAIN LANDSCAPE

SPRING SNOW (61)

(62) ROCKY MOUNTAINS IN SNOW

(62A) MOUNTAIN RODEO

WINTRY PEAK (63)

(64) HILL AND CLOUD

HIGH VALLEY (65)

(66) EROSION

FOOT OF THE RANGE (67)

(68) IN THE ROCKIES

(68A) CHALK CREEK

THE BARN-DOOR (69)

(70) THE GULCH

MIDNIGHT, CENTRAL CITY (71)

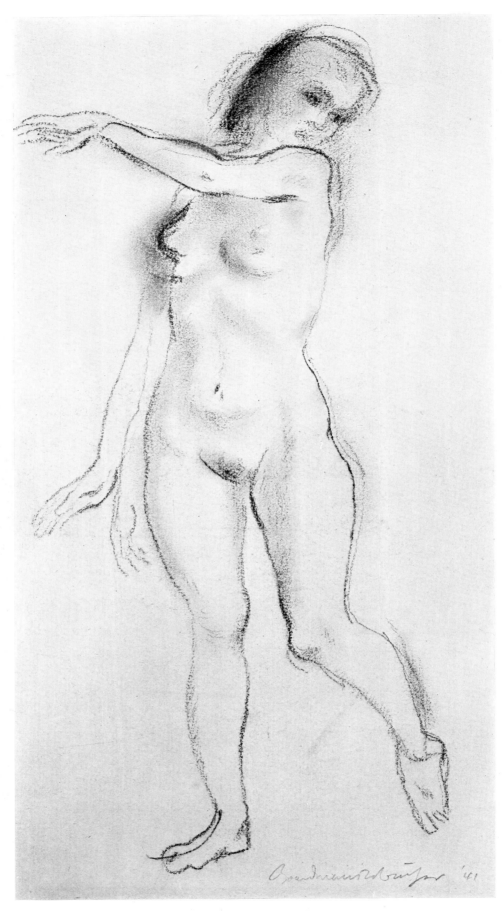

(72) WALKING NUDE

NUDE (73)

(74) NUDE TORSO

BATHER—STUDY (75)

(76) DANCER

DANCING NUDE (77)

(78) DRAPED NUDE

NUDE (79)

(80) NUDE

Boardman Robinson '27

NUDE (81)

(82) WOMEN OF THE LOIRE

KNEELING SCRIBE (83)

(84) SQUATTING FIGURE

(84*A*) CROUCHING FIGURE

SALLY (85)

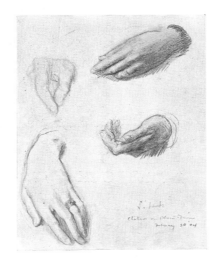

SALLY'S HANDS (85*A*)

(86) LUCINDA MATLOCK

GIRL'S HEAD (87)

(88) LAUGHING GIRL

NEGRO GIRL (89)

(90) HEAD

STUDY FOR CHRIST (91)

(92) LAUGHING COWBOYS

(92A) ROUGH CHARACTER

CIVIL PRISONERS (93)

Ciril

John Same as Capheus
in
Aria da Capo

B.R

(94) COTHURNOS

ANTONIO AND GRATIANO (95)

STAGE DESIGN (95A)

(96) ONE-STEP

TWO-STEP (97)

(98) READING HIS MOUTH

STREET CAR (99)

(100) WEIGHT HANDLERS

BOXERS (101)

(102) JO DAVIDSON

SINCLAIR LEWIS (103)

(104) DE VALERA

(104*A*) BERTRAND RUSSELL

SAMUEL GOMPERS (105)

GEORGE BIDDLE (105*A*)

(106) PERCY HAGERMAN

DR. CHARLES W. ELIOT (107)

(108) MARY McLANE

PORTRAIT (109)

(110) MADAM HOHLAKOV

Society Dame

Boardman Robinson

SOCIETY DAME (111)

(112) TRIAD

TRIAD (113)

(114) FOUNTAIN VALLEY SCHOOL MURAL

(114*A*) RAILROAD WORKERS

EXCAVATION (115)

(116) MENES, MOSES, HAMMURABI

(116*A*) HANDS OF HAMMURABI

QUIXOTE AND SANCHO (117)

(118) A HISTORY OF COMMERCE

(118A) SKETCH FOR MURAL

THE CLIPPER-SHIP ERA (119)

FIGURE STUDIES FOR MURAL (119*A*)

(120) COMMERCE ON THE MISSISSIPPI

(120*A*) FIGURE STUDIES FOR MURAL

COLORADO HORSE SALE (121)

STUDY OF COWBOY HEAD (121*A*)

(122) THE UNBURIED DEAD, GUCHEVO

THE RETREAT FROM MOSCOW (123)

(124) ANOTHER KNOCKOUT

THE MAN-EATING STATE (125)

(126) HENRY C. CALHOUN